PRAISE FOR VICT

'A richly crafted novel that graphically depicts life during those harrowing years. A touching tale and an enthralling read.' —*Reader's Digest* on *The Women's Pages*

'A powerful and moving book.' —*Canberra Weekly* on *The Women's Pages*

'Once again, Victoria reeled me in to a richly imagined (and meticulously researched) world. I loved the characters and slowed down in the final pages, reluctant to finish the book and leave them behind.' —*Better Reading* on *The Women's Pages*

'Seamlessly merging historical facts with fiction, Purman's focus is on exploring the post war experiences of women in this enjoyable, moving, and interesting novel.' —*Book'd Out* on *The Women's Pages*

'Victoria Purman has devoted plenty of time and research to *The Women's Pages*. I came way feeling educated, informed and more than little inspired.' —*Mrs B's Book Reviews* on *The Women's Pages*

'an engaging tale from a foundation of extensive research that deserves its place in the canon of Australia's wartime-inspired fiction.' —*News Mail* on *The Land Girls*

'Moments of great sadness and grief, as well as moments of pure, radiant joy, unfold in this gentle, charming tale … the genuine heartfelt emotion and the lovely reimagining of the way we once were … makes *The Land Girls* such a rich and rewarding read.' —*Better Reading*

'a well-researched and moving story.' —*Canberra Weekly* on *The Land Girls*

'a moving tale of love, loss and survival against the odds.' —*Better Homes & Gardens* on *The Land Girls*

'This is a beautifully written story that was obviously so well researched, I cried bucket loads of tears and I smiled as well as I journeyed with Flora, Betty and Lilian and the many other girls.' —*RBH Blogspot* on *The Land Girls*

'A heartwarming novel ... The story of Bonegilla is a remarkable one, and this novel is a tantalising glimpse into its legacy.' —*The Weekly Times* on *The Last of the Bonegilla Girls*

'Victoria Purman has researched and written a delightful historical piece that will involve its readers from the first page to the last ... written with empathy and understanding.' —*Starts At 60* on *The Last of the Bonegilla Girls*

'Victoria Purman has written a story about people exactly like my family, migrants to Australia ... I came to this novel for the migrant story, but I stayed for the wonderful friendship Victoria Purman has painted between the four girls ... The story is written in such a friendly, welcoming style that you can't help but be embraced by the Bonegilla girls and become one of them ... don't be surprised if you find yourself crying at the end.' —*Sam Still Reading* on *The Last of the Bonegilla Girls*

'A story told directly from the heart ... *The Last of the Bonegilla Girls* is a wonderful ode to the bonds of female friendship and the composition of our country.' —*Mrs B's Book Reviews*

'... a moving and heartwarming story [and] a poignant and compelling read, *The Last of the Bonegilla Girls* is ... a beautiful story about female friendship and how it can transcend cultural and language barriers.' —*Better Reading*

'... so rich with emotion, detail and customs that are almost unheard of these days, and thankfully so [because] the best way to get to know these characters is to read their story for yourself.' —*Beauty & Lace* on *The Last of the Bonegilla Girls*

Victoria Purman is an award-nominated, bestselling Australian author. She is a regular guest at writers' festivals, has been nominated for a number of readers choice awards and was a judge in the fiction category for the 2018 Adelaide Festival Awards for Literature. Her most recent novels are *The Three Miss Allens* (2016), *The Last of the Bonegilla Girls* (2018) and Australian bestseller *The Land Girls* (2019).

Also by Victoria Purman

The Boys of Summer:
Nobody But Him
Someone Like You
Our Kind of Love
Hold Onto Me

Only We Know

The Three Miss Allens
The Last of the Bonegilla Girls
The Land Girls

The
Women's
Pages

Victoria Purman

FICTION

First Published 2020
Second Australian Paperback Edition 2021
ISBN 9781867208020

THE WOMEN'S PAGES
© 2020 by Victoria Purman
Australian Copyright 2020
New Zealand Copyright 2020

Published by
HQ Fiction
An imprint of Harlequin Enterprises (Australia) Pty Limited (ABN 47 001 180 918), a subsidiary of HarperCollins Publishers Australia Pty Limited (ABN 36 009 913 517)
Level 13, 201 Elizabeth St
SYDNEY NSW 2000
AUSTRALIA

® and TM (apart from those relating to FSC®) are trademarks of Harlequin Enterprises (Australia) Pty Limited or its corporate affiliates. Trademarks indicated with ® are registered in Australia, New Zealand and in other countries.

A catalogue record for this book is available from the National Library of Australia
www.librariesaustralia.nla.gov.au

Printed and bound in Australia by McPherson's Printing Group

To Jo, with heartfelt thanks

PEACE

The Sun, 15 August 1945

Chapter One

The day the war ended, Tilly Galloway sat at her desk on the second floor of the *Daily Herald* building in Sydney's Pitt Street and cried with delirious joy.

She held a sodden handkerchief in her left hand, smeared with what was left of her foundation and mascara, and a cigarette was gripped tightly between the middle and index fingers of her right, the imprint of her Regimental Red Helena Rubinstein lipstick like a kiss on the cork tip end. She dragged hard, filling her lungs with heat and smoke, and her blood with the rush that had kept her going for so long now she couldn't imagine getting through a day without it. When the tears stopped, when her shoulders stopped shaking, she lit another from the butt of her fourth that morning and leant back in her chair, eyes closed, feeling her heart knock against her ribs.

The whole bloody thing was really over.

She opened her eyes with a quick blink as the cacophonous sounds of victory swept right through her. The phone next to her typewriter rang but it took her a moment to hear it amid the crying and shrieking laughter all around her in the women's newsroom. She tugged off her marquasite earring, reached for the black receiver and pressed it to her ear.

'Galloway.'

A song blared from the wireless in the corner—something triumphant with trumpets and stirring strings—and her colleagues, police reporter Maggie Pritchard and Frances Langley from courts, were spinning each other around an imaginary dance floor, Maggie's blonde curls bouncing at her shoulders and Frances's glasses slipping to the end of her large nose and in danger of toppling to the floor as they threw their heads back gaily and hooted and hollered.

'Hello? Are you there?'

Tilly looked back across the sea of empty desks and abandoned Remingtons. Cups of tea were going cold. Someone had pushed open one of the windows overlooking Pitt Street and a gust of wind whipped through the floor and unsettled stacks of copy paper, which swirled into the air like joyously thrown wedding confetti.

'I'm having trouble hearing you, whoever you are,' she yelled down the line. 'In case you haven't heard, the war's over. We're celebrating.' Tilly puffed on her cigarette and flicked the ash into an overflowing ashtray on her desk.

'Tilly! Can you hear me now?' Tilly recognised the voice of her flatmate and dearest friend, Mary.

She covered her free ear with a cupped hand. 'I can barely hear you, Mary.'

'Can you really believe it's over?'

Agony aunt Betty Norris, always called Dear Agatha on account of it being the name of the column the newspaper had been running since the dawn of time, beckoned Tilly to the wireless. 'The prime minister's about to speak,' she implored, then stopped and cleared her throat, her voice choking with emotion and her eyes filled with tears. 'Hurry!'

'Wait on, Mary. Chifley's on. I'll call you back as soon as I can.' Tilly dropped the receiver into the phone's cradle with a hard thunk, grabbed her ashtray and ran over to join the huddle around the wireless.

Tilly and Mary had left their Potts Point flat so early that morning that Kings Cross had still been asleep. They'd been too excited to stay in bed, as rumours had swirled for days that the war in the Pacific might be over that very day and they hadn't wanted to miss a minute of it. As they'd walked hurriedly through Hyde Park—they were far too excited to stand in the crush on the tram—and then all the way down Pitt Street to the *Daily Herald* building, expectation had crackled in the winter air. Nine days before, the B-29 Superfortress bomber, the Enola Gay, had dropped an atomic bomb on Hiroshima. The bomb was codenamed Little Boy and Tilly had tried not to think about such an innocent name being used for a weapon of such destruction. And then another dropped, three days after that, on Nagasaki.

The war had been over in Europe since May, but the Japanese had fought on in the Pacific until the bombs had all but wiped out two entire cities.

Now, after so much devastation and loss and grief, the end felt close, real, final.

Maggie slipped two fingers in the corners of her mouth and let fly a piercing sound. Frances laughed and elbowed Maggie in the ribs. Just then, fashion editor Kitty Darling arrived and sashayed directly over to her colleagues. 'It is true? Everyone on the street is saying it's over.'

Tilly nodded. 'Yes. It's about to be announced.'

Kitty tugged at each fingertip of her white gloves and slipped them off, clutching them in her hand as tears welled in her eyes. Kitty had never let wartime rationing hinder her ability to look ravishing. She was sporting a tan, tailored, square-shouldered suit with a pleated skirt and a silk flower was pinned to her left lapel.

'Thank goodness,' she said. 'I hope I never have to see khaki *anything* again as long as I live.'

Prime Minister Ben Chifley's stoic tone filled the air, the reception crackling with static.

'Where's Mrs Freeman?' Dear Agatha gasped, enquiring after the editor of the *Daily Herald*'s women's pages. 'She should be hearing this, too.'

'She's up with Sinclair, I expect, planning the victory edition of the paper,' Frances replied.

'Hush! Or I'll whistle again,' Maggie threatened and the women were finally quiet.

'Fellow citizens,' the prime minister started, sounding as exhausted as everyone in the country was by six years of fighting. 'The war is over.'

'I still expect to hear John Curtin's voice when someone announces the prime minister is about to speak.' Dear Agatha dabbed at her eyes with a dainty embroidered handkerchief. 'Poor man. Imagine living through all this and dying a few weeks before it's over?'

Maggie lunged forward and twiddled with the tuning knob. 'Sshhh.'

'Turn it to the left, not the right, Maggie,' Dear Agatha instructed, which earnt her a look of reproach from Maggie.

'Oh, for goodness sake, be quiet.' Frances held a finger to her lips and looked sharply at Maggie.

The women leant in, holding their collective breath.

The radio crackled. 'The Japanese Government has accepted the terms of surrender imposed by the Allied nations and hostilities will now cease. At this moment let us offer thanks to God. Let us remember those whose lives were given that we may enjoy this glorious moment and may look forward to a peace which they have won for us.'

Dear Agatha crossed herself and then blew her nose loudly. Cookery editor Vera Maxwell, sitting at the desk nearest the wireless, dropped her head into her crossed arms and sobbed.

Tilly found herself saying in a whisper, too disbelieving to utter it out loud in case she jinxed it, 'The Japanese have surrendered.' Chifley himself had said it. There really was to be victory in the Pacific.

A strange sort of hush overcame Tilly and then they all succumbed to it as the news sunk in that right had endured after so many years of despair. A hard-fought victory had finally been achieved, at a brutal and terrible cost. The unspeakable human suffering of the war would come to an end. The men and women who'd been so far away for so long would be coming home. Some families and loved ones would be reunited.

'To victory,' Maggie shouted.

'To peace at last,' Dear Agatha said through her sobs.

Around her, her colleagues' stunned silence suddenly gave way to laughing and cheering and singing. Frances began to bellow 'Rule Britannia' and everyone joined in. The world's darkest days were over and life might finally return to what it had been before Hitler and Hirohito and Mussolini. Tilly's head was filled with a loud buzzing, and for the first time since 1941 she didn't immediately assume it was the sound of Japanese Zeros flying low over Sydney Harbour. She picked up her ashtray and went back to her desk, reaching for her Craven As. She tapped the pack against her palm, pinched the last cigarette between her trembling red lips and struck a match, hoping one more puff would still the shudder working its way up her body, from her toes past her roiling stomach to the end of each strand of pinned and curled brown hair.

It was over.

She looked up and wished she could see the sky instead of the old and yellowed plaster ceiling. Her vision blurred and she imagined it shattering into a million pieces and flying into the atmosphere, and the grey lampshades hanging from it disappearing into the azure sky as if they were being pulled by a puppeteer's strings. Then the black Remington typewriters on each desk began to sway and float as light as feathers on a warm breeze, the clouds above them soft as the cotton bolls she'd seen freshly picked in Gunnedah when she'd reported from there back in 1942.

An enormous weight had been lifted from Australia's shoulders but Tilly still carried a burden which sat like lead in her stomach.

Then someone was calling her name and she turned. Mary was running towards her, wearing a smile as wide as Sydney Harbour. Tilly swept Mary up into her arms and lifted her off her feet, which made Mary giggle before they hugged each other breathless. Mary was quivering with excitement.

'You didn't ring me back, you rat.'

Tilly lowered Mary to the floor. Her cheeks were wet from Mary's tears. 'I meant to. Honestly.'

'It's really over, Tilly,' Mary cried. 'It really is peace. I can hardly believe it, can you?'

'I can and I do.'

'Everyone in Sydney's heading out to the streets. Come and see. Can't you hear it?' Mary grabbed Tilly's hand and pulled her across the floor to the windows. Pitt Street was already overflowing with people, wave after wave of them, and from their vantage point they saw hats and Union Jacks and the Stars and Stripes fluttering above people's heads. Shreds of paper were falling from the sky in intermittent bursts and they swirled and spun in the blustery sunshine of that Sydney winter day.

'Our dear boys will be coming home now, Tilly.' Mary's arm was around Tilly and she squeezed her tight.

Tilly nodded, overcome.

And then Mary's tears became laughter and joy. 'Bugger this for a joke. No one in their right mind will be wanting to call in a classified ad today. Let's get out there and celebrate, too. Because we deserve it, don't you think?'

The most important story of her career was unfolding all around her. A surge of adrenaline set her trembling. It took Tilly half a minute to grab her hat, her jacket and her reporter's notebook, and race Mary to the stairs.

She had never in her life seen crowds so enormous. Was it possible that every single person in Sydney had marched into the street for the victory celebrations? There were soldiers and sailors, American and Australian and English, and girls in their navy WAAAF uniforms walking arm in arm, striding towards peace and their hopes for a brighter future. Women kissed policemen. Horses pulled carts filled with revellers, and became skittish as they were daubed with lipstick, the word 'victory' smudged into their coats. Any vehicle that made it through the crowds was soon swamped with pedestrians hitching rides on its running boards. Schoolchildren in short pants and hand-knitted jumpers darted in and out of the crowds and people burst into spontaneous song everywhere she looked, dancing the hokey-pokey and forming conga lines to the music blaring from any nearby wireless.

At the Cenotaph in Martin Place, there were tears of joy and sombre prayers and the laying of flowers to honour the war dead. Young women with flags poked into their hats like sprays of flowers marched alongside soldiers. Every piece of paper people could get their hands on high up in office buildings—including telephone books and old posters—had been shredded and was being thrown out of wide open windows, paving the streets bright white. Outside the Ministry of Munitions in Castlereagh Street, a group of men in suits stood in foot-high piles of shredded paper, grabbing great handfuls of it and throwing it into the air like hay. On Campbell Street Tilly walked through clouds of smoke wafting from fireworks and crackers let off by the Chinese community, and laughed in joyful surprise when she stumbled upon a thirty-foot long paper dragon worming its way through the throng, lit up by Catherine wheels. In Elizabeth Street, a smart-looking man whirled with his hat in his hand, and seemed to float on air as he danced, as weightless as Fred Astaire, the road under his feet strewn with paper.

And the sheer roaring noise of it, the laughing, shouting, crying-with-joy sound of it, was like waves, bouncing off the city's sandstone buildings and echoing down one street and up another, the vibrations so powerful Tilly wondered if they had created whitecaps in the water down at Circular Quay.

The sight and sound of pure jubilation, such a gleeful communal outpouring of joy, made her cry too, and Tilly had let herself enjoy the moment, her tears washing away her fears for just a little while.

Chapter Two

When Tilly had finally battled her way through the crowds and made it back to her desk, she sat with her fingers poised over the keys of her typewriter for a moment. She was suddenly nervous with the pressure to do justice to the freshly minted peace; and filled with pride that she had been a witness to such an historic day. She took a deep breath and began, recounting every moment she'd witnessed out on the streets, the tips of her fingers growing numb as she slammed the keys on the old Remington, the words flying onto the page as she took time to fully describe everything she'd seen and experienced in a way that would honour the day and the sacrifices people had made and the futures they had put on hold.

And when she turned the platen knob and pulled her final paragraphs from the typewriter, a hovering copyboy scurried upstairs with the pages in his inky hands to take them to one of the mole-like subeditors whose task it was to combine them with all of the other reports that were set to fill the victory edition of the next day's paper.

Tilly leant back in her chair, lit another cigarette and surveyed the empty desks all around her. When she and

Mary had raced out into the streets earlier that day, the other women had followed in a happy convoy and they hadn't returned. Courts and crimes and advice and fashion and cookery stories wouldn't find a place in the paper tomorrow among all the stories about the official end of the war.

When the war had broken out in September 1939, Tilly had been secretary to the newspaper's editor, Rex Sinclair. If she had written about her trajectory and put someone else in the story, she might not believe it had ever happened, that a waterside worker's daughter from Millers Point had found herself in such a position at Sydney's bestselling daily newspaper.

She would have headlined it 'Girl From Wrong Side Of Tracks Makes Good'.

She'd been a smart girl, dux of her primary school, soared through her leaving certificate at high school and then finished top of the class at her secretarial college with the fastest and most accurate typing speed and excellent shorthand. She'd been recommended to Mr Sinclair by her shorthand teacher, who knew how important it was in the newspaper business, and when Mr Sinclair had discovered she hailed from Millers Point, his eyes had sparkled and he'd offered her the job, after a quick shorthand exercise to settle his mind that he'd made the right call. She had passed with one hundred per cent accuracy. She would be forever grateful to the bootmaker's son who had given a young girl an opportunity others might not have been afforded. He had opened a door to another world, one she had never imagined in a thousand years would be open to someone like her, a young woman with little else to recommend her but her intelligence and her dreams.

She had learnt so much working for Mr Sinclair, sitting at a desk outside his office up on the prestigious third floor where he had a view over every desk and therefore every man in the newsroom. From her perch, she had grown to know him, the newspaper and the city. She'd learnt when he was pondering a decision by the way he strode in circles around his oak desk and when to avoid him when he was about to roar at a reporter or a subeditor or, by phone, the typesetters. She had reminded him to put on a tie when the Chairman of the Board Robert Fowles swept in, a man who barely ever cast an eye in her direction. The chairman always sported a pristine gun-metal grey homburg and a greatcoat about his shoulders, as if he had just led a battle on the Western Front. He was delivered to Pitt Street in his shining black Wolseley by his driver, inevitably to share his views on the paper's coverage of some such issue or other, usually industrial unrest among the perverted communists working on the waterfront or down in the coal mines. Tilly had observed that there always seemed to be shouting from behind closed doors when the chairman visited.

Then there were the section editors shuffling past her desk for editorial meetings, who appeared harried and aged, because they were. Their daily editing challenge, to keep stories short, had become more pressing than ever with newsprint in such short supply during the war years. Every so often, the father of chapel—the printers' union's senior delegate—would emerge from the incessant roaring clickety-clack of the typesetting machines on the printing floor to raise the concerns of his brothers over one problem or another downstairs. There would also often be shouting when he visited, too.

The editor of the women's pages, the ever elegant and unruffled Mrs Dorothy Freeman, whose office was down on the second floor, had a regular weekly appointment with Mr Sinclair and they would always have tea and scones because Mrs Freeman liked them and Mr Sinclair believed it was important to keep her happy. He was well aware of the newspaper's imperative to attract women readers so advertisers would be enticed to buy space to sell rayon stockings and cigarettes and make-up and antacid powders and children's summer sandals and dress patterns and satin nightgowns for six shillings and eleven coupons.

Tilly had become familiar with all the managerial routines of a daily newspaper, including the weekly editorial conferences and daily editorial councils. She knew everyone and took it upon herself to remind Mr Sinclair about Peter McDougall's sick wife and to arrange a delivery of flowers; to purchase something from the gift registry at David Jones for the upcoming marriage of Dorothy from Sales.

She knew that each morning a conga line of reporters would cross the reporters' room and make a beeline for Mr Sinclair's office, just as soon as they'd had their first smoko, to argue about why their yarn was bloody well buried on page eight, or to gossip about what the other papers in Sydney were covering and how those other blokes had missed the real story and no doubt been hoodwinked by some minister or other or the army or how they were down in the gutter again with the crooks and the spivs. That criticism was most usually levelled at the scandal sheet *Truth*, full of racing and adultery and crime when it appeared on newsstands every Sunday.

The *Daily Herald* prided itself on the fact that it was Sydney's newspaper of record and it would never lower itself to run those kinds of stories. Its reporters wore that pride as a badge of honour too. Which didn't mean they didn't pore over the *Truth*'s stories every Monday morning with gleeful sneers and sly winks, and place their racing bets according to the tips within its sports pages.

Tilly had been like every other secretary in the place, a young woman simply dressed in a tweed suit with freshly applied lipstick and short hair neatly curled around her face and pinned back at the nape of her neck in a roll. Brown hair, brown eyes—although sometimes when she wanted to feel sophisticated she claimed them to be hazel—perhaps slightly taller than average but nothing out of the box.

Until the day she witnessed a robbery at a pharmacy on Castlereagh Street during her lunch break. She'd been having a quick lunch at Repin's Coffee Inn with Dorothy from Sales to hear all about Dorothy's honeymoon at Thirroul and had just finished her cup of coffee and a toasted fried egg sandwich when she'd heard screams and had seen the shop assistant bolt into the street shouting, 'Help' at the top of her lungs.

She had rushed straight over, asked the panicked shop assistant if she was hurt, instructed Shirley to fetch her a cup of tea from Repin's and waited with her while the police arrived. When they did, Tilly passed on a description to the officers (the assailant was short, blond, wore a flat cap over his short hair, sported brown trousers and a dark grey overcoat, and had a limp), and then listened on as they questioned the poor woman, who by this stage needed to be sent to hospital on account of a nervous attack.

When she explained to Mr Sinclair the reason for her tardiness in returning from lunch, he'd listened transfixed.

For years, she'd listened intently to the reporters from the newsroom selling stories to their editor, as they fought their colleagues for prominence on the news pages, so she could learn everything she possibly could about the news business. When she found herself in the position to pitch one of her own, she was well-versed in how to sell it. She infused the robbery with all the drama and fear one might expect from a street stick-up, and when she'd finished, Mr Sinclair had leant back in his chair, thrown her a smile and nodded. 'That's quite a story, Tilly.'

And as she'd walked back to her desk that day, feeling six feet tall, she knew that his smile and his nod of approval meant more than he would ever give away.

Tilly had been waiting for a chance to prove herself, to show that she could do more than take appointments and answer phone calls, and she'd known in that moment that she had met the challenge with flying colours. She had for some years, perhaps ten, known full well that she was wasted as his secretary, but it wasn't the done thing to go around pointing out how smart you were in the company of copyboys related to the senior newsmen. She didn't have those connections and she was a woman, two strikes against her from the very beginning.

When the Federal Government had removed journalists from the reserved occupations list in February 1942, a flurry of patriotism and careerism exploded in the newsroom, and the newspaper soon had its own manpower crisis on its hands. A week after the robbery on Castlereagh Street, two reporters up and enlisted with the AIF and another two abandoned the Sydney newsroom for the excitement and danger of London and the glamour of war reporting, forcing

Mr Sinclair to urgently fix the gaping hole in his reporting staff. He had emerged from his office one afternoon, after a rather loud row on the telephone, looked around the newsroom with a resigned stare and when his eyes met Tilly's he'd pointed at her and said, 'You'll do.'

She'd leapt to her feet, knocking over a cup of tea. In that moment, she hadn't cared a jot where it had spilled. 'Me?'

'Yes, you. Think you can handle it?'

'Of course I can,' Tilly had declared.

A chorus of jeers rose from the men in the newsroom, who'd been hanging on every word, always on the lookout for newsroom gossip to trade at the Sydney Journalists' Club, a place Tilly and her colleagues were not allowed to join on account of their sex. Information was power and there was always a tussle to have the latest, the juiciest, the freshest; and that game of reputation-building and influence-peddling was one only the men could play.

'You've got to be kidding.'

'Not the secretary, Sinclair. Surely you can do better than that.'

Tilly didn't need to turn to know who'd made the comment. She would know Donald Robinson's voice anywhere. The senior reporter had always made a point of sauntering by her desk whenever he had a spare minute and perched himself there, waiting for her to engage in conversation. When she hadn't, ignoring his smirks and his long stares at her breasts, he would respond in whispers and taunts. 'Have a drink with me tonight, Tilly. You're a very attractive girl. You know, I've been sitting behind my desk over there wondering if you're wearing lingerie under that sensible suit. The fancy French kind. Are you?'

She despised him.

At the sound of his supercilious chuckling, Tilly had glared sharply in his direction. Robinson was leaning back in his chair, his feet on his desk crossed at the ankles, his head cupped in his hands. 'She'll never make a reporter, Sinclair. She doesn't have what it takes. I mean, look at her. Who'll take her seriously?'

Mr Sinclair had turned his back on his male reporter and smiled at Tilly. 'Make me proud, Tilly.'

And just like that, she'd been promoted to a reporting position. She'd quickly packed up all her things and galloped downstairs to the women's newsroom where Mrs Freeman already had a desk waiting for her. Tilly might have been the *Daily Herald*'s newest reporter but she was a *woman* reporter and no woman had ever had a desk up in the main newsroom and, according to the newsmen of the third floor, no woman ever would.

The main newsroom had always been a male domain— except for the secretaries, of course—and the newspapermen liked it that way. Women reporters weren't trusted up there, Tilly knew, from all her years spent overhearing the ways the men talked about the women reporters downstairs.

'That's one for the sob sisters,' they would snigger at the merest suggestion that one of their colleagues should follow up a story with any hint of a woman's angle in it. In effect, that meant that every story in which a woman featured, unless of course the story was about Tilly Devine or Kate Leigh and their sly grog-running years or their razor gangs. They were mysteriously the men's stories to write.

Relegated to the second floor, Tilly had learnt the ropes from the women around her. She'd shadowed Maggie

Pritchard on the police round, covering break and enters, petty crime and the exploits of dodgy wartime conmen. She'd trailed along with Frances Langley, scurrying after her galloping strides, to the Monday morning magistrates' court appearances of those caught up in too much weekend tomfoolery, drunkenness and violence.

She'd covered everything during her twelve months as a general reporter on the paper, from city floods to state parliament's question time. If a man in his cups fell into the harbour and drowned, she filed the story. And when, back in 1943, she'd been called into Mr Sinclair's office and been told of the decision to appoint her the newspaper's first woman war correspondent, she'd beamed with pride. And although he'd tried to hide it, because a newsman didn't show such emotions, she'd seen the gleaming twinkle in his eye.

'I won't let you down, Mr Sinclair,' Tilly had murmured into the lapel of his smoky suit jacket after she'd rounded his desk and thrown her arms around him.

'Yes, yes,' he'd replied gruffly. 'Don't make me regret it.' And while he huffed, Tilly had noticed she had been the first to release herself from their embrace.

When Tilly had told her parents, her mother had cried too at the idea that her daughter was to be sent off to the war, but she needn't have worried herself, as it turned out. Much to her frustration, Tilly had written about the war without ever leaving the country or interviewing a soldier.

After three years working in the women's newsroom and observing her colleagues, she knew them well. If there was a scent of Tosca Eau de Cologne in the air, she knew Dear Agatha was at work. The advice columnist sprayed it liberally at her neck and wrists while talking to herself as she typed answers to readers' letters, attempting in the kindest way possible to solve their complicated life dilemmas in three neat paragraphs.

"'While you may believe your new mother-in-law to be interfering, she is likely missing her son terribly and most keen to ensure he is comfortable in his new home and circumstances.'"

She then lifted her fingers from the keys, leant back in her chair and announced in an exasperated fashion, 'For god's sake. Leave your daughter-in-law alone, you interfering old busybody. Does it really matter if she doesn't iron her tea towels?'

If the smell of Woodbines drifted across the floor, it was Maggie, who smoked incessantly at her desk while she transcribed from her shorthand notes stories of the wartime crimes and misdemeanours of the populace of Sydney. Nothing seemed to faze Maggie. She didn't blink when covering bodies dragged out of the harbour, or backyard abortionists arrested after the death of a patient, or raids on upmarket gambling dens or men arrested for wilfully and obscenely exposing themselves in a public lavatory, often in the new men's toilets at Lang Park near Wynyard Station.

If something smelt delicious, it was Vera, who had been experimenting with another of the ration recipes she insisted her colleagues judge before she put them in her column. The best, by popular acclaim, had been meatloaf with boiled egg. The worst by a unanimous vote was choko marmalade. With one taste, Tilly had vowed to never eat marmalade again until it was made from real fruit, even if it meant she would have to wait until the end of the war.

While Maggie and Frances and Tilly answered to Mr Sinclair, the women of the women's pages worked for Mrs Freeman. Tilly had always thought Mrs Freeman to be quite formidable. She'd been at the paper forever and had edited the women's pages even longer. Tilly knew her, of course, from her time as Mr Sinclair's secretary, when Mrs Freeman had walked by so lightly on her feet that sometimes Tilly swore the woman was barefoot. She was always immaculately dressed. She wore her hair in a trim bun pinned at the nape of her neck, which emphasised its length and her high cheekbones. Her make-up was always flawless, lightly powdered and pale pink lips, not too much for her age and not too little. Mrs Freeman's exact age was a closely guarded secret, but Tilly guessed she was perhaps in her sixties, judging by the fine lines that had settled into the corners of her eyes and the back of her hands, which, while sheathed in white gloves during the day and black of an evening, were a gentle landscape of ridges and sunspots. She wore a simple wedding band on her left-hand ring finger and every day a string of pearls around her neck.

The women of the *Daily Herald* worked at the oldest desks in the building, and typed their copy on typewriters with the stiffest keys, which Maggie swore were as old as the paper itself, and ribbons that had been turned over so many times that if they were held up to the light, stories announcing the beginning of the war might be seen. They were surrounded by the detritus of life on a busy daily newspaper: old reporters' notebooks, torn pages scattered near ashtrays and stained teacups and crushed cigarette packets; wartime information booklets telling the women of Australia to eat more lamb, to do it for the boys, to make do and mend, reminding them that loose lips sunk ships, to keep their legs closed and deny men regular intercourse to banish venereal disease, to refrain from drink in case it might lead to intercourse, to keep a clean home to ward off infection, to not be too nervy lest it affect your children, to get your share of air and sunshine. The men may have carried the major burden of fighting the war on foreign shores, but the women had carried their own burdens at home, there was nothing surer.

Chapter Three

At midnight on VP Day, Sydney's streets were still bursting with victory celebrations but Tilly was almost home. It had taken her two hours to make her way up Pitt Street and then through the crowds of Hyde Park, many still trying to get to the joyous celebrations around the Anzac Memorial. William Street and Kings Cross heaved with people, the trams and buses having given up hope of ever making their stops much earlier in the evening. She had elbowed her way through crowds singing 'Parlez-Vous' and 'God Save the King' and 'Waltzing Matilda'. The searchlights that had been erected on tall buildings when the war was at its bleakest were not trained on forbidding dark skies any longer but on revellers below, like those that might shine on a starlet at a Hollywood opening night. They almost blinded Tilly as they arced in delirious streaks across the crowd, following her up Darlinghurst Road and down Macleay Street to the flat.

She arrived home exhilarated. The air had crackled with stories and she'd caught as many of those threads as she'd been able to and written her heart out. As she locked the front door, yawning, she took a moment to let herself bask in the knowledge that every copy of the hundreds of thousands of special victory editions of the *Daily Herald* that had been at that exact moment rolling off the presses had her words in it.

But as she slipped out of her coat, that exhilaration drizzled out of her like blood from a fresh wound. She looked around for Mary, but the only sound in the flat was the faint ticking of the clock on the wall. She and Mary had lost each other somewhere in Martin Place almost the minute they'd left the office and Tilly had no clue where Mary had ended up.

Tilly dropped her handbag on the settee and dragged her feet to the wireless, tuning it to the ABC. She tried to keep her eyes open as she listened to a repeat of the new British Prime Minister Clement Attlee's broadcast from London.

The reception in the apartment building had always been patchy and she turned it up loud to make out his address over the static and hiss. 'Japan has today surrendered. The last of our enemies is laid low. Taking full advantage of surprise and treachery, Japanese forces quickly overran the territories of ourselves and our allies in the far east and at one time it appeared as though they might even invade the mainland of Australia and advance far into India. But the tide turned. First slowly, then with an ever-increasing speed and violence as the mighty forces of the United States and of the British Commonwealth and Empire and their allies, of finally Russia, were brought to bear. Peace has once again come to the world. Long live the King.'

She needed to sleep. She was as weary as worn-out shoes. She'd been on the streets for hours and hours that day to properly capture the sights and sounds of victory, knowing that if she didn't make it back to the office in time for deadline the typesetters would scream at the subeditors who would then scream at her.

Tomorrow would be another day and there would be more news to report. Tilly decided, respectfully, that another item should be added to Benjamin Franklin's assertion that the only certainties in life were death and taxes.

There would always be another story.

The voice she heard wasn't a subeditor screaming at her. It was far too caring and kind.

'Tilly?'

She blinked open her eyes to find Mary kneeling by her side. The living room light was still on and excited voices continued to broadcast from the wireless. Tilly's head felt thick and her tongue was furry with thirst.

How many hours before had she fumbled with the lock in the darkness of the hallway and dragged her weary self inside?

'Tilly?' Mary looked down at her.

Tilly slowly sat up. 'What time is it?'

'It's two in the morning,' Mary whispered. 'I've just got in. How long have you been out here? Why didn't you go to bed?'

'I must have fallen asleep, I suppose. Where did you get to?'

Mary sighed, deep and exhausted, and then her bare lips parted in a pretty smile. 'I was swept up in a conga line and found myself in Martin Place. 2UW was doing a live broadcast with Alwyn Kurts, Tilly. Alwyn Kurts!' Mary burst out laughing. 'And suddenly the crowd became an enormous choir—louder than anything I've ever heard in church—and it felt so jolly, I didn't want to leave.'

Mrs Mary Smith, nee Houghton, was a neat and particular thirty-year-old woman from the *Daily Herald*'s Classified Advertisements department who loved fresh flowers and went to bed each night with her wet hair in pin curls.

She and Tilly had been born within a day of each other, in June 1915, almost a month after the landing at Gallipoli which the family would only months after discover had claimed Tilly's uncle Herbert, her father's oldest brother. Mary was a grocer's daughter from Forster on the Central Coast who'd come to Sydney in 1939 looking for a job that didn't involve turnips. She'd landed a position at the paper the week she arrived, the typing skills she'd acquired at school proving most useful, and within two years she'd married Bert, a fine young man with a barrel chest and a winning smile. Once Bert joined the army in 1941, Mary hadn't fancied living on her own, so she'd moved in with Tilly.

In every respect but one, Mary was as neat as a pin. The exception was her shoes. Every evening when she walked in the door, she would slip off her coat and fold it neatly over the crook of her elbow before going to the fireplace and toeing off her low-heeled brogues, where they would lie until the next morning.

'They need an airing, Tilly. They've walked a long way, those things,' she always said. It had only taken one day for Tilly to realise that Mary's habit had more to do with taking a long and loving look at the photograph in the silver frame right there on the mantelpiece and kissing her fingers and pressing them to Bert's lips than it did with damp brogues. Bert had been captured in his uniform, his slouch hat proudly askew, and from there he perpetually smiled down at his wife. In four years, his expression had never changed; he hadn't aged a day, and his dark eyes remained as handsome as any film star's.

In four long years, and despite knowing for most of that time that her husband was a prisoner of war in Changi, Mary had never had a skerrick of doubt that Bert would come home from the war. 'He'll be back, safe and sound,' Mary had told Tilly, more than once, with unflappable optimism and unshakeable confidence.

'You don't know Bert like I do,' she'd said. 'He's a larrikin, that one, and I know that'll see him right. The Japs won't know what to do with a bloke like him, Tilly. He's strong and smart and works hard. One day, when the war is over, he's going to march up from Kings Cross Station, knock on the door and sweep me into his arms. I'm going to kiss him like there's no tomorrow and then we'll be able to get on with things. To make up for all the years he's been gone. Just you wait and see.'

Every morning, she sat at a switchboard, slipped on a headset and took down advertisements that members of the public called in for the newspaper. For births, engagements and marriages; flats for let; situations vacant; motor cars and lorries and pianos for sale; glasses and teeth and school blazers lost and found; employers looking for young girls for the boot trade; and, inevitably, deaths. War deaths. So many had died, their lives memorialised by their families and loved ones in five brief lines on page eleven of the newspaper. How many calls like this had Mary taken? Tilly wondered about the inner strength it required to come home each evening wearing a smile.

So many had grasped on to the slimmest slivers of hope even when there seemed to be none. Tilly's younger sister Martha had always expected that her husband Colin would walk off his ship after his service and resume being a father to their three young boys, just as he'd promised in every letter he'd written home to his family during his time in the navy. Sometimes Martha's stoic insistence on Colin's safe return had been too much for Tilly to bear. And now, Mary was staring at Tilly with a clear-eyed belief that her own happy ending was now one step closer.

How could they know? How had they not given up hope?

Tilly stretched and flopped back in her armchair. 'That sounds marvellous. I went back to the newsroom and then had to fight my way home. All those people ...' she trailed off, yawning. 'And I seem to remember I decided to sit here for a minute to listen to Attlee's speech again. And next thing I know, here you are.'

Mary sat on the chair's wide and flat arm. 'I'm exhausted, but who on earth will get a wink of sleep tonight?' Her cheeks were rosy pink and her bright blue eyes looked even brighter in the dim light of the living room. Her pale lips had lost their lipstick much earlier in the evening and her straight blonde hair, which she'd coaxed for years into gentle curls, had turned limp.

She laid a hand on the top of Tilly's head. 'Don't look at my hair, whatever you do. It's a disaster, I know. A few drunken fellows were splashing in the Pool of Remembrance in Hyde Park and I copped it as I walked past.' Mary began to dig the pins out of her formerly elaborate rolls. 'Truth is, Tilly, my mind's been racing like a hungry greyhound since this morning. Bert's coming home. I can barely believe it.' She glanced at his photograph. 'It's truly going to be over. For all of us.'

Tilly found a smile. 'I know. It's the best news. And now, I really must go to bed.' She stood slowly, wincing at the ache in her back. 'Goodnight. Sleep tight.'

Mary responded in a light, singsong voice, with the words she always did. 'Don't let the bed bugs bite.'

Tilly changed out of her clothes wearily, making sure to hang her suit to air overnight, and slid between the sheets, as thin as muslin on her single bed. Her limbs were heavy but her mind spun like the Catherine wheel she'd seen on the dragon in Chinatown earlier that night. Outside, the rest of Sydney seemed to be experiencing the same problems settling. The voices of revellers floated up through her closed window and flashes of light from The Roosevelt Club across Orwell Street shone bright every now and then, like a policeman's searching torchlight.

'Nothing to find here,' she whispered into the dark as she began to cry softly. Nothing but a girl reporter with a half-broken heart. She'd shed so many tears since 1942 they could have filled Sydney Harbour four times over. How was it possible she had any left?

Tilly moved to sit and pressed her back to the headboard. She shivered and rubbed her hands back and forth over her arms, but she couldn't get warm. Then the shiver became a shudder and she shook and her teeth chattered against each other, the sound echoing in her ears like a rat-a-tat-tat.

She switched on her bedside lamp, reached for a cigarette and smoked it tremulously. Then another. And when she was calmer, she looked around her bedroom. It didn't contain much and most of it had been in the flat when she had moved in. Her bed with its lumpen mattress had always been pushed into one corner and a decent-sized rug covered most of the rest of the floor. A three-drawer dresser with a swing mirror on top sat by the window, and in front of the mirror rested her hairbrush and comb, a glass bowl full of hairpins, her deodorant cream and the dram of perfume she'd bought from the French perfumerie on Orwell Street when she'd desperately needed cheering up. She'd had to wait behind a queue of Yanks buying gifts for their Australian girls. When they'd left, the shop assistant behind the counter had sneered in their direction and turned to Tilly. 'Who'd step out with a Negro, I ask you?'

On the wall opposite the window a two-doored gentleman's oak wardrobe with a broken hinge held her suits, a couple of pretty dresses and her wedding gown in a calico bag.

This was not the life she had imagined for herself when she'd married Archie Galloway on Saturday 9 November 1939. That was the day she'd said goodbye to the home she'd lived in all her life, her parents' rented terrace on Argyle Place at Millers Point; to the attic room she'd shared with Martha, her younger sister by two years; to the small dark spaces and wood stove downstairs; to a house full of coal lumpers and watersiders; and walked into a rented flat in Bondi on the arm of her new husband. She'd gasped when she'd seen its full view of the ocean. The ocean! For almost eight months she'd basked in the sun, in days with sand between her toes and in blissful married life with the caring and kind fellow she'd dreamt she would spend the rest of her life with.

When they'd met, Archie had been a clerk in an insurance office in Macquarie Street, with a very bright future according to his boss. She'd first seen Archie at a supper dance at The Trocadero, a venue that promised never a dull moment. Back in the day, it had been a respectable place for young ladies to be seen and she'd hurriedly handed over her two shillings at the door and made her way inside. She'd found a position on the edge of the dance floor and, with a lemonade in her hand, she'd stood with a smile hoping to be asked to dance. She hadn't been very good back then but had told herself that the only way to improve was by practising. She took in the couples and almost immediately became spellbound at the sight of Archie. She understood with the merest glance that he was someone who knew what he was doing. He twirled his partners like ribbons; they stepped out and back to him with the merest guiding hand on the small of their backs. He made them look good and Tilly wanted to look good.

When he escorted a partner back to the table near her, she took her chance.

She'd gulped her soft drink, set the glass down on the table among the teacups and ashtrays and reached for his arm.

'Excuse me,' she'd said.

Archie had stopped, glanced at her hand on his jacket and slowly lifted his gaze to meet her eyes. Was it possible that in that moment she knew she would marry him?

'Good evening, Miss,' he'd said and nodded his head.

'You're a wonderful dancer,' she'd told him and he'd blushed, and then she'd blushed, too.

'That's very kind of you to say.'

She stepped closer to him to be heard above the band, which had just begun another number. People began to move out to the floor and someone bumped Tilly right into him.

'Can you teach me to dance like that?' she'd asked. 'I'm not very good at the moment, you see, and I need some practice.'

He'd reached a hand out to her. 'The name's Archibald Galloway. Everyone calls me Archie.'

'Matilda Bell,' she'd replied. 'But I'm Tilly.'

Neither of them had danced with another partner that night or any other night. Carried away with a new passion for each other and an uncertainty about what would come next for themselves and the country, they'd had a quick courtship before Archie had proposed. Tilly had hurriedly accepted, but then Archie had enlisted in July 1940, and that life had been folded up and put away like winter blankets at the first warm hint of spring.

'Tell me again why you have to go back to Melbourne to join up?' Tilly had asked, aching at the thought of him leaving one day sooner than he had to.

'Family history, Tilly,' he'd told her with a grin. 'It's my father's division, you see.' He'd paused and leant down to kiss her quickly. 'I told you he served in the 22nd in the Great War, didn't I? Gallipoli, the Somme, Flanders, all that. Came back with nothing but a scratch. You know me, Til. Strong as an ox and smart as a whip. It'll all be over bar the shouting by the end of the year.' And so he'd left on the train to Melbourne for the Victoria Barracks. By September 1940, the 2/22nd had marched one hundred and forty-five miles on foot to Bonegilla, near Wodonga on the New South Wales–Victoria border, to continue their training at the camp.

They'd only had one more night together before he'd gone to war. The entire battalion had arrived in Sydney by train in preparation for heading off to New Guinea, and Tilly and Archie had spent it together in her new flat in Potts Point. She hadn't been able to afford the Bondi rent on her own, stubbornly determined to save all Archie's wartime pay for a house of their own when he returned, and anyway, she'd found the sudden loneliness unbearable.

'I don't need to see the sights,' Archie had told her, as they'd lain together, entwined in the dark, having made love one last time. 'I know what the Coathanger looks like. I want to be right here, remembering what you feel like in my arms. You'll get me through this, Tilly. The idea of you in this bed in this little room. I'll think of you every day and every night. You will write to me, won't you?'

'Of course I'll write to you,' she had answered hurriedly and desperately. 'It's what I do. Write.'

'And perhaps when you're a reporter, you might become a war correspondent and come and see me in action. You're always talking about that. Writing about the war, I mean. Wouldn't that be marvellous! I might get my picture in the paper.'

She'd only shared her dream with one person and Archie had been a cheerful supporter of her ambition. But that had been before Pearl Harbor. Before Singapore had fallen. They had fought a very different war after those catastrophes.

The day Archie left Sydney, on 17 April 1941, Tilly had sobbed as she'd waved him goodbye at Circular Quay. By the time the SS *Katoomba* finally departed two hours later, she was at Embarkation Park in Potts Point watching him sail away towards the Heads and on to the war. She remembered now with great humility her expectation, and the whole country's, that the war would be all over by Christmas and that all the boys would soon be home.

Their Potts Point landlord, who was as flash as a rat with a gold tooth, had taken their details and quickly judged Tilly and Mary to be good prospects, being two women of twenty-six years of age with husbands doing their duty to the king and no little 'uns to squawk at all hours and annoy the neighbours. He was used to letting share flats and bedsits to women, he'd told them.

'They make good tenants. They look after everything much better than the blokes do. Have you seen the state of some of those boarding houses in the Cross? It's a bloody disgrace,' he'd expostulated as he'd stuffed their bond money into his wallet then his wallet into the inside pocket of his suit jacket. 'Pity about all the ladies, though, wouldn't you say? Old spinsters, you understand. There weren't enough blokes to go round after the Great War and they missed out.'

Tilly reached for another cigarette and knocked the pack off her bedside table and onto the wicker basket on the other side. She could unpack that basket now. Years before, when a Japanese invasion was all anyone in Sydney could talk about, when people in harbourside houses and flats who had the means moved to the Blue Mountains to get as far away from torpedoes as they could, she'd assiduously taken the very precautions she'd read about in her own newspaper. Pack supplies in the event you have to evacuate in a hurry. Include a torch. A candle with matches. Some money. A warm cardigan and a pair of slacks in case you need to get dressed in a hurry and in the dark. While it was frowned upon to wear trousers at the newspaper—something Frances had never given two hoots about—the authorities had advised women they would be a sensible choice if one was forced into an air-raid shelter.

Next to the wicker basket was a case filled with a roll of bandages, cotton wool, drinking water, sticking plaster, a bottle of iodine, a pair of low-heeled shoes and another change of clothes: they were the essentials one would need if one's home was destroyed.

Back then, Mary and Tilly had carefully read the new instructions issued each week by the authorities on how to stay safe in case the Japs invaded.

'We have to fill the bathtub with water in case incendiary bombs destroy the rest of the flat,' Mary had announced.

Tilly read on. 'And it says here that we should cover all our food. "Plates will protect the contents of basins against flying splinters of glass. Food in airtight tins or jars is protected against gas."' They exchanged wary glances.

Tilly picked up the case and slipped back in bed, lifting it onto her lap and snapping open its clasps. She unfolded the emergency cardigan that held wrapped in its warm embrace an Arnott's biscuit tin filled with her most precious things: envelopes containing telegrams from the army, all Archie's letters and their framed wedding photo.

She slowly shuffled the letters in her hands. There were only forty of them. Perhaps if she was more careful, if she didn't sort roughly and hurriedly through the pile as she'd done in her worst moments, as if she were shuffling cards in a game she didn't want to play, there might be one she'd previously missed. Perhaps one had been caught up under the flap of another, and she would open it to find fresh declarations of love, observations about the weather and some new, humorous stories from the husband she hadn't seen since 17 April 1941.

Twice each day since then she'd checked the letterbox set into the curved brick entrance to the apartment block downstairs, and twice each and every day for the past three years there had been nothing more from Archie. She only had forty letters from her husband. There were the letters from Melbourne and Bonegilla and then his first few from New Guinea, which were filled with greetings and messages of love, about how much he missed her, telling her not to worry, that he was well and surrounded by blokes who would look after him. It was hot, he had written, and the jungle was dense and humid. He'd seen some kind of monkey, which had amused him no end. 'He wasn't that keen on our bully beef, I can tell you. Come to think of it, neither are we.' And on that weekend, Tilly caught the ferry to Taronga to study all the primates to try to figure out which one Archie had seen in the verdant jungle so far away.

On the back of each envelope, he'd written OOLAAKOEW: Oceans Of Love And A Kiss On Every Wave. Or HOLLAND and EGYPT: Hope Our Love Lives And Never Dies, and Ever Gives You Pleasant Thoughts. The acronyms had made her laugh once upon a time. Now they made her weep.

Archie's last letter was postmarked September 1942. In it, he had informed her that he was a prisoner of war of the Japanese.

Things had gone badly in the war that year. In the months after the attack on Pearl Harbor and the entry

of the Americans into the war, Singapore had fallen on
15 February 1942. Mary's husband Bert had become one
of the fifteen thousand Australians captured there by the
Japanese. And then when Darwin had been attacked four
days after Singapore, it seemed the darkest days of the war
in the Pacific had only just begun.

Archie had been in New Britain for just eight months
when the Japanese had invaded. They'd bombed Rabaul, a
town north-east of Port Moresby, and taken all the remaining
troops and local civilians prisoner. When Tilly had heard
the news, she'd run to the bathroom and vomited.

Shortly after, in February 1942, she'd received a
telegram informing her that her husband was missing,
believed prisoner of war. And then nothing from Archie
until September. How much she had grieved for Archie in
those dreadful, lonely months.

That final letter from Archie, the one that arrived in
September, had been confusingly dated 5 June. It was brief
and to the point. And then there had been nothing in the
three years since. Not a word. Not a line in any story her own
newspaper or any other in Australia had run. The soldiers of
Lark Force and all the Australian civilians in New Britain
had disappeared into Japanese hands.

Lark Force, as it was called, had been sent to Rabaul
to protect Allied airfields and to provide advance notice of
any Japanese movements through the islands to Australia's
north. It had been a disaster. Mr Sinclair had heard rumours
that the commander of Lark Force had declared every man
for himself when the Japanese had invaded, and there were
rumours that a few soldiers had made it out of New Guinea
and had returned to Australia to tell the tale. That detail had

never been in the papers. Mr Sinclair had told her things about the war no one else knew.

Rumours had swirled in Sydney like smoke during the war. Tilly needed to see Archie with her own eyes, to hold him in her own embrace, before she would truly know he was still alive. When she was desperate with missing him, she would sit in bed and read each letter over again, whispering along with every line that she knew by heart after all these years.

In his neat hand, between 'Dearest Tilly' and 'As always, your Archie', there wasn't much detail about what he was up to and no purple protestations of love or of missing her. Censors read every letter, they both knew that, and anyway, she hadn't needed words back then to be reminded of how much he loved her.

She regularly dreamt of him in his khaki uniform, his pack on his shoulders, his blond hair glinting in the Sydney sun just the way it had that departure day when he'd lifted his slouch hat to kiss her one last time. In her dreams he was tanned and shirtless because of the New Guinea heat but smiling, always smiling. Or he was joking with one of the mates he'd written about from his battalion. Mates like Tugger and Bega and Spiller who were in the 2/22nd with him.

Tilly wiped away tears with the back of a hand and stared at Archie's last letter. He'd scrawled it on pale yellow paper, about eight inches by ten, folded it twice and slipped it inside an envelope of the same colour. There were three long stickers on the envelope, about a third of an inch wide, which were printed with the words *Opened by Censor* in bold red type, almost the exact same colour as her lipstick. And then, another sticker. *Passed by Censor*. It pained Tilly to think of all the people who had read Archie's precious words to her before she had had the chance to, how something private between them had been studied by a man wearing an army uniform and wielding a sharp blade.

The postmark on the envelope said 30 September 1942, and the letter began, as his letters always did, with 'Dearest Tilly'.

It is with the greatest relief that I write to tell you that I am well and there is no need to worry. I am a prisoner of war and I'm being held at Rabaul under the Japanese—.

Tilly smoothed her right index finger over the paper on which a censor had wielded his pen knife. A rectangular hole had been spliced into Archie's handwriting just after the word 'Japanese'. She held it closer to the lamp and watched the light bleed through the gap in the page.

I can only imagine how anxious you are but I am in excellent health and good spirits. Could you let mother and father know that I'm all right and that I look forward to seeing them again when I get home?

It's good of the Japanese to let us write a letter home and this might be my last chance for a while. Don't worry. They're treating us well.

Let us hope that it won't be long until you and I, darling, are reunited once again.

As always, your Archie

There had not been another word from Archie, nor any of the Japanese prisoners of war in Rabaul in New Guinea, since that letter had arrived.

She'd wished every night for one more letter. Just one, in his familiar handwriting, neat and practised from his insurance work, telling her that he was alive. She would have begged to God if she were a believer.

But nothing had ever come.

All around her, Sydney was celebrating the end of the war.

Tilly let herself think the most selfish of thoughts. When would her war be over?

Chapter Four

When the attack on Pearl Harbor in December 1941 had brought the Americans marching into the war and sailing into Sydney, Tilly suddenly realised the city she loved was under real threat. Like hundreds of thousands of other Sydneysiders, she had agreed to the drastic measures the government had decreed must be put in place if they were to keep themselves safe from attack.

Just twenty-four hours after the announcement that the country would go dark at night, Tilly's mother Elsie Bell had arrived at the flat in Potts Point lugging two carpet bags with enough expertly made blackout curtains to cover all six windows.

'What on earth are they?' Tilly had asked when Elsie bustled in and began tugging on folds of fabric, which had unfurled like a magic pudding.

'It's for the brownouts, Tilly. The Japs are in Singapore and North Borneo and the Philippines and soon they'll be marching into Malaya, just you wait,' her mother had answered her indignantly, propping her fists on her hips and staring at Tilly with a dumbfounded expression.

'No wonder you and Mary pay such cheap rent. That navy base Kuttabul is just down the road. Everyone around here must be scared out of their wits. And with good reason, too. These curtains will do the trick. Give me a hand to take down those old ones. Now, make sure you keep some newspaper aside to stuff in the cracks so you can keep every skerrick of light in. You hear me, young lady? Or your father will never forgive me.'

Although the government had advised residents along Sydney's eastern seaboard to evacuate, how could Tilly have left her family and her job? And anyway, even if the coast wasn't safe, most people didn't have the means to leave, unless of course they were the families living in the mansions of Elizabeth Bay. Bondi, Coogee and Manly beaches had been strung with barbed wire and impaled with iron stakes, and giant wire coils like hair rollers had been laid out along the sand. Other suburban beaches had been closed and every day on the way to work Tilly and Mary passed by another air-raid trench dug in Hyde Park. Car headlights were covered with hoods like droopy eyelids to subdue them, streetlights had been dimmed and street signs had disappeared from beachside suburbs to confuse the Japanese should they invade. All those threats of invasion became frighteningly real after the Japanese midget subs slipped into Sydney Harbour and attacked on a cold, moonlit night in May 1942.

From that day, Sydneysiders had well and truly been drawn into the front line of the war.

A street in Bellevue Hill had been shelled and another shell had exploded beside a block of flats in Rose Bay, gouging a crater that men stood around and stared at. Tilly and Mary had tugged on some clothes and headed to the harbour and had seen and heard it all: the heavy gunfire and the depth-charge detonations, the sweep of the searchlights across the water, and the terrific explosion of a Japanese torpedo. Tilly had filled her notebook as residents came out in their hundreds, not all quite so fussed as she had been about getting dressed. They were in dressing-gowns and slippers, hair in curlers and wrapped with scarves and hairnets, setting aside any embarrassment at being seen that way in the arc of the searchlights, which lit up parts of the harbour as bright as day. Shrapnel from bursting shells had rained down on the water like fireworks. It had been fantastic and terrifying all at once.

Tilly had raced back to the flat to phone the newsroom and had dictated her story to one of the late-night copytakers, but it was days before anything had been able to be reported.

Mr Sinclair had been apoplectic about the army's censorship of the story. All the reporters had heard that the chairman of the board of the newspaper himself had got right on the blower to the Navy Minister Mr Makin to express his fury that his own paper had been prevented from printing what Sydneysiders had been able to see, as it was happening, with their very own eyes.

What made it worse was that news of the attack in Sydney's own watery backyard had been reported first in America, and by the BBC in London, and only then, officially, out of Melbourne. Tilly's eyewitness account, and those of other newspaper reporters and photographers and broadcasters, had appeared in papers in every other state in the country and in radio reports broadcast all over the world.

Finally, the Commander in Chief of the Allied Forces in Australia, General Douglas MacArthur himself, made the announcement that the enemy's attack had been completely unsuccessful and damage had been confined to one small harbour vessel of no military value.

Three days after the Sydney Harbour attacks, when the names of the twenty-one dead naval ratings had appeared in the newspaper with an announcement they would be buried at Rookwood Cemetery with full naval honours, Tilly had read each one aloud. They were boys from Medindie in Adelaide and Paddington and Penrith in New South Wales and Brisbane and Redcliffe in Queensland. She imagined their crooked smiles, their pride at wearing a navy uniform, their family's grief and loss at losing their sons so close to home in a place they would have believed to be safe.

After that, she had followed her mother's advice and had stuffed every gap in the windows in the flat with newspaper as soon as darkness had fallen. It wasn't just her mother's urging which had her swinging into action; she and Mary also had to contend with the eagle eyes of the local air-raid warden who lived in the flat next door.

Mr Kleinmann had never been backwards in coming forwards, rapping his knuckles on their door the minute the sun set.

'Ladies,' he would call. 'It's dark already. Make the lights out. We must be safe here. Make hurry.'

Tilly had always bitten her lip and sucked in a deep breath before opening the door to him. On the day he'd told her that if Archie was listed as missing it meant he was already dead, she had decided she hated him. If she so much as heard his front door closing or the sound of a violin coming from his flat, she found herself swallowing bitter rage.

'Yes, Mr Kleinmann. We're just getting to it now,' she would say through gritted teeth.

He was in his seventies if he was a day and Tilly had imagined he had only become air-raid warden because he was the only one left standing when the local defence committee had asked people to volunteer for the position. He was a little hunched over, he shuffled when he walked and he wore glasses with thick lenses. She had glimpsed gnarled knuckles too, and wondered if it was arthritis that made him so cranky with the world.

But the women were both good citizens who wanted to stay safe, so they'd dutifully drawn Elsie's curtains closed and stuffed every possible gap with newspaper. It was fortunate they had a ready supply.

Most of those brownout restrictions had been lifted by July 1943, when the tide was turning and the Japanese were on the run in the Pacific. Tilly and Mary had celebrated the Minister for Home Security's announcement by pulling down those horrid blackout curtains and ceremonially burning them in a forty-four gallon drum in the laneway behind their block of flats. The ugly grey things had been blankets that had once warmed the coal lumpers and seamen who boarded at Tilly's parents' house in Argyle Place. No matter how often they'd been aired by the breezes warming the city, they'd continued to reek of tobacco and exotic travels and coal dust.

As Tilly hopped off Thursday morning's early bus to Millers Point, walked down Argyle Street past the Garrison Church and crossed the verge into Argyle Place, she wondered if there would ever be a good time to tell her mother about the curtains. She decided to think on it a little longer.

The streets bore witness to the celebrations of the day and night before. Cigarette butts were strewn like confetti and shredded newspapers had been blown by the wind into tree canopies and fences, wrapped around the wrought-iron posts as if they'd been glued there. Chairs had been left out on footpaths and it seemed at least one person was still asleep on the verandah of number thirty-five, a shapeless lump covered with an overcoat. Tilly paused a moment for proof of life and was relieved to hear a snoring snuffle.

At the gate to her family's terrace, she paused before going downstairs, taking a moment, as she always did, to look north past the Moreton Bay figs and the London plane trees to the bridge in the near distance. The street curved left and it was a trick of the eye, she knew, but it had always seemed to her as if she could walk to the end of Argyle Street and step directly on to the bridge's arches and cross right over to the other side of the harbour.

Tilly had been ten years old when construction had begun on the bridge and almost eighteen when it finished in 1932. During those years, every second house on the peninsula was filled with someone working for Dorman Long and Co, the British firm that had built the bridge: engineers, boilermakers, blacksmiths, painters, ironworkers and riveters. One of the McCartney boys, Bill from down the street, had scored a job as a riveter. He'd been blinded in one eye when a red-hot rivet had been tossed at his face instead of into the steel bucket he was holding for the express purpose of catching it. Some of the stonemasons working on the project had travelled all the way from Italy to help create the masterpiece and they'd all lived together in a house on Hickson Road. It was the first time Tilly had heard anyone speaking Italian and it had sounded mysterious and exotic.

When the bridge officially opened, everyone in Argyle Place, including half-blind Bill McCartney, went down to The Rocks in a big convoy to watch the proceedings and marvel at what had been created out of thin air.

Tilly pushed open the wrought-iron gate, skipped down the flight of steps to the kitchen and swung open the back door to find her mother at the sink, elbow high in suds and breakfast dishes.

Elsie turned and gasped as she hurriedly dried her arms on her apron. 'Tilly! It's over, love. I can't believe it.'

Tilly opened her arms and swept her mother up in a warm and familiar embrace. That morning's paper, tucked under her arm, fluttered to the ground at Tilly's feet.

'Isn't it wonderful news, Mum?' Tilly didn't let go of her mother for the longest time. In the comfort of her embrace, she remembered every skinned knee, every splinter, every heartbreak, the joy of Archie's proposal, the nerves of her wedding day, her pride the day he'd enlisted and the unutterable dread of every day of his captivity. Her mother had comforted her through all of it.

'He'll be coming home now, won't he? Archie and Martha's Colin? He'll be sailing home any day now. The boys will be over the moon, they've missed their father so much. He won't recognise them, I bet, what with how much they've grown. I bet Bernard's nearly as tall as his father now.'

Tilly laughed. 'Mum, he's only ten years old.'

'But I swear those boys are growing like topsy. Faster than you and your sister ever did. Well, your sister at least. And Brian's lost his baby teeth. And Terry, he's not the little one Colin left, is he? Eight years old and as cheeky as a monkey, that one.'

'He'll be home just in time for cricket season. They'll be thrilled.'

'Won't they? And Archie. Your poor Archie. The Japs will be releasing all those prisoners now, won't they? They've got to. They've surrendered. Our troops will be going in to all the camps and freeing them all, I'm sure of it. That's what they were saying on the wireless. Did you listen to the wireless last night, Tilly? Chifley announced it. Oh, if only Curtin had lived to see the day. Imagine. The worries about the war killed him, as sure as I'm standing here. Just like that Roosevelt.'

Tilly let her mother talk as she had no answers to her rapid-fire questions. Would Archie come home now? She had hoped too much and despaired even more and neither state of mind had given her the answer she craved.

'Oh, look at me.' Elsie tugged a handkerchief from the pocket of her clean white apron. 'I don't know if I've stopped crying since we heard the news. The whole street came out, did you know that? All the ships down at the wharves were blasting their sirens all day and night and Frank from two doors down stood right out front here in the middle of the road with his squeezebox and your father sang "The Internationale".'

'Of course he did.' Tilly chuckled as she picked up the paper from the floor.

Elsie laughed through her happy tears. 'He might start up again if you ask him.'

Tilly had adored listening to her father sing. He was so good he might have been a vaudevillian, if his life had taken a different direction, if he'd been born someone else or somewhere else. He'd had the matinee good looks for it and he could dance, too. He'd been quite the catch when Elsie had noticed him in the crowd at a musical extravaganza at the Tivoli Theatre in 1914. Wylie Watson and Celia Gold had entertained the audience with their slapstick, but Stan had made Elsie's heart sing and they'd married a month later.

Elsie reached for cups and saucers sitting neatly on the shelf by the fireplace. 'Hitler hated that song, you know, "The Internationale".'

Tilly was puzzled. 'I didn't know that.'

Elsie began to sing. '"So comrades, come rally, and the last fight let us face. The Internationale unites the human race." Hitler didn't want people to join together and fight tyranny, did he? He hated organised labour and he hated socialists. And when they turned up at his Nazi rallies to sing that song in protest, he'd send the stormtroopers to kick their heads in. That's what he did to workers, Tilly.'

The lyrics of the song drifted back to Tilly, as familiar to her as the fairy tales her mother had told her when she was a child, tucked up with Martha in the single bed they shared in the attic upstairs. '"On tyrants only we'll make war. The soldiers too will take strike action, they'll break ranks and fight no more."'

'Precisely.' Elsie huffed and her chest puffed out in pride. 'Well, then. That's a turnabout for the books, isn't it?

Me telling my smart young daughter something she doesn't know. Why don't you put that in that newspaper of yours next time it takes a crack at your father and the union?'

'Mum,' Tilly sighed. 'Not today. Please?'

Elsie planted her fists on her hips. 'It still gets my goat that they said our boys down in Port Kembla sabotaged the war effort. They fought Hitler and Hirohito and Mussolini as much as any other man. Who tried to stop that pig iron being loaded into ships for Japan back in '38? It was the union boys, that's who. What was to stop it all coming back as bombs and guns and ships? But the bosses from BHP didn't care and neither did that attorney general, that Menzies.'

In Tilly's parents' house, his name was always through gritted teeth.

'But we remember who was on our side. That's right. The Chinese right here in Sydney. They sent fruit and veg and even money, what little they had, to make sure those strikers' kids were fed. They knew what the Japs were up to. They'd seen it with their own eyes back in '37.'

Tilly didn't want to think about Japanese bombs and guns and ships and her mother quickly realised when she was met with silence.

Elsie nudged her in the side. 'But today's a day for celebrating. Isn't it?'

Tilly smiled, glad of the change of subject. 'I wish I'd been here to hear him sing.'

'Your father's no Bing Crosby any more.' Elsie laughed. 'But he did all right for an old bloke.'

It was only natural that Stan had followed in the footsteps of his father and his two older brothers by becoming a watersider. Working the wharves and the ships was the business of the men of The Rocks and Millers Point, all born within spitting distance of the wharves along Hickson Road, who'd grown up being woken by ships' horns instead of alarm clocks. Stan had run the streets of the peninsula as a child until he was old enough to work. He'd been the tallest and strongest fourteen-year-old in the whole of Sydney, according to his father, and it soon became his turn to try his luck among the adults who gathered along that stretch of Hickson Road, the Hungry Mile as it was called by men desperate for work and their anxious families. The work was shift by shift and day by day, a cruel lottery of *you, you and you* as the men from the stevedoring companies stood at the gates like lords with an arm outstretched, casting their scrutinising eyes over the crowds of men, self-satisfied with the luxury of choosing only those who looked strong enough and tough enough to haul and heave and hunger until a boat was loaded and out, even if it took twenty-four straight hours.

Stan had been a bull, one of the strong ones, standing head and shoulders above the rest. During Tilly's childhood, her father had seemed like a giant. Tall, strong and as tanned as a Bondi lifesaver, his shoulders were broad from work and his forearms were like hams. He could haul Tilly and Martha up onto his shoulders, one in each arm, in a deft move that left them giggling and breathless and he'd carry them down Argyle Place all the way to the Cut. Tilly had felt like a princess atop a prancing pony.

But that couldn't last forever. It was said that Australia was built on the sheep's back, but Tilly knew it was really built on the backs of men like her father. He'd spent his working life crouched in the bows of ships hand shovelling soda ash and superphosphate and coal and sulphur with a bare face, the sulphur clouding in a yellow fog, his eyes burnt by the acrid stench. When sulphur caught fire, the holds of ships became pits of poisonous smoke. He'd humped two hundred pound bags of wheat across his shoulders, his lungs clogging with wheat dust as thick as a Sydney fog. He'd worked shirtless in the heat on the docks and then almost frozen down in the holds of ships where all he'd had to keep himself warm was scraps of hessian tied around his shoes, while frostbite had claimed other men's toes and fingers. He'd lugged wet animal hides imported from South America that were rotten and oozing with maggots. Asbestos and fibreglass wool had given men like her father severe skin rashes, which he'd scratched at until the skin was raw, and at other times bone dust had made him vomit blood for days.

The work was tough, dangerous and it broke good, hardworking, healthy men in their droves. The watersiders were treated no better than the horses harnessed to pull carts along the docks. They were meat, not men, to the stevedores and the international shipping companies.

And by his mid-fifties, Stan was mutton.

'If I was a greyhound, they would've put me down by now.' Tilly knew his mantra by heart.

'None of that talk now, Stan,' Tilly's mother would always reply. 'We can't afford to bury your bones.'

Tilly's father had had a cough for two years that he couldn't shake and more than once his doctor had told him that his twin maladies of arthritis and high blood pressure meant he would qualify for a disability card so he could be relieved of some of the heavier work on the wharves. But her father had been too proud. Being a wharfie and a union man was built into him as fundamentally as a hull on any of the ships he loaded. And anyway, any man who turned up for work half broken had Buckley's and none of getting a shift on the wharves. That's the way it had always been, until the war had stolen away the youngest and the fittest.

There were heavy footsteps on the narrow wooden stairs leading up to the ground floor and Tilly heard in the slow and limping rhythm that one leg bore more weight than the other. Her father was shuffling now, more than striding.

'"So comrades, come rally..."' His voice echoed down the stairwell, thin and breathless.

'Any excuse,' Elsie grinned. 'I told you.' And Tilly saw by the expression in her face, that she tried to hide from her daughter by turning away to fuss at the sink, that her mother heard the rasp in his voice and the weakness in his lungs.

'Hello, Dad.'

'Hello, Tilly girl.'

Tilly went to her father and they held each other gently, lovingly. He smelt like soap and shaving cream and his cheeks were cool and smooth.

'I hear you were annoying all the neighbours with your singing last night during the victory celebrations,' she said into the warm and worn shoulder of his hand-knitted cardigan.

'Me?' Stan wheezed as he laughed. 'It was that Frank Thomas from two doors down with his squeezebox. He scared all the dogs in the street. Howled all night, they did.'

Tilly had always found comfort in this house, even if her father's name would never be on the title, even if the kitchen table wobbled and the chairs didn't match, if the carpet runner in the hallway was threadbare, if the settee in the living room was already wearing through its second reupholstering. During the storm of her life during the war, it had been a place of refuge and a reminder of where she had come from, the streets that had helped raise her, and the politics of her parents and all their friends, which had guided her and helped her understand the world. The kitchen table was the centre of it all. When she'd won the position working for Mr Sinclair at the *Daily Herald*, Elsie had sewn her a dropped waist knee-length maroon wool ensemble with a matching cloche hat right here but her parents had given her something much more useful. At that very spot, she had learnt about all the vicissitudes of fortune, of the ongoing and seemingly interminable struggles of ordinary people and their battles to simply live a decent, ordinary life. She had learnt it because they had lived it.

'Do you want breakfast, Tilly? The porridge is all gone, but there's fruit cake if you're hungry. Eat some even if you're not. You're looking far too scrawny for my liking. Like a racetrack greyhound, you are. Did you get any sleep last night? I wouldn't be surprised in the slightest if the answer is no. I don't think anyone in Sydney got a wink.'

'Not much,' Tilly replied. 'I didn't get home until past midnight. I was right in the thick of everything.'

'Was that yes to a cuppa?' Elsie asked, distracted.

Tilly checked the time. 'A quick one, Mum. I just wanted to stop by for a tick. I'm reporting on the big victory parade today. There'll be forty bands marching through the city and the RSL says there'll be more than one hundred thousand servicemen and women taking part. We hear there's going to be a one hundred and one gun salute. If anyone is still sleeping after last night, that's sure to get them out of bed.'

Stan smiled at his daughter with teary eyes and covered her fingers with one of his big, callused hands. 'Any day now, love. He'll be home.' And with such economy, her father had seen through her jittery rambling.

'Thanks, Dad.' Tilly unfolded the newspaper and turned it so her father could read the front page. 'It says so right here in my own newspaper so it must be true. Hospital ships are ready and waiting to go into Singapore to get our boys from the prisoners of war camps.'

'That's bloody good news.'

'He'll be home before Christmas. Won't that be a miracle?' Elsie said. 'And that's not long now, is it? You two will be able to get on with things. Put this whole war behind you and start again. You didn't have much of a married life before he went off, did you?'

'No, not really.' Tilly shrugged, suddenly uncomfortable at the idea that the hard-fought victory was only about her. 'But I was hardly alone in that, was I? Everyone's lives were turned upside-down. Not just me. Martha and Colin and the boys. Mary. Every second person I know. Half of Sydney. The rest of the country. The whole world. We're no different.'

Elsie focussed on a spot in the distance as she spoke again. 'Archie will have his war pay all saved up, won't he? And you'll be able to get one of those soldier's loans. Imagine that. You and Archie with a home of your own. A proper backyard with a vegetable garden and plenty of room for children to play. Fresh air. And they can all have a bedroom of their own and a front yard with a tree and some roses.'

Tilly had had this conversation with her mother a thousand times before, about Archie's return, about children and what that future would look like. How on earth could Tilly raise the elephant in the room when it would crush her mother's hopes for her eldest daughter? And how would her mother react at the knowledge that Tilly's hopes for his safe return had faded like curtains in the summer sun; that her loyalty to Archie had been tested during his long absence? Tilly knew that three hearts in her family would shatter if Archie never returned so she pretended, held on to that thin skerrick of hope, for her mother's sake as well as her own.

Stan hacked out a cough, crossed his elbows on the table and studied the front page, lifting his head back to focus on the fine print.

'Where are your spectacles?' Elsie fussed.

'Upstairs,' Stan wheezed. 'I can read plenty without them.'

Elsie and Tilly exchanged knowing glances and suppressed smiles.

'What do you think of that front page, Dad? "Huge crowd in gay city carnival"?'

Elsie came to the table, pressed her hands on Stan's shoulders and leant over to look. 'Are you in that photograph, Tilly? Can't say as I can see you, but it's hard to make out anyone, really.'

'No, it's not that. Some of the words there are mine. Look here.' Tilly ran her finger down the column inches. 'This part here. "Crowds gathered for an unrestrained demonstration of gay bedlam, singing and dancing to celebrate the declaration of peace." Oh, and here's another sentence of mine: "Thousands of men—and not just those in uniform—walked the streets with lipstick smears on their faces."'

Elsie beamed. 'Well, how about that, Stan.'

Tilly's swell of pride flushed her cheeks.

'Don't you get to have your name right there on the page if you wrote it, Tilly?'

'You mean a by-line? Reporters don't usually get them and certainly not women,' Tilly explained with a sigh. 'Unless you're a regular columnist or a famous correspondent. Dad? I know you don't usually read the *Daily Herald* but—'

Stan slowly closed the paper and made an elaborate and purposeful show of folding it in half so the sports page faced up. 'Only decent thing in it is the racing results.'

'Dad—'

'I'm sorry, Tilly girl. I won't forget what that paper called me and every other bloke like me. "Lazy, incompetent, drunken thieves." They even accused some of my comrades of rifling through all the soldiers' mail and nicking anything they could get their hands on that was stuffed inside those envelopes. How low can you go? Calling us traitors to the country for fighting for better conditions on the wharves.' Stan's wheeze hissed through his tight lips. She remembered his outrage then and it clearly still burnt in his belly. Those heinous insults and accusations had put fire in the wharfies' bellies when they had barely any food to put there instead.

Tilly remembered and had fumed when she'd read it. Was there a greater insult during the war than to accuse Australians of undermining their fellow citizens? Her father and his mates had felt it keenly and would never forget it.

'It makes you sick to your bloody stomach.' Stan coughed and his voice grew hoarse. 'Now that it's over, that'll all be forgotten. They'll go back to hating us for something else. You know that it was members of the Seamen's Union who sailed those merchant ships all over the Pacific, delivering supplies to our lads? And to the Americans and the British. They weren't wearing uniforms like your Archie and Martha's Colin, but they were loyal blokes all the same, hit by Jap mines and submarines and planes. Right here off our coast and all the way up to Queensland and all through the Pacific. I met one lad who came back.' Stan paused, the emotion almost getting the better of him. 'His ship was hit by a torpedo and he spent eight hours in the sea waiting to be rescued, watching a Jap sub surface and circle around that sinking boat. Eight hours and he didn't know if another hit was coming. Or the sharks. Bloody Japs.'

It was a long moment before anyone spoke. Her father had quickly swept them past the euphoria of yesterday's victory celebrations to stocktake what had been lost and at what price. Tilly looked up from her entwined fingers. Her father's attention was focussed on the street and the morning light cast shadows in the deep lines on his ruddy face.

'That's the truth of it, Tilly. I don't see much of that in that newspaper of yours.'

What was the truth?

The censorship war had been raging as fiercely as the real one. Mr Sinclair had pinned telegrams from the State Publicity Censor in the Department of Information on a board in the newsroom to remind reporters and subeditors about what was forbidden. When Darwin had been bombed, newsrooms had been cautioned: 'All publicity media are advised that, unless officially stated by the Air Board, reports concerning Japanese air raids against objectives in

Australian defence areas must not contain any indication of specific military, naval or air force targets. Reference must be confined to areas only and not targets.'

Tilly reached for her handbag and her packet of cigarettes. She lit one, smoked it. Tired, anxious, exhausted by the war and by the years of inescapable grief, she shook with frustration but her voice was controlled, her rage contained, because she wasn't angry at her father, not really.

'I'm not a mouthpiece for the bosses *or* the big end of town, Dad. They're my words right there on the front page. I thought you might be proud of me. Who in a million years would have thought the daughter of a communist wharfie would ever be allowed to write sentences for the front page of the capitalist press?'

Her father sipped his tea and gently returned the cup to its saucer. 'He'll be home soon, love,' Stan said, his voice gruff.

Tilly hesitated and was suddenly overcome. She dropped her head into her crossed arms on the table and wept.

Chapter Five

'Tilly Galloway speaking.' When the telephone on her desk rang with a shrill tone, Tilly tugged off her earring and pressed the receiver to her ear. She heard the crackle and static she recognised as an overseas connection. 'Cooper?' She gripped the earring tight in her fist and sat bolt upright in her chair. 'Where in heaven's name are you?'

She covered her other ear and waited for the delay and then his voice.

'Tell me, Mrs Galloway. Are you still hungover from VP Day celebrations? I hear there were a million people out on the streets of Sydney the other night.'

A laugh bubbled up inside Tilly. 'You know what they say about us girls. Stick to two drinks and you'll remain a lady. After that, all bets are off. So no, not hungover in the slightest. I was out there, along with every other reporter and photographer in Sydney. The ABC even did a live broadcast from Martin Place. I waved to Talbot Duckmanton as I bustled past. So, where the heck are you, Cooper? You didn't say.'

'Work it out, Mrs Galloway. Last night I was sitting in a hotel and I couldn't see the floorboards for cracked peanut shells. There's no sneaking out of a joint like that. It sounds like you're walking on broken glass. Pity the poor blokes who have to sweep it all up. I'm rubbing shoulders with English brass weighed down with double-barrelled surnames and pompous self-importance, and correspondents from around the world are nursing very sore heads. And yes, you should definitely include me in that number.'

'Well, you're in Singapore, obviously.'

'Funniest thing, cobber. I woke up this morning to see some of the staff out in the Palm Court garden with shovels. Thought they might be burying a body. But they were digging up all the hotel's silverware. They buried it all, apparently, so the Japs wouldn't get their hands on it. How bloody enterprising.'

'Very clever indeed,' Tilly replied. 'And here's another story for you. Rumour is that the last white tiger in Singapore was shot right there at the hotel.'

'Poor tiger. So, how's everything with you?'

'Fine,' she lied. 'Busy. And you? I bet you've forgotten what Sydney looks like.'

'Not all of it,' he answered and then there was silence. He liked speaking in riddles, liked testing her, and although from anyone else it might have felt like a condescending exam, it had never felt that way to Tilly. From the very first time they'd met, back in 1940, George Cooper had always treated her with the respect that very few women in the newsroom had been afforded.

Perhaps that was because he hadn't worked his whole life in the Sydney newsroom of the *Daily Herald*.

He'd spied her on his first day at the paper, as he'd crossed the newsroom to see Mr Sinclair. In front of her desk, her guard station, he'd paused, thrown her a sideways glance, and then stopped and doubled back.

'How do you do.' He'd flashed a charming smile and offered his outstretched hand. 'George Cooper. Brand-new foreign correspondent. I don't believe we've met.'

In most respects, he'd looked like every other dishevelled reporter on the paper: rolled-up sleeves on shirts that had perhaps last seen an iron in 1929, suits that carried the stale odour of spilled beer, a rolled-up newspaper in a front jacket pocket (most often the racing pages), and sharpened pencils in every conceivable spot, including behind his left ear. But it was the twinkle in his blue eyes that had caught Tilly's attention. She was rather used to being ignored by the other reporters. He wasn't like them at all. A tall, slim man with swept-back blond hair and a strong jaw, she imagined he set hearts aflutter wherever he went. She figured that's why he'd had a brilliant career—she'd heard the gossip about him even before he'd arrived—because he simply beamed that charming smile at people like headlights on a car and they couldn't help but tell him everything.

Tilly had shaken his hand politely. 'Nice to meet you, Mr Cooper. Tilly Galloway.'

It had been quite a coup for the *Daily Herald* to entice him up to Sydney from Canberra where he'd been covering federal politics for one of the Melbourne newspapers. He'd been known as Menzies's least favourite press gallery reporter, which Tilly took as a recommendation rather than a mark against his character. He'd come with a strong reputation as a top newsman, armed with intelligence, persistence, a kind of reckless bravery and a prodigious work ethic.

'It's *Mrs* Galloway, I see.' He'd held on to her hand and made a dramatic show of inspecting the plain gold band on her left ring finger. She and Archie hadn't had the money for a fancy wedding ring and Tilly hadn't minded. Jewellers' displays had grown sparse during the war, and no one wanted to waltz around Sydney wearing a fancy bauble when the boys were away fighting.

'Yes, it is.'

He'd perched himself on the opposite side of her desk. 'Who's the lucky chap, then?'

'That's a rather personal question, Mr Cooper. We've only just met.'

He'd played at looking affronted but his grin had given him away. 'This is the business I'm in, Mrs Galloway. I ask personal questions for a crust.' He'd leant in, lowered his voice and raised one eyebrow. 'He's not a spy, is he?'

She'd suppressed her laughter and replied, 'His name is Archie and he works in insurance.'

He'd studied her then, taking in her curls and her lipstick, her buttoned shirt and the brooch on her lapel. Later, when she knew him better, she would recognise this as a technique he often employed. Ask a question, wait, think on it, hope the person being asked might nervously say something else, take an answer just a little bit further, give something away that they hadn't intended to. If there was space, some people felt obliged to fill it with conversation, and Cooper would always pounce when they did.

She hadn't taken the bait.

'Archie Galloway. That's a solid name. I bet he's a solid kind of bloke, too. You're just married.'

She'd met his confident statement and his gaze with a defiant none-of-your-business stare. 'No comment, Mr Cooper.'

Cooper had raised his hands in mock surrender and stood, righting the pile of papers he'd bumped with his thigh. 'It's been a pleasure to meet you, Mrs Galloway.'

Two years later, on the day Tilly had been promoted to reporter, Cooper happened to be back in Sydney from an assignment in London, and Mr Sinclair, in the manner he regularly employed, had walked into the newsroom, seen him conferring with some colleagues and called him over.

'You'll do,' he'd said. 'Teach Tilly the ropes, will you?'

At Cooper's insistence, they'd left the newsroom and taken to the streets of Sydney and the sunshine. They'd bought cheese and pickle sandwiches from a lunch bar on Pitt Street and walked down to Circular Quay, where they'd sat on a bench in the sun and looked across the Quay to the Botanic Gardens and over their shoulder at the bridge.

'There are six things you need to remember,' Cooper told her, tapping his cigarette ash onto the ground by his feet.

He counted them off on the fingers of one hand, plus his thumb on the other. 'Who. What. Why. Where. When. And how. If you ask those questions, you'll get the whole picture, every time. Then all you need to do is get back to the office, come up with a cracking lead, and put all the rest of the facts in the right order.'

'The lead is the first sentence, isn't it.' Tilly's pencil hovered over a fresh notepad.

'You learn fast, I see.'

She had rolled her eyes. 'You forget I've worked for Mr Sinclair for nine years. I have managed to pick up a few things.'

Cooper had narrowed his eyes, intrigued. 'Like?'

There were secrets Tilly knew that she would never tell, especially to a newsman. 'Like the fact that you always overspend your travel allowance and that you always seem to get away with it. You must have something on Sinclair but I can't figure out what. He's a family man with no skeletons, not that I've ever heard. But you, on the other hand.' This time, Tilly turned to focus back on Cooper, studying his expression and his reaction.

He grinned. 'No comment, Mrs Galloway.'

She waited, listened. And he recognised that tactic and smiled at her. 'So, your slug is the nub of the story and it goes right at the top of your copy so the subs know what the story is about.'

Tilly held her pencil to her lips and pondered. 'Mmm, you mean like, "Newsman overspends travel allowance"?'

He'd burst into laughter. 'Who's teaching who here?'

'Go on,' she'd said, lowering her pencil, poised to record everything he told her.

'You've got your slug. Now, you need a first sentence to grab the reader's attention but that's only the beginning. Then you need the human interest. That's what makes the reader remember the story.'

'That sounds simple enough.'

'And remember. Everyone has a story. You just have to listen long enough to hear it.'

He'd been right, of course, and from that day on, Tilly had listened more than she'd talked when she was interviewing people. And as for Cooper, he'd become a mentor, friend and respected colleague, and she'd genuinely missed him when he'd flown off to be a war reporter. In February 1942, he'd gone to Townsville as one of the first Australians to be licensed by the Australian Army as a war correspondent. During the rest of the war, he'd reported wherever Australian troops were facing action and she had a drawer full of postcards and telegrams from all over the world, each one signed cynically and ostentatiously, *Captain George Cooper*, which she of course teased him about every opportunity she could.

And now he was in Singapore, which was safely back in Allied hands. Prisoners of war were being released, more every day, and war correspondents were there to capture all the drama and joy and glory of their service and their freedom.

Tilly could picture him. He was probably wearing a white shirt rolled up to the elbows. Khaki trousers. His blond hair pushed back off his tanned face, his blue eyes bright with the adrenaline rush of his latest assignment. He would have a lit cigarette dangling from his lips, and his long, lean frame would be slouching as it always had, a casualty of too much time hunched over the portable typewriter he'd carried with him all over the world.

Tilly lit a cigarette and leant back in her chair, crossing one leg over the other. Their friendship had, in the years since they'd met, been built on a match of wits, of humour, of truth. 'When did you get to Singapore? I thought you were still in Malaya? Something about a rubber plantation?'

The line was silent.

'Cooper? Are you still there?'

There was another crackle. '... a plane out of there. This is where all the action is, Mrs Galloway. Here and in Manila, of course, but the gin's better here. Everyone's cracking on to find all their missing POWs.'

Tilly squeezed the receiver so hard she thought it might shatter in her hand. If anyone could get to the truth of those missing men and women, George could. He had connections in the government and among defence officials in Canberra and in South-West Pacific Headquarters, as well as among the Americans and British. He knew what had been really going on, the truth that would never pass a censor's pen. He had information that might have shaken Australians' confidence in the progress of the war, in the idea that the Japanese would never win, if it'd been printed.

'Mrs Galloway.' George's voice was low suddenly, as though he was trying not to be overheard. 'Listen. I've been into some of the prison camps. I've got lists of survivors. The other fellows have too, and we're putting them together into master lists from each division. We've got names, service numbers, the whole lot. The army brass is bloody annoyed. They want us to hold off running them until they get official notification from Japan but bugger that. We've seen the blokes with our own eyes.' When there was another silence, Tilly feared for a moment that the line had dropped out again. 'People at home deserve to know they're alive.'

Tilly sat bolt upright. 'Are you telling me ... have you found Archie? Archibald Henry Galloway.' Tilly reeled off his service number, the letters and numerals of which had been tattooed on her heart all these years. 'Have you seen him? Where is he? How long's he been there? Is he alive, George?'

'Wait a minute now.'

Tilly tried to breathe and listen and concentrate all at once.

'We haven't found him. Not yet. I wanted to tell you about the lists before you saw the names in the paper tomorrow. Before you got your hopes up.'

Tilly jammed an elbow onto her desk and dropped her forehead into her open palm. Her head pounded and her heart hurt.

'Mrs Galloway? You there? Damn this phone line, if I—'

'I'm here,' she replied quickly.

'Did you hear me? You heard what I said?'

'Yes,' she murmured. 'But ... but what about General Blamey's office? You know people there, don't you? His press officer? They'll be able to find him, won't they? Ask them, George. They'll tell *you*.'

His sigh was audible and frustrated. 'I have. They know even less than we do. The Japanese have refused to cooperate in any way, shape or form when it comes to tracking people down. They wouldn't even let the Red Cross provide any skerrick of humanitarian aid. It's been abominable. They haven't handed over any nominal rolls to the Allies so our side can track prisoners of war. And forget all about letters and parcels. The eight thousand POWs in Europe, poor bastards, at least got sustenance from the Red Cross and letters from home. The Japanese POWS, almost nothing. Complete radio silence. Thousands and thousands of men and women haven't been heard of at all, officially or unofficially. That's what we're facing in finding your Archie, Mrs Galloway. It's like a needle in a fucking haystack.'

Tilly squeezed her eyes closed, trying not to hear what Cooper had just told her. All her letters and parcels and fruitcakes, written with care, baked with love and hope, wrapped tenderly. Archie had probably not received any of them. Had he thought she'd given up on him? Had he started to believe she didn't care, that she'd given up hope? It was all so unthinkable and unbearable.

'Mrs Galloway? You there? Can you hear me?' he asked and there was an urgency in his tone.

'Yes. I can hear you,' she managed, her heart in her throat.

'I promise I'll keep searching. You know what my promise means.'

'I know.' She had survived this long holding on to the merest sliver of hope, and the news from Cooper meant that she would have to keep waiting. She would have to continue getting out of bed each day, putting one foot in front of the other and breathing in and out as if everything was normal.

'Thank you, Cooper. I really do appreciate everything. I'll make you a cake when you get back. At least—' she found a chuckle to try to lighten the mood. If she didn't she would burst into tears right there in the newsroom '—I'll ask my mother to bake one.'

'Everything good with my two favourite communists, Elsie and Stan?'

Tilly laughed. 'Yes, and I'll tell them that their second favourite running dog of the capitalist press says hello.'

'It's a badge I wear with pride.' Cooper had met her parents the summer before at the Australia Hotel on Martin Place. Mary had thrown Tilly a surprise birthday party at the fancy establishment and Stan and Elsie had walked through the entrance foyer, full of black Carrara marble and black glass and mirrors, and gawped. It was the fanciest place they'd ever seen. Stan had even borrowed a suit for the occasion from one of his wharfie comrades. As Tilly and Mary and the women of the newsroom chatted and sipped glasses of sherry, Cooper had arrived, much to Tilly's surprise. He'd kissed her on the cheek and presented her with a box of chocolates.

'Happy birthday, Mrs Galloway,' he'd said and his eyes had sparkled with warmth and something else Tilly couldn't define.

She had opened her mouth to speak but had been suddenly lost for words. It had been so long since she'd felt the warm and intimate press of a man's lips on her skin, had felt the solid grip of a man's hands on her shoulders, that it had rendered her speechless and guilty and filled with longing all at once.

Cooper must have interpreted her silence as embarrassment as he seemed overly relieved to have found another man in the gathering looking as uncomfortable as he was. That's how her father and Cooper had met.

'Mum's fine. Dad is ...' She couldn't say the words out loud in case the mere act of saying them might make them true. 'We're all waiting for news.'

'Give them my best, won't you? I'm here in Singapore for another four weeks. The military's preparing for the war trials, here in Singapore and in Morotai and Rabaul and Darwin. I'll get a few yarns out of that then I'm coming home for a break until they get underway, early next year we think. The war might be over but the story's not, Mrs Galloway. I'll call you the minute I find out anything.'

'Thank you.'

'You have my word.'

She knew what he meant. 'Stay safe, Cooper.'

'Be good, Mrs Galloway.' Tilly hung up and slowly finished her cigarette, trying to disappear into the smoke, and turned when she heard her name called.

It was Maggie, the police reporter, waving a piece of paper in the air.

'What's that you've got there?' Tilly asked.

'I've just been up to Sinclair. He wants something on this for tomorrow and asked me to give it to you. See if there's a local angle.' Maggie handed Tilly a printout from the teletypewriter, a story from the Associated Press out of London.

'I don't know if I'll have the time today. I've already written two stories and I've got to file this for tomorrow.' Tilly waved a hand over her notebook on the desk beside her typewriter.

'What's the yarn?' Maggie perched herself on the edge of Tilly's desk.

'I've interviewed the Deputy Director of Posts and Telegraphs. They're holding postcards at the GPO from prisoners of war that they haven't been able to deliver to anyone. They've given me the names and addresses to see if printing them in the paper will bring people out of the woodwork.'

'I hope so. Why haven't they been able to find people?' Maggie looked as perplexed as Tilly had been when she'd interviewed the deputy director, Mr Malone. The idea that such precious letters were in a mailbag unclaimed, when families would have been so desperate for news, was an agonising and unfathomable mystery.

'Officially, "various reasons". Unofficially, they haven't been able to track down the addressees. In some cases, it's a surname and a suburb. Like,' Tilly checked her notes. '"Mrs D Sannsen, Tullamore."'

Maggie's brow furrowed. 'That's out in the central west. Surely everyone there knows everyone. Especially the posties.'

'You'd think. Anyway, what does Mr Sinclair want me to follow up?'

'Something out of London? I've got to scram. Someone's shot himself in Redfern.' Maggie winked. 'In the back of the head. It's a miracle.'

'Thanks, Maggie.' Tilly looked up at her colleague with a weak smile. Fifteen years Tilly's senior, Maggie was an enigmatic presence. She'd never married and took great delight in telling the girls she never wanted to. Tilly admired her but did not understand her at all. Maggie had both the street smarts and resilience needed to survive when dealing with the toughest cops in the city. And, to Tilly's great admiration, she had never exhibited any fear of going into the back streets and dives of Surry Hills and Darlinghurst to track down a story. Maggie slung a leather satchel over her shoulder, saluted Tilly and strode off.

Tilly scanned the Associated Press article and the date, 17 August. 'Wave of "peace" ailments sweeping London', the headline read. It was being reported that now the whole world was finally at peace, a new wave of sickness was driving Londoners into chemists' shops in search of cures. 'Chemists report a record demand for tonics at a time when, with holidays over, the sickness rate usually falls. Women are the principal sufferers.'

The rise in anxiety and frustration, according to a doctor, was a result of women's failed expectations about what the end of the war would bring. They'd been hoping to get a bit extra out of life after the war, he believed, and they were not getting it at all. It was all the fault of queuing, which was giving them neurosis.

Tilly flicked the telex on her desk and rubbed a hand over her face, trying not to scream. What she really wanted to do was to shred it into a million pieces and toss them out the windows. She splayed a hand across her chest, right on the spot where her heart was beating like a drum. *Oh, dear doctor.* If only you'd taken the time to speak to just one of those women and really listen to what they were trying to tell you, you would discover what was ailing them. And it wasn't queues or clothes rations or the lack of red lipstick.

It was too many years of fear; of being on high alert to danger and death and the threat of hearing the worst news imaginable. It was years of not enough sleep. It was the terror of hearing a knock on your door and fearing it was someone from the post office. It was too many pitying looks when people found out your husband was a prisoner of the Japanese and hadn't been heard of in a year, in two years, in three and then four. It was the air-raid warden telling you that your husband must already be dead. It was the lonely nights full of demons, of stomach-turning thoughts about where Archie was and what he was possibly enduring at the hands of those brutes in the camps. It was the daydreams that Archie would return and then the shame at daring to imagine a future that might have already slipped through your fingers.

Her own newspaper was filled with advertisements for
Beecham Pills and laxatives and liver cleansers and salts for
kidney disorders and Chinese herbalists, and drops for tired
eyes and Dr Mackenzie's Menthoids for high blood pressure
and kidney problems and Clements Tonic for waking up in
the morning with a song. Tilly would have tried them all
if she believed for just one moment that they might have
relieved her agony.

The men of Sydney, in uniform or out, didn't need such
tonics or potions. They found their pick-me-ups in the bottle.
If Tilly left work early and happened to walk through the
throbbing heart of Kings Cross before six o'clock, she was
witness to the swill, the crowds, the desperation of that urge
for just one more glass. Cigarette smoke billowed onto the
street from windows that had been flung open so men could
pass beer upon beer to their mates in the street, everyone
crawling over each other to get one last one in before the
clock struck.

She'd been drunk only once, at the wedding of an old
school friend. It was gin and she'd vomited in the gutter
out the front of her parents' house. It hadn't been anything
she'd ever wanted to repeat and she'd been teased about
it for months. When she and Archie were married, her
father-in-law had brought them a bottle of Great Western
champagne as a gift and she and Archie had sipped from
their glasses, entwined their arms, and then kissed each
other with tingling lips.

Tilly reached for another cigarette and lit up. She
smoked the whole thing down to a butt, ground it out in
the ashtray on her desk, and then reached for her notepad.

There was a chemist nearby she knew she could speak to, and a doctor in Kings Cross who'd prescribed some pills to Mary to help her sleep.

She was a reporter and she would do her job. She would put one foot in front of the other and wake up tomorrow and do it all again.

What other choice did she possibly have?

Chapter Six

'Is that you, Tilly?'

With a hip sway worthy of a Tivoli dancer, Tilly closed the front door to her flat and set two hessian shopping bags on the floor.

'I'm home,' Tilly answered wearily.

In the dim light of the living room, she stretched her fingers out, flexing and contracting, rubbing at the red welts with the opposite thumbs. In that moment, she longed for the luxury of a car. She had coveted a two-tone Buick in white and silver blue she'd seen once, glistening as it drove through Potts Point, catching the sun and reflecting its light just as the harbour did on a beautiful day, no doubt on its way to one of the fancy homes in Elizabeth Bay that also sparkled, that were so fancy there was room to park not just one vehicle but ten in long driveways that curled around houses like snakes. On Sydney days like this, when rain beat down from the skies like bullets and soaked you through to your bones, Tilly thought it would be lovely not to have to walk home with the squelching of your toes in your shoes like the cymbal crash of a percussive backbeat of a jazz song.

Tilly wearily toed off her sodden shoes and sighed. She'd forgotten her umbrella on her desk at work and it had begun to pour as she'd been walking through Hyde Park so she'd trudged the rest of the way, drenched and exhausted, with an uncharacteristically bitter August cold chilling her through. Surely spring would arrive soon. In the front gardens of the houses around Potts Point there were already signs of new life, as if the plants too realised the war was over and were bursting to celebrate. Buds were about to blossom, leaves were on their way to unfurling, but that day's rain and gloomy grey skies hanging low over Sydney had dragged Tilly back to the darkest days of winter. All she wanted was a bath and a cigarette, preferably at the same time, and then toast and tea while sitting by the wireless. And then to her bed to curl up in the blankets and disappear.

Mary's lace-ups were by the fireplace, one lying flat on its side revealing a hole in the leather almost as big as the ball of her foot. Tilly smiled at the simple familiarity of Mary's shoes.

Mary was an optimist by nature and her surroundings reflected her sunny outlook. From the minute they'd moved in to the flat, Mary had worked to turn it into a home. No matter what time of year, it was always decorated with fresh flowers, which wasn't easy during the war. Flower growers had given over their land to the cultivation of vegetables so blooms had become frightfully expensive, which is why Mary was so careful with the flowers she surreptitiously stole from rosebushes and from the shrubs in the fancy front gardens of the houses along Victoria Street and Elizabeth Bay. She would arrive home with a shopping bag that smelt like a florist's and would artfully arrange the blooms in little glass jars all over the flat: on the two window sills in the living room; on the kitchen table and on the kitchen sill to distract from the view over Orwell Street. Tonight, two deep purple freesias sat in an old perfume bottle on the mantelpiece by Bert's photo.

Mary tended the cuttings as if they were in her own garden instead of empty aspirin bottles. Each day, she took care to snip the stems just a little and refresh the water.

'It makes it homely, don't you think?' she'd asked Tilly, admiring her own work with an entirely deserved sense of pride.

And it wasn't just the flowers. Mary had laid antimacassars over the back of each headrest on the settee and on the armchair by the fireplace. She plumped the couch cushions every night when they were about to turn in to their respective bedrooms for their restless sleep.

The flat was a home to her, a haven she kept carefully prepared for Bert's imminent arrival home. In the darkest depths of the war, throughout '43, Mary had knelt at the side of her bed every night and prayed to God for Bert's return. Each Sunday, she would rise early, dress in her finest winter suit or a day dress with hat and white gloves in spring, summer and autumn and join her fellow Anglicans in humble and confident prayer at St Mary's Cathedral, from which she would return revived. Tilly hadn't wanted to remind Mary that her floral habit was actually thieving and that God probably wouldn't look too kindly on it because the perfume went a small way to masking the hint of mould creeping up the bathroom walls and, anyway, it seemed to bring Mary so much joy it would be like revealing to a child that Father Christmas wasn't real.

As the years went on, Mary's faith in God and in Bert's return had strengthened, in inverse proportion to Tilly's growing fears about the unthinkable.

'How can you be so sure God is listening, or even if there is a god?' Tilly had asked her once.

'Because I feel it in here.' Mary had covered her heart with a hand. 'Right here. Every time I think about Bert I simply feel … safe. I know that probably sounds strange to you but I know God is watching over him and that he'll bring him back to me. Don't you feel that about Archie, Tilly?'

Tilly hadn't found God anywhere, not that she'd been particularly searching for him. God hadn't had a seat at the table in her family when she was growing up. In fact, her father's suspicion of faith and the church had rubbed off onto Tilly in ways she was only now beginning to realise. She didn't cross herself for luck or look to the heavens for any kind of absolution and she hadn't felt that the St Christopher's medal Archie's mother had given him would make any difference to whether any bullet missed him or not. Tilly's mother had once been a regular churchgoer, more as an opportunity to catch up with her Millers Point neighbours than anything, but Tilly remembered the day Elsie had lost her faith. Tilly's Uncle Ern, Elsie's only brother, had been crushed by a load of wheat at Dalgety's Wharf, leaving behind a devastated wife and six young children.

'It must be God's will,' the priest from the Garrison Church had told Elsie and Stan when he'd come by to offer his prayers.

Elsie had flamed red in the face, picked up her broom and waved it at the clergyman as if he were a swooping magpie. 'Why on earth would God want my brother's wife and his six little ones to lose their father? Why would it be God's will to have him die like that?' Elsie had shrieked at him and he'd cowered on the front verandah of the terrace. For every step forward Elsie took, the priest stepped back until he found himself in the middle of the street. 'I don't see God saving any of those men down there on the wharves, working themselves to death so other men can make a profit from their blood and sweat and pain. Why would God want them to beg for work, to fight each other to get a shift so they can put food on their families' tables and pay the rent? If that's your God, you can have him.' She'd slammed the front door so hard a pane of glass in the front window had shattered and fallen in jagged pieces onto the verandah. After Ern died, his widow and Tilly's six cousins had moved in with Tilly's own family for a while, all crammed together into the attic room. They'd brought with them Ern's six chickens and a fawn greyhound called Ned that he'd raced at Harold Park. Tilly had loved Ned as if he were her own, but without Ern to race him, the dog became a burden they couldn't afford to feed and he was sold off to an old mate of Ern's from Glebe.

'Tilly?' Mary called again, her voice high and almost a shriek.

'Of course it's me,' Tilly replied sulkily. 'I'm sodding wet and freezing cold so I bloody well hope there's some hot water left.'

'Tilly! Tilly!'

Mary appeared from the hallway and rushed Tilly, rivulets of mascara forming long lines on her cheeks. 'This just came. Twenty minutes ago. It's good news, Tilly. The best news. Look!' Mary was at her side, her chest heaving with sobs and laughter all at once. Tilly wiped the raindrops from her forehead and her eyes with the forearm of her jacket. It happened so quickly. The flicker of hope that it was news about Archie, the glance to Mary's face to see those hopes dashed, and then a crushing weight against Tilly's chest.

Mary thrust the telegram at Tilly, who took in the typed words and what they meant.

'"L/Cpl Albert Smith is in the 2/10th Australian General Hospital in Singapore",' she read aloud.

'He's coming home, Tilly. Isn't it a miracle?'

Mary threw her arms around Tilly and held on for dear life. Tilly felt only the purest joy for her dear friend, who had never given up hope that Bert would survive, that he would one day walk through the front door of the flat, throw off his slouch hat and sweep his wife into his arms with a kiss that would last for weeks. Tilly was thrilled for her, deliriously thrilled. But at the same time as laughter and words of congratulations fell from her lips, the leaden sensation in her chest grew heavier.

Archie was still a ghost. It was almost two weeks since the war had ended and she'd not heard a word. Cooper had tried, she had tried, but nothing. 'Be patient, Mrs Galloway,' she'd been told when she'd begged the army for more news. 'Do you know how many men were taken prisoner? More than thirty thousand. And there are camps everywhere: Japan and Borneo and Malaya and New Guinea, and in Italy and Germany. The Japs and the Germans moved them around willy-nilly and they're not being especially helpful in giving us those records. Something to do with losing.

We're doing all we can. It's only been a fortnight. We'll be in touch.'

No one had been in touch.

Every day, Tilly had pored over the lists of names printed in the papers that had been compiled by George Cooper and the other war correspondents in the field. They were no longer reliant on the defence forces to supply them with information and were talking directly to soldiers and freed prisoners themselves, taking the names of the living and the dead. Archie's name hadn't yet appeared on any of them. Tilly's feelings of dread at all the possibilities grew worse every day as she read, chilled to the core, the news reports of the appalling cruelty inflicted on prisoners of the Japanese. The stories grew more detailed now that the army's censors had put down their knives and pens. The truth was finally being revealed. Six hundred Australians had died at Sandakan in Borneo in just six months. They'd been whipped, beaten, starved, worked to death. Every day, the newspapers had been filled with more horrors. The atrocities of the Nazis at Belsen. The murder of Jewish people in gas chambers. It seemed as if the world had descended into hell.

How lucky was Mary that Bert was coming home from all that horror.

'I knew he would come home to me. I just knew he would.' Mary released herself from Tilly's embrace and wiped her eyes with her sodden handkerchief.

'You never gave up, Mary. That has to count for something.' The two women shared a silent acknowledgement of all they had endured, that which they'd shared and that which had been too painful to articulate, the kind of heartbreak that could only be relieved by sobbing alone at night, in their own bedrooms, when the not-knowing had become too much to bear for both of them.

'When's the big date then? When's he coming home exactly?'

'It doesn't say, but it can't be long, can it? If Bert's in hospital they're probably giving him a once-over to make sure he doesn't bring any of those horrible tropical diseases back home. Malaria and the like. That's all it can be. I'm sure of it.'

'I bet he's just bursting to get home to see you.'

Mary nodded and smiled but when her bottom lip wobbled, she launched into Tilly's arms again, her body racked with heaving and happy sobs.

'There, there, Mary. You're allowed to cry. I can't think of a better reason.'

'I'm so happy, Tilly. So happy.'

Tilly patted her back and then held Mary at arm's length. 'Look at me. I've gone and made you damp. Why don't you put the kettle on while I change out of these wet clothes? Check the shopping. I have two eggs, a loaf of bread, a block of cheese, two very small pork chops from Alberto's, a bottle of milk, a tomato and a cucumber if you fancy them. We'll have a feast to celebrate Bert's homecoming.'

Mary reached for Tilly's shoulders and spun her around towards the bathroom. 'That sounds wonderful. It's just what I need. And yes, to answer your earlier question, there's plenty of hot water left. Go and have a bath first.'

Tilly tugged off her still-damp tweed suit, rolled down her rayon stockings and padded to the bathroom in her dressing-gown. As she waited for the bath to fill, she smoothed Ponds cream over her face to remove her make-up, carefully avoiding the mirror above the sink. The black spots blooming behind the glass obscured her face anyway and she didn't need to see her reflection to know how she appeared to the world. War weary.

She tossed her stockings into the water and slipped in herself while it was still running. She breathed deep, letting the hot steam warm her from the inside, and watched the water level rise as it covered her hips, her knees, her breasts and her shoulders. The heat prickled her skin and she closed her eyes to the sensation of it coming alive one nerve ending at a time.

There had been a loneliness she had never shared with Mary, because even though they were close, they had never shared details of the intimacies of their marriages. They'd shared almost everything else: deodorant cream, toothpaste, stockings if either of them had found a hole on the calf or ankle that couldn't be hidden with a skirt or shoes. They'd shared their daydreams of children and a future, and of having rosier cheeks and longer eyelashes and shinier hair, of the teenage dreams of marrying a rich man and voyages to London and perhaps even seeing the dancers' high kicks at the Moulin Rouge. But they had never talked about sex.

On the day she'd married Archie, Tilly had been a blushing bride with wide innocent brown eyes and rouged cheeks. She still had the stick of red lipstick she'd worn that day, the lipstick they'd smudged over their lips that night, when they'd tentatively shared a bed for the first time as husband and wife, young and curious and scared and inexperienced, both of them. She'd understood nothing of sex, other than knowing it was her job to make her husband happy that night, so she'd spent all the coupons she'd saved to buy a new rayon nightgown from David Jones. When they'd both taken off their clothes and lain naked with each other under the sheets, she'd liked the warmth of his body next to hers. When he'd entered her, and thrust inside her, she'd remained completely still and waited and when he was finished, he'd kissed her and asked her if she needed to go and clean herself up, so she had, not knowing that this was expected of her. When she had wiped herself, she'd seen blood and felt stickiness and then they'd put on their nightgown and pyjamas and slept.

Things had improved after that first time, as they had become more familiar with each other's bodies and desires, but not long after Archie had left for the war and Tilly had spent the past four years untouched. For a time, she had remembered the heat of Archie's body, the strength of his arms around her, the passionate way he kissed her every night when they returned home from work, what it felt like when he'd moved inside her, as if they were joined in ways other than at their intimate core. But those memories had worn away like the soles of Mary's shoes.

When Archie had enlisted, Tilly had vowed to herself that she wouldn't use that red lipstick again until he was home, when he would be able to turn his eyes to her and everything in that red stain on her lips would signal, *It's me. I'm still here. I've not changed. I'm still the woman you married. I'm your bride. We can get on with our lives now. I've missed you and I love you more than ever.*

Archie had already missed three Christmases, four of her birthdays and four of his own. He'd missed his own father's death from lung cancer and his mother's stroke. His brother still wrote to Tilly asking for news and she had had to reply with a heavy heart that there was none.

That Mary had sustained her faith was a mystery to Tilly. Is that why Archie was still missing? Had Tilly not prayed hard enough? Did God know, in his omnipotence, that Tilly had lost faith in him too, and had decided to reward only those who supplicated themselves to him? And if that were true, what kind of a God was that?

After her bath, Tilly stood at her bedroom window, her short brown hair wrapped in her threadbare towel like a turban. She shivered in her chenille dressing-gown, her bare feet cold on the floorboards. She moved the net curtain aside and looked down over Orwell Street and the Roosevelt nightclub. It was doing brisk business. A queue snaked all the way to Macleay Street and shadows gathered on the balcony, despite the weather, glamorous figures backlit by the low lights from the inside, the ends of their cigarettes bright little sparks in the darkness. Sculpted topiary pot plants in a neat row on the street side provided both a buffer for those at risk of tumbling over the edge and discreet places for illicit conversations and liaisons.

It seemed as full tonight as it had been in 1943 on the night it opened. Mary and Tilly had looked across at it from their eyrie, queues full of American troops enticed by the titular nod to their president and the opportunity to take Australian girls somewhere fancy and American. In the end, and despite widespread fears about the Japanese, the only foreign troops to invade Australia had been the Americans, with their smart uniforms and their silk stockings and their big smiles and polite manners and their bulging wallets. Tilly had had plenty of invitations from Americans to walk through that narrow door, but she'd declined every one. She let herself regret it sometimes, for a moment or two, when she realised how much she missed dancing and the musicians who seamlessly turned individual notes into jazz and swing tunes, and for the many lonely nights when she missed being held in someone's arms.

The last time she'd danced with a man she'd been a long way from home and a million miles away from the life she'd created with Archie. George Cooper had held her close in an Officers' Mess on a steamy night in Darwin back in February 1943. Tilly had tried not to think about it too much in the two-and-a-half years since. She had had far too much else to worry about without letting confusion and guilt have their own seats in the front row of her life.

Tilly still sported her towel turban when she joined Mary in the kitchen. A pot of tea was brewing, Mary had created a Scandinavian-style smorgasbord and the pork chops were sizzling on the stove.

'This looks delicious,' Tilly said hungrily.

'Tuck in,' Mary replied. 'I'll be a minute.' She sat at the table, her elbows propped, her chin in her hands and her eyes closed. At first glance, Tilly thought Mary was praying, but her hands weren't pressed together in silent repose. Her palms cupped her cheeks and her middle fingers were massaging tiny circles at the outside corners of her eyes.

'What on earth are you doing?' Tilly giggled.

Mary's eyelids fluttered open for a moment and then lowered again. 'I'm massaging away the wrinkles. I was so much younger when Bert left. He still thinks the twenty-six-year-old me is the one he'll find when he comes home, not this wrinkled old woman.' It wasn't just the passing of the years that had lined their faces and hollowed their cheeks. There had been too many sleepless nights and too much worry.

'Oh, Mary. Don't be ridiculous. Bert will still love you. Even if you look like a wrinkled-up old prune.'

Mary dropped her hands and laughed, the joy lighting up her face in a way that ridiculous finger massages never would. 'I'm just nervous. And excited. Aren't you, Tilly, at the thought that Archie will be home soon? Because I know he will.'

Tilly couldn't describe what she was feeling. Not to Mary. 'I'm nervous and excited. Of course I am.' She found a smile, more to cheer Mary than to reflect the state of her own heart.

'To the end of the war,' Mary said.

'Hear, hear. And to our husbands.'

They clinked their teacups against one another's.

Tilly sighed. 'I wish this was some kind of fancy French champagne. The kind they're probably drinking across the road right now.'

'I don't think anyone's had French champagne at all during the war. You'll have to make do with Great Western.'

'Then Great Western it shall have to be for Bert's welcome home party. Tell me everything. What do you have planned?' Tilly lifted her cup and wrapped her fingers around it. She'd needed to feel the warmth of it. She was so cold deep down that the bath on its own hadn't defrosted her. She blew across her milky brew, watching the waves in it.

'How did you know that's what I've been thinking about?'

'That and your wrinkles, obviously.' Tilly reached across the table and covered Mary's hand with hers. 'I know you, Mary Smith. Bert deserves to have the biggest party he's ever seen. As do you. I'll help you organise everything. I could ask my mother to make a cake or two. I'm sure she'd love to. We'll get some beer and sherry. What if we make a banner and string it over the fireplace so it's the first thing he sees when he comes home?'

Mary clapped her hands together and beamed. 'That would be marvellous! It could say *Welcome Home Bert* in huge letters.' Mary traced an arc in the air and formed the letters with an index finger.

'I don't think it'll matter one bit what the banner says. Bert won't see anything or anyone but you. You could be wearing a housecoat for all he's going to care.'

'A housecoat? Bite your tongue. I've already chosen my outfit. I'm going to wear my red dress. You know, the one with—'

'The white trim on the matching jacket?'

Mary nodded excitedly.

'Perfect.'

'I hope so,' Mary said. 'I hardly know what to think, Tilly.' Her voice grew quiet. 'It's as if I've been asleep for the longest time and I've woken up suddenly and the world has changed all around me and I can't keep up with its spinning.' Her eyes filled with exhausted tears. 'How have we managed to go on for so long? How have we survived it all?'

'All I know, dear Mary, is that we have.'

'And it's over for me and I feel so happy about that and I want you to feel this happiness I feel, Tilly. I'm wishing that for you more than anything.'

They held each other's gaze for the longest time.

'When Archie and I were first married,' Tilly said after a moment, 'we went to Luna Park. I hadn't been since it had opened in 1935 and Archie said it was about time. I'd thought it was a place for children, you see, but it was packed with people. Adults. Girls with soldiers on their arms, carrying prizes from the sideshow attractions. We had the most wonderful time, eating hot dogs and hot peanuts and forgetting about the war for just one night. Archie hadn't wanted to, but I dragged him to the Big Dipper and we crowded into that wooden carriage and off it went.' Tilly laughed at the memory. 'I had no idea what to expect. I'd seen it from across the harbour and it looked high and slightly scary, but being up close? It was so much bigger than I thought. When you're standing at the bottom of it with your ticket in your hand it seems as high as the flags fluttering on the top of the bridge. But Archie was with me and I didn't want him to think I was a chicken, so I tried not to scream.'

Mary listened intently, her smile familiar and comforting.

'And it's hard not to scream, I'm telling you, when the carriage crawls to the top and you can hear the mechanics underneath you whirring and catching and then you're almost at the top and you stop for just a moment and then, whoosh. You fly down into the dip and you've left your stomach on the other side and you're hanging on and trying not to scream and inside you're terrified but you can't show it because you have to be brave. But Archie was beside me, one arm about my shoulders, the other holding my hand. And I knew I'd be safe.' Tilly closed her eyes, afraid to tell the truth. 'And that's how I've felt ever since his last letter from Rabaul, Mary. I've been hanging on, trying not to scream every day. The difference is, Archie's not beside me, one arm about my shoulders, keeping me safe. I'm still trapped on that rollercoaster.'

Mary began to cry. 'I've prayed for you, too, Tilly. You'll get a telegram. I know you will.'

Chapter Seven

Tilly Galloway wore it as a badge of honour that she had been appointed the *Daily Herald*'s first official woman war correspondent, although, she thought begrudgingly, perhaps a badge of dishonour might have been more appropriate.

Because the truth of it was she had never left Australian soil. The by-lines on the stories she'd written during her one and only war correspondents' tour in February 1943 carried only the vaguest description 'Somewhere in Australia', for security reasons. And if she hadn't argued with Mr Sinclair until she was almost blue in the face, she might not even have been given permission to go.

That January, she'd heard from a colleague on the *Daily Telegraph*, whom she'd run into covering a shop fire in Elizabeth Street, that a women war correspondents' tour was being planned. A group of journalists from other newspapers and the ABC had been pressuring the army to allow them to cover the real war. They were tired of being restricted to covering the women's angle and stories from the home front. They'd been hounding the army since 1939 for permission to be sent overseas just like the male war correspondents— George Cooper, Damien Parer, George Johnston, Chester

Wilmot and Osmar White. These women were serious reporters, as determined as the men to tell the truth about the war, to report the reality of Australia's war effort, but the army had been fiercely opposed to the idea. They'd refused women reporters permission to accompany troops on manoeuvres or to be anywhere fighting men were. The excuses for the restriction had flown thick and fast: that women were natural gossips and would struggle to keep wartime secrets; that there wasn't enough separate accommodation for them; that it was too dangerous at the front.

As soon as Tilly heard on the grapevine that the tour had been approved, she'd marched upstairs to Mr Sinclair's office and insisted she be one of the party.

He'd looked up at her over the rims of his glasses and blustered, 'You want to go where, Tilly?'

'The war. Well, as close as I'm allowed to go.'

He'd almost spilt his tea all over the messy pile of copy on his desk.

'Whatever for?'

She'd held back the urge to stomp her feet in indignation at the ridiculousness of his question. Had he ever asked George Cooper why he'd wanted to cover the war? She'd enjoyed working for Mr Sinclair, and still admired him very much, but he was a relic, really, a man who'd been born in the previous century with ideas that sometimes reflected that, no matter how hard he tried.

Mr Sinclair slipped off his glasses, tugged a handkerchief from the pocket of his trousers and cleaned the lenses with gentle circles. 'Mothers, wives and sweethearts are desperate to know what their loved ones are doing, Tilly. How they're living. Women are the ones best suited to telling this dramatic side of our war effort, I believe. The woman's angle, Tilly. Only you ladies can do it justice.'

Tilly's mind whirred and spun. She was well aware she only had one chance to convince Mr Sinclair. She had to give him a story he wouldn't be able to resist.

'We are fighting for everything we hold dear, Mr Sinclair. Our very liberty. Our democracy. For the freedoms of enslaved people who are counting on us to be victorious so they may once again live in peace. We're fighting against nationalism and pure evil. Young Australians, both men and women, are sacrificing their lives every day for this great and just cause. Why wouldn't I want to cover such a story?'

It took Mr Sinclair a moment to collect himself. He whipped off his glasses and wiped his eyes. 'Damn you, Tilly Galloway,' he muttered. 'Write me some copy like that when you're away, won't you?'

She'd almost raced around his desk and kissed him.

It had been the first time Tilly had flown in a plane. She'd been thrilled at taking off, seeing Sydney's harbour from above for the first time, the wharves she'd run past as a child like fingers reaching into the water. The bays and small peninsulas looked astounding and beautiful, as if drawn freehand. Windows in waterside houses glittered in the sun like jewels as she looked down and, her war correspondent's uniform khaki and stiff, her portable typewriter in the hold, she felt as if she was finally going to be a real reporter.

Tilly and Denise Stapleton from *The Sun* were the youngest of all the women correspondents and they soaked up all they could from the doyennes of Australian women reporters. She'd had the great good fortune to share supper and an in-depth analysis of the state of the war with Elsie Jackson from the *Australian Women's Weekly*, Connie Robertson who was covering the tour for the *Sydney Morning Herald*, the *Age* and the ABC—she didn't know how that woman ever slept—and the glamorous Iris Dexter from *Woman* magazine. Tilly had always believed that her own perceptive and curious personality and George Cooper's advice had prepared her for this kind of reporting, but spending time with the other women on the tour was an education she had never forgotten. They were forthright and determined and Tilly came to understand that by hiding those aspects of her character she had done herself a disservice.

A peculiar kind of solidarity had developed between the women, even though they worked for rival publications and broadcasters. While they would have stepped over each other as easily as any man to get a scoop, they'd quickly come to realise that their strength lay in numbers and in the fact that the armed forces and the government wanted more women to sign up for war work. What better way to do that than to have women write inspiring stories about the work the country needed Australian women to do?

The four-week tour of army, air force and navy centres throughout New South Wales, Queensland and finally Darwin had been exhausting and exhilarating and the best four weeks of Tilly's life.

She had blossomed in the tropical heat like the verdant vegetation she saw everywhere. On the long and ear-splitting flights and over meals and bus rides, the correspondents had shared cigarettes and gossip about things that would never be in any of their publications. The stories about editors and male reporters and politicians and businessmen and criminals. Those with wandering hands and more; those who thought it perfectly acceptable to put conditions on promotions or scoops; or who had made threats. These women's secrets were powerful information and Tilly soaked it all in.

In Queensland, they'd landed in Cairns and she'd interviewed young women from the Australian Women's Army Service. Dubbed ack-ack girls, they guarded the coastline and adeptly handled anti-aircraft instruments. Their colleagues worked in plotting rooms mapping out targets hidden in the tropical clouds that hung heavy overhead.

There was one problem that had arisen early on in the trip. The women correspondents had been anticipating interviews with soldiers who were on leave or who were back in Australia for training or R and R, but they weren't allowed near any of them. This led to a general crankiness among the travelling troupe that couldn't be quelled by deliciously catered Country Women's Association lunches. The officer escorting them had informed them more than once that they should feel honoured they were able to do something male reporters could not.

'You are innately attuned to women's stories,' he'd said, unaware that condescension dripped from him like the sweat from his forehead in the dense Darwin humidity. 'It is only women reporters who have the sensitivity to the particular work of women on the home front and to the importance of their role in wartime.' Tilly hadn't been alone in feeling infuriated at those oft-repeated comments but the army and its officers were not for turning.

When the travelling troupe had arrived in the tropics, Tilly had tried to imagine what Archie had seen, smelt, heard.

The energy-sapping humidity, the constant symphony of dripping water, of condensation and rain, the undergrowth and the canopy, so lush and fecund it felt as if the leaves were growing as you held them between your fingers. And the rain, oh the rain. It flooded down like a widow's tears. In Bowen, they'd been stranded by rising floodwaters and the group had to fly out to Cairns in two Catalina bombers and a Tiger Moth before heading west to Darwin. It had been exhilarating.

Upon landing in Darwin, she'd turned her eyes to the sky and imagined what it had looked like to locals when it had been filled with Japanese planes, with vessels on fire lilting in the harbour, billowing black smoke in toxic clouds as they sank. She could only imagine the terror of those left behind after the evacuation and in the troops there to defend it. Then she turned slightly north-east, imagining the Arafura Sea and to the north-east, Rabaul, a place fifteen hundred miles away that she'd never heard of before the war. Now she knew them all: Rabaul and Morotai and Lae and Wau and Salamau and the Huon Peninsula and Milne Bay and Madang and Finschhafen and Shaggy Ridge and the Owen Stanley Ranges. She knew those places as well as she knew the streets of Millers Point. Her schoolgirl atlas had been her only connection to her husband and she had sat, tracing her fingers over the lines of longitude and latitude, whispering, 'Where are you, Archie?' until sleep overcame her.

When the women war correspondents arrived in Darwin, the garrison town was almost entirely populated by men—and men in uniform. Tilly believed the arrival of the women war correspondents had just about doubled the female population. On the streets, in the shops, at the base, there was barely a feminine voice to be heard nor a child to be seen. She remembered why: just after Pearl Harbor, most of the civilian women and children—two thousand of them—had begun to be evacuated, and by February 1942, just before the bombs had dropped on Darwin, they were all gone. By then, Darwin's military capabilities had dramatically expanded, with eight times more military personnel in the city than civilians.

When Tilly and her colleagues landed, they were silent in the face of the crippling damage from the Japanese air raids. No one said a word on the bus ride in, as they all seemed to take in how close the war had come. House roofs had been torn to shreds, the wooden beams exposed like broken ribs. Debris still lay in piles on the streets and as they passed the Darwin Post Office, Patricia Knox of the *Argus* in Melbourne, who was sitting next to Tilly, nudged her gently.

'There was a trench behind the post office. When the raid started, all the workers inside ran out to take shelter.' She paused and Tilly saw tears in her eyes. 'It took a direct hit. All ten of them were killed.'

Despite the heat, Tilly shivered. She thought of London and the Blitz, and realised that if what she had seen was only a small taste of what they had endured for so long, how unbearable it must have been for the English.

They weren't allowed to report anything of the damage, however. In one important respect the women war correspondents were given equal treatment to the men: they faced the same strict army censorship provisions. The Director-General of Public Relations for the army had absolute control over what any newspaper could publish and since he was the one ultimately authorising their presence there, they had little choice but to comply. However, there were grumbles that every single word they wrote for publication had to be approved by field censors. Even their private mail was subject to redaction and the scalpels. Nor were they allowed anywhere near a real soldier or a nurse or any other military type who hadn't been schooled in what to say to them. Military personnel were strictly forbidden from talking to the press without permission, and Tilly and the other reporters had no doubt they'd been forcibly and officially warned as such before the arrival of the travelling female press corps.

'The Americans and the English let women on the front line,' Connie Robertson had argued with their army escort. 'There are British Spitfire pilots stationed in Darwin. There's a story there, you know, about who those boys helping protect Australia are.' He simply smiled and shrugged his shoulders. The women were carefully shepherded, taken to the places and shown only what the army wanted them to see and had joked with each other that the only hardships they'd had to put up with were the mosquitoes and melting make-up in the heat. After a long three weeks of travelling, and limited opportunities for meeting anyone else bar members of the Country Women's Association, the travelling troupe had been taken in jeeps to RAAF Base Darwin and a party in their honour at the Airmen's Mess. It was a celebration to mark the end of their mission and after showers and many attempts to tame their hair made uncontrollable by the humidity, they wore their own clothes and smiles at the thought of jobs done as well as they were able to in the circumstances.

That was where Tilly had seen George Cooper for the first time in a year. Tilly and her colleagues had just walked into the mess when a raucous cheer arose from the bar. A wag called out in a booming baritone, 'The lady reporters have arrived!'

Tilly looked over.

It was George Cooper and he was on his feet, waving at her to join him, a look of pure disbelief on his face, a cigarette dangling from his lips. She could barely contain the thrill at the sight of him, and found herself firmly planting her feet on the wooden floorboards of the mess to stop herself from running over and throwing her arms around him. A familiar face and a friend, so far from home. What a wonderful surprise.

The newspapermen surrounding him burst into boisterous applause as the women headed over.

'Look out,' someone behind Tilly said, and it might have been Alice or Iris. 'I reckon they've got a head start on us.'

'Which is exactly where I plan to be as soon as possible,' said another, and the click of their heels on the floor was soon drowned out by the scratchy intro to a song blaring from a radio in the corner.

Tilly walked towards Cooper, his laughing smile a magnet.

He slowly took the cigarette from his mouth as he stared at her. A smile curved his lips and his blue eyes crinkled in the corners. 'What the hell are you doing in Darwin, Mrs Galloway?'

'Working.' Tilly beamed. 'Tell me something. You haven't caught anything from any damn mosquitoes, have you?'

'Bloody hell. I hope not.'

'Good. Then I can kiss you.'

He raised an eyebrow at her.

'Oh, come on, Cooper,' she laughed, punching him on the arm. 'I'm so thrilled to see a familiar face from home. I can't believe you're here.' She gripped his shoulders and pressed her lips to his left cheek. He smelt musty and sweaty and of beer.

'You need a haircut, Cooper. And a shave.' She screwed up her nose. 'Not to mention a shower.'

He held his chin and rubbed his thumb and forefinger over the stubble. 'Guilty as charged. We only arrived two hours ago. Cleaning up will be my second order of business, after this.' He upended his beer and wiped his mouth with the back of his hand. 'I think I need another. A shandy for you?'

Tilly scoffed. 'A real beer, if you don't mind, and make it as cold as you can possibly get it.'

Cooper caught the attention of the bartender and held up two fingers. Then he looked her over slowly, from her sandals to her crumpled floral dress, which had been crushed by notebooks filled with shorthand at the bottom of her suitcase for three weeks.

'So are you going to tell me what you're doing in Darwin, Mrs Galloway?' Cooper called out above the music.

'This is the final leg of the women war correspondents' tour.'

'The what now?'

'Didn't you get my letter announcing the big news? I've been covering the war.' She rolled her eyes and sighed. 'Well, the women's war on the home front. They won't let us anywhere near the troops. This is the closest we've got.' She glanced over to a crowd of men in uniform sitting around a table by the doorway. 'And they're American. It's so damn ridiculous. We haven't been let near a soldier. Or a pilot. This whole thing was organised to stop us complaining.'

'Doesn't seem to have worked then, does it?' Cooper grinned.

'Oh, it's been infuriating but what can we do? No one wants to derail the war effort or accidentally let anything slip. Things seem to be going well, finally, don't they? The Germans have surrendered in Stalingrad. The Brits are thrashing Rommel in Africa. And we've won Guadalcanal. I'm feeling more hopeful than I have in a long time. Aren't you?'

'Who wants to talk about the war? It's Saturday night. There's lukewarm beer. I might actually get a hot shower sometime soon and you're here. This is a bloody good day, I reckon.' He took a long drag on his cigarette and met her gaze.

'I want to talk about the war. Tell me everything. Where have you been and what did you see?'

'We've just come from Port Moresby.'

She reached across and laid her hand on his bare arm. His eyes flickered there for a moment. Cooper had been closer to Archie than she would ever be.

'Please, Cooper. Tell me.'

He upended his beer and stared into the frothy remains. 'You've still not heard anything?'

Tilly shook her head. 'Not a word.' And loss and grief and pain roiled inside her again, making her feel seasick. She gripped harder.

Cooper met her searching gaze. 'New Guinea is the greenest place on earth.' He stared off into the distance, lost in thought for a moment. 'Even the water looks green. It's lush and thick and undulating with huge tall trees and ferns and plants, mangrove swamps and tropical rain forests. It's muddy and the humidity is so thick you imagine you could slice it.'

Tilly closed her eyes and saw Archie in that peaceful and beautiful place, and imagined he might struggle with Sydney's winters after living in such warmth for so much time. And she remembered the jumpers she'd knitted for him, one for each winter he'd been away, and thought how he'd laugh when he came home at the idea of needing one again.

Cooper's glass hit the bar with a thud. 'There must be birds but I didn't hear them.' His eyes were glassy, his lips pulled tight. 'Our troops are shut in by that godforsaken jungle. The poor bastards have to hack their way through it with machetes to create supply lines and it's damn slow and excruciating work in that heat. That lush jungle? Perfect for hiding snipers.'

Cooper paused and then whispered hoarsely, 'All that fucking rain.' His eyes darted to Tilly's, a question in them. Was he wondering if she was shocked by his language—no wharfie's daughter could be—or was he hesitating out of concern about how she would react to the truth?

'They're wet all the time and the skin peels off their feet in thick clumps. The mosquitoes that share their malaria

with you are as big as the bats you see flying over Sydney.'
He shakily lit another cigarette. 'So that's what you've missed
out on, Mrs Galloway. Dragging your portable typewriter
into the middle of the jungle to sit on a tree stump and bat
away the mosquitoes while writing about our brave troops
as the sweat drips from your forehead and you're looking for
the nearest latrine because by god you've got the trots from
some bloody thing or other, whether it's the bully beef or
the water you're warned not to drink or some godforsaken
tropical disease.'

Tilly felt a chill. George Cooper made cynicism an art
form but this was something more. Bitterness dripped from
his every word and she couldn't help but feel it was aimed
somehow at her and her questions. Was he trying to teach
her a lesson that she should be careful what she wished for?
She felt as if she'd been chastised and it was hurtful and
discomforting coming from someone she'd considered a
colleague and a mentor. And a friend. Why was he trying to
put her back in her place? She had asked for the truth and
he'd delivered it to her with cutting words that felt like a
slap in the face.

Did he know he'd just ripped open her heart and
shattered every wish she'd had for Archie and his captivity?
That he might bear it well enough to come home to her?

'I can't write the truth for the paper, Mrs Galloway, but
I'm not going to keep it from you. It's a shithole. And look
around. We get to leave it. We write some bullshit about
bravery and courage and the resolve of our diggers and send
it off to the censors who hack out any hint of what it's really
like and people at home are none the wiser about what's
really going on. And those poor bloody blokes, kids really,

getting by on bully beef and biscuits and rice, are still there.' He raised his beer and clinked it hard against Tilly's before she could react and frothy liquid spilled out of the glass and down the front of her dress.

'Bloody hell,' Cooper groaned. 'Bartender. A cloth.'

Tilly looked down at the damp stain across her breasts and felt the wet coolness soaking through her bra to her skin. It was her only frock and now it would smell like stale beer. Anger flared and became an unspoken rage that rampaged inside her, sending her pulse thudding in her ears. She opened her mouth to speak but the words choked her.

Archie was still there.

Cooper had articulated her rage so succinctly it was as if he was in her head. How did he know? Why did he know that about her?

Tilly was still, a cigarette in one hand and her other wet with beer. Cooper held a clean cloth towards her and she met his gaze. Slowly, he came closer and pressed the cloth against the wet fabric of her cotton dress. The gentle pressure of his fingers pressing into her flesh, despite the cotton in between, made every nerve tingle and she imagined it to be a caress on her body and she closed her eyes and breathed in deep, trying to savour that long-forgotten feeling of a man's hand on her, of an urgent kiss on her mouth, of desire flaring and crashing over her.

It had been so long.

Cooper's eyes met hers and lingered there, soft and enquiring, before lowering to her mouth.

Archie was still there.

And Cooper was right here.

She watched his hand pressing into her and saw Cooper, not Archie, and while that thought might once have scared her, she was beyond that. The past was so far away and the future was unknowable. All she had was that moment to feel alive.

By the wireless in the corner, couples had begun to dance and Tilly gave in to the need for someone's body pressed against hers. She took the cloth, set it on the bar and took Cooper's hand.

'Dance with me, George Cooper.'

'Dance with you?'

'Is your dance card full or something?' She tasted beer in her mouth and her pulse thudded at her temple.

Cooper's smile faltered and was replaced with something far more serious. He held out his other hand and Tilly rested her pale fingers there. Sixteen steps and they were facing each other in the middle of the crowd. He stepped into her, slipped an arm around her waist and pulled her in close. She held on to his shoulder with her left hand and looked up into his eyes.

She didn't recognise the song that was blaring from the wireless but she recognised the look on his face. She'd seen it from other men, from her husband, but never from Cooper. His eyes flickered from her mouth to her eyes and then back to her mouth and she bit her lip. She felt his shoulders draw up as he inhaled deep and long and she knew in that moment she had a decision to make. If she held his gaze, he was going to kiss her. There was nothing surer.

Was it the beer or Darwin or the war or Cooper or a combination of all of them wrapped up in her longing and loneliness?

She paused and at the moment she felt his breath on her lips, she turned and rested her head on his chest. She could not give in to this. Not now. She listened to his heart beat instead of the song and held on for dear life.

Chapter Eight

'Excuse me. Pardon me. *Daily Herald*. Coming through.'

Tilly elbowed her way through a Sunday sea of trilbys and homburgs and porkpies and flat caps; of elaborate and decoratively curled French rolls and freshly painted red lips; of worn but clean trousers; of greasy overalls and schoolboy pants and ribboned ponytails. The air was thick with cigarette smoke, special occasion perfume and the scrubbed, soapy scent of young children.

She checked her watch. Two forty-five. She'd just hopped off the tram on New South Head Road before Elanora Street and was following the curve of Rose Bay to the waterfront and the wharf. She cut through Lyne Park, which was so crowded with people that it was impossible to make out exactly where the Anzac Memorial was, quickened her pace and sharpened her elbows.

The Allies had declared victory in the Pacific four weeks earlier and diggers had been steadily returning from theatres of war each week to heartfelt celebrations in every home, every street, every town and every city in the country.

And still no word of Archie or any of the other Lark Force boys or the Rabaul civilians.

In years past, the flying boats that were about to land in the choppy waters off Sydney Harbour had carried first class mail all the way from London. During the war, they had taken flight, filled with ammunition bound for the battlefront. Now, they were carrying the most precious cargo imaginable: the first one hundred and thirty prisoners of war who'd been liberated from the Japanese. Bert Smith, unfortunately, wasn't one of them. Mary had had further word that her husband was still being treated for malaria in a Singapore army hospital and she had taken the news with the same sense of optimism she had displayed during his entire captivity. He was alive and he was well, and the letter that had just arrived this week, written in his own hand that made her weep, had reassured her. His time would come, he said, as soon as he was well enough to make the journey home.

The whole country had been avidly following the news in the papers that four days before, nine Catalina flying boats had left Singapore filled with men. They'd stopped in Darwin to refuel and four days and so many years later, the diggers were about to arrive home.

Tilly moved around people, twisted herself sideways and bobbed under tall men waving their hands, inching closer and closer to the gates of Rose Bay Airport.

'Excuse me. *Daily Herald.*' She was going to need the crowds to part like the Red Sea if she was ever going to get any closer to the gates.

'Tilly!'

At Tilly's left shoulder stood Denise Stapleton from *The Sun*.

They threw their arms as wide as they could and embraced.

'How are you, Denise?'

'I'm very well indeed,' she replied. 'How about you?' She leant close to ask quietly, 'Any news about Archie?'

Tilly shook her head and bit her lower lip to stop it wobbling.

'You're probably sick and tired of being asked, but I couldn't not.'

'I know. And I appreciate it, I really do.'

'I don't think I've seen you since Leeton when we interviewed the Land Army girls.'

Tilly smiled at the happy memory. 'Only the tastiest apples I've ever eaten. Picking them fresh off the tree made so much difference, didn't it?'

When they'd returned to Sydney after their war correspondents' tour up north in 1943, they'd continued to report on the war at home, still barred by the army from doing anything else. Whether it was the work of the Land Army girls, or women in munitions factories all over Sydney who worked on massive production lines making bullets and shell casings, or stories about nurses and knitting circles, if it involved women and the war, the women war correspondents were assigned those stories.

And while Tilly had found it fascinating that women were doing all sorts of jobs they'd never been allowed to do before—and in some cases being paid the same as men—the irony wasn't lost on her that she still wasn't allowed to do the same job that men on the paper were doing.

When Tilly had pushed Mr Sinclair to be allowed to cover stories that didn't only involve a feminine angle on the war, he'd stared at her as if she'd asked to be sent to the moon.

'Wasn't Darwin enough?' he'd responded, exasperated.

'Not in the slightest.'

'You can't cover the real war, Tilly. We've got the blokes doing that. Cooper and Farris and that pain in the arse Dalton who still won't account for that week he went missing in Palestine. They can embed with the troops, see battles firsthand and really get a feel for what a soldier's life is like. You couldn't bunk in with the men, for god's sake. You know the army won't let you anywhere near a fighting man. Your job is to cover the human interest angles. How the ladies back home are coping. The home front. You know, how we need more women to sign up for the auxiliary forces and munitions work, that sort of thing. I've got enough on my mind keeping track of the boys without worrying about you getting into trouble in a war zone.'

She had continued to push, arguing with Mr Sinclair that she could be sent overseas as a special war correspondent to cover the real and incredibly dangerous work of Australian nurses, and again he'd knocked her back.

'But Mr Sinclair,' she'd argued. 'Other women have done it. Lorraine Stumm went to Rabaul, you know. General MacArthur invited her himself. And Elsie Jackson from *The Australian Women's Weekly* has been overseas, too.'

Rabaul. That's where Tilly really wanted to go. If she was able to set foot on the same soil as where Archie had last been seen, she might be able to find the real story of what had happened to him. Wasn't that a possibility?

But Mr Sinclair had scoffed. 'Stumm only got there because of the Americans. And Jackson's the bloody editor! The Australians don't want women anywhere near the front and they're the people I have to deal with. Give it up, Tilly. There are plenty of stories right here in Sydney.'

As it had turned out, Tilly's fight was for naught. After Stumm's and Jackson's trips, the army had withdrawn all its accreditations for women war correspondents to enter operational areas. She was to be stuck reporting on gung-ho gals in munitions factories and all the women back home who were making do and mending.

'What do you think?' Denise asked Tilly, glancing over each shoulder to survey the people crowded onto the Rose Bay foreshore. 'Forty thousand people?'

'I'd say fifty, at least,' Tilly replied.

They slowly inched forwards.

'Trouble is,' Denise said, 'if I tell my editor the *Daily Herald*'s running with fifty thousand, he'll insist *The Sun* run with sixty.'

'Mine will be exactly the same,' Tilly conceded with a laugh.

'Let's ask the navy's press officer. He'll be here somewhere with whichever colonel is greeting the diggers.'

'It's Major General Eric Plant, I believe.'

Denise elbowed Tilly good-naturedly in the arm. 'Oh, who cares any more? We won't have to do the bidding of those men in uniform much longer, will we? We'll be back to doing the bidding of men in plain old cheap suits bought from Foy's.' Denise winked. 'You doing the families?'

Tilly sighed. 'All the happy reunions. The colour. The women's angle.'

'Consider yourself lucky, Galloway. I'm doing frocks and hats. Oh, look. I spot a broad-brimmed white hat with a net veil. I'll see you. A coffee soon?'

'Definitely.'

Denise waved and disappeared into the crowd.

Tilly tried to move forward but came to an impasse.

'Sorry, pet. There doesn't seem to be much room to move.' An old man looked back at Tilly over his hunched shoulder. He was hemmed in on both sides by office girls waving white handkerchiefs to every seagull flying and squawking overhead. His rheumy eyes sparkled in the September sunshine and the skin folds under his chin wobbled as he spoke. 'My grandson's coming home today.' He clutched a handkerchief in his hand. His knuckles were misshapen and swollen, his fingers crooked. When he dabbed his eyes, Tilly spotted a set of initials embroidered at one corner: HC. 'More than three years he's been gone, our John.'

Tilly pulled her notebook and pencil from the pocket of her jacket and extended her free hand. They shook, almost pressed up against each other in the crush. 'Tilly Galloway, the *Daily Herald*. How long's he been gone, sir?'

'February 1942. Since Singapore fell.'

Tilly didn't need to write down that date. 'So he's in the 8th Division.'

The man nodded. 'The Lost 8th.'

'One of General Bennett's boys.'

The old man pulled his lips tight. 'Bennett. Yes. That bloke who told our troops to stay put at the same time he was on a boat out of Singapore. Our boy's been a prisoner of war for three-and-a-half years because of that ... that man.'

Tilly never let down her guard when she was reporting. She had learnt to remain impartial, to ask questions and then listen, to not be scared of offending or upsetting. Some days that was harder than others.

'What's your son's name, sir?'

'He's my grandson. Casey.' The man's voice faltered, almost broke. 'Private John William Casey. We've raised him, me and my wife, since our daughter passed in '36.'

Tilly resisted the urge to pat him on the shoulder, to provide him some comfort. Everyone in Australia needed comforting of one kind or another these days; to be reassured that their loved ones were alive, that they were safe, that they would be the same men they were when they went off to war.

'You must be so proud of him.'

'Too right. Bloody proud.'

Tilly wrote in shorthand: *tears of joy at the prospect of a happy reunion between grandfather and grandson.*

'And your name? So I can put it in the paper? I'd like to tell everyone in Sydney how happy you are to see your John home.'

'The name's Herbert Casey.'

'And your suburb, Mr Casey?'

'Newtown.'

Tilly's pencil skimmed over her page. 'And Mrs Casey? Is she here?' Tilly wondered where her photographer was. She was due to meet him but he was nowhere to be seen in the crush.

'She's at home baking a sponge cake. Just for John. He can eat the whole thing, have it all to himself, that's what she said. She saved up weeks' worth of butter rations specially. She wanted to wait at home, not come down here. You know.'

Tilly's pencil hovered over her notebook. 'What if I say she's preparing a special party at home? That's why she couldn't be here. Would that be all right?'

Mr Casey nodded and started to speak but his words were lost as the crowd around them erupted in a roar. Tilly was squeezed in a surge of hats and sharp elbows and bodies. She gripped her pencil tight in her fist.

'Look! Look!' A woman's voice was shrill in Tilly's ear.

'Can you see them?' A man with a wiry grey moustache and round silver glasses looked skyward, his hand flat to shade his eyes. 'It's one of them Catalinas!'

Tilly shoved forward through a chorus of cheers and hollering and made a bolt for the gate to the flying boat base and then turned her eyes to look back at the crowd. She would need to remember it all to describe it when she was sitting behind her typewriter. People were packed, shoulder to shoulder, more bare legs than she could count dangled over the lip of the stone wall at the harbour's edge, rows and rows and rows of people standing behind like an enormous choir. Young men were aloft, as if they might be sitting on someone's shoulders, and the buzz of anticipation and excitement sparked in the air like electricity. Fifty thousand chins lifted. Fifty thousand breaths were held, and one hundred thousand eyes squinted towards the sky, waiting to get the first glimpse of the Catalinas.

The flying boat's long flat wings, each bearing two propellers, slowly came into more distinct view, a low white bird against the blue of the water and the grey-green of Georges Head on the other side of the harbour and then there was a splash of foam and it landed like a tremendous gull.

Fifty thousand joyous voices behind her lifted in celebration. Waving handkerchiefs looked like a million white dancing butterflies.

Tilly ducked and bobbed towards the airport's main gate. The five destinations marked on it—Brisbane, Townsville, Darwin, Singapore and London—were now announcing arrivals instead. Beyond it, dignitaries and officials were milling, kissing cheeks and shaking hands, waving towards the plane in the harbour.

'Tilly Galloway,' she said quickly to the soldier guarding the gate to the wharf. '*Daily Herald.*'

Her rush was not his. He looked her over.

Behind the guard, she spotted her photographer, Peter Burton, freely snapping, his camera aimed out at the Catalina, which was bobbing now. She rummaged in her pocket and thrust her war correspondent licence as close to his eyes as her patience allowed. 'Correspondent Tilly Galloway from the *Daily Herald*. My editor assigned me to cover the return of the POWs. It would be very useful if I could get down there on the pontoon to meet them.'

He studied her licence. 'No reporters allowed down there, Mrs ... Galloway. Only photographers. Out of respect for the men.'

'C'mon, digger,' she implored. 'I'm from the *Daily Herald*. All I want is to ask our heroes if they're glad to be home. How much they've missed their sweethearts. What they'd like to eat as their first meal. If they had a good flight from Singapore, that kind of thing.'

From the wharf, engines throbbed and three barges pulled away from the dock and headed out towards the Catalina in a convoy.

'Dignitaries and photographers only.' The soldier held up a hand.

'Go back up to New South Head Road,' the guard told her. 'The buses will be taking the boys to the 113th Australian General Hospital at Concord. Yaralla. That's where they're meeting their families. You'll get your story there.'

Her story. The women's angle. The feminine touch. She ground her teeth in fresh frustration. 'Talk to the wives,' Sinclair had said. 'Find out how long they've been waiting for their husbands to come home. Ask them what they'll be cooking for that first meal. Meatloaf or pork chops? Have they sewn up a special frock for the welcome home? Describe the dresses and the hats and the colour of their lipstick. Ask the young boys if they're sorry they missed out on going to war. Ask how many kids were born while the husbands were away. Colour, Tilly, colour. The boys upstairs will talk to the diggers and the generals. You do the wives and families.'

She waited among the crowd while the barges motored towards that first Catalina, while they were loaded with their precious cargo. When, ten minutes later, the boats returned to the wharf, a roar went up around her that was almost deafening.

Her pencil flew over the next page in her notebook.

Fourteen heroes on each barge were met with rousing cheers. From Changi to the calm peaceful waters of Rose Bay. Clean khaki uniforms. Smiling healthy faces. Met by Major General EC Plant and Colonel H Walker.

A sailor threw a rope and lashed it around one of the wharf posts and a minute later the first soldiers set foot back on Australian soil.

Tilly scribbled in her notebook. *How impressed they must be with this welcome.*

She looked to the gangplank as the first former POWs stepped off onto the wharf.

Almost four years in Japanese captivity. Against all odds, they look healthy. Fresh new uniforms. Too big for them. Smiling. Eyes bright, Clean-shaven. Tanned. Strode with strength and purpose. Greeted by hearty handshakes and waves.

Peter was staring down the lens of his camera. He was right there on the gangplank. Seeing up close what she should be seeing for herself.

After handshakes and the official welcome, the soldiers were ushered into the terminal building on the base. The crowd around Tilly was expectant, jittery.

'I think that was Robert. Did you see him, Mum?' a woman called.

'I don't know, love. I think so.'

Peter headed out of the gate and greeted her with a wave. 'Tilly. Fancy meeting you here.'

'Did you get your shots, Pete?'

He grinned. 'Don't I always?'

'Listen, the diggers' families are waiting at Concord. We should head over there. If we can get through the traffic. New South Head Road is blocked with people.'

'All in hand.' Peter reached into the pocket of his trousers and jangled his car keys.

It was an hour before the returned prisoners of war and the group of dignitaries left Rose Bay. They boarded a red-and-cream double-decker bus sporting a calico banner draped across the top of it which read *8 Div. AIF PRISONERS OF WAR FROM SINGAPORE*.

Police cars led the procession and Peter nudged his car into the cavalcade right behind the bus. The huge crowds made the journey very slow going, which gave Peter every opportunity to grip the steering wheel with his knees and shoot out the car window. As the conga line crawled up along New South Head Road, he snapped the surging crowd, seeing the detail others didn't: a sobbing wife, a beaming father, a mother and siblings with a sign held aloft saying *Welcome home boys.*

Police on foot along the route warned onlookers to keep out of the line of traffic but their warnings to the assembled crowds were of little use as the buses inched past Rose Bay's crowded footpaths. In Kings Cross, people showered the buses with confetti and torn paper from the flats looking over Darlinghurst Road and children waved little paper Union Jacks. Cars that had been forced to pull over because of the surging crowds tooted their horns in celebration not annoyance. As the convoy approached the city, throngs of people lined Queens Square and Macquarie Street. At Martin Place, Tilly heard someone shout, 'Good on you, lads.' Then 'Well done,' and 'Glad you're back'.

From the buses, the bronzed diggers waved new handkerchiefs through the open windows. On Parramatta Road, houses were decorated with Union Jacks, children waved excitedly from front yards and people of all ages waited on their verandahs to pay tribute to the men from Singapore. Tilly heard them all say it, the words falling from in the air around her like the torn paper had on VP Day: 'They're home.' She wrote all the details in her notebook, already working on the story in her head, what the lead sentence would be and the details she would include for colour.

At Concord, the returned soldiers were welcomed by hospital staff and members of the Red Cross before they were engulfed in the embraces of their loved ones. Watching on, Tilly's mind was in a thousand places as she wrote everything down. In one corner of the large reception room, a young soldier was swept up in the arms of four women, who Tilly took to be his three sisters and his mother. Every single member of the family began to sob. An older soldier announced to anyone who would listen that he'd served in both wars but his proudest moment was being able to hold his three-year-old granddaughter for the first time. His wife had rushed over to Tilly and instructed, 'Write that down and put that in the paper, won't you, that my husband is home?'

Wherever Tilly looked, there was another joyous reunion and fresh tears. She went from group to group, asking for names and rank and suburbs for her story. Peter snapped away at her side.

It wasn't long before a nurse announced that the men needed their rest. 'We expect they'll all be ready to go home tomorrow or the next day,' she said. 'And be assured we'll be in contact with families.'

As the soldiers filed out with last waves, there was another burst of applause and then quiet sobs, peppered with excited conversations about what would be prepared for dinner when Clarrie came home or what Francis would think of the new curtains in the living room or how much taller young Dudley had grown since his uncle had been away.

Tilly tucked her notebook and her pencil into her handbag and followed Peter back to the car parked by the sisters' quarters off the main entrance. Above them, the Union Jack, the Red Cross and the Australian flag fluttered in the mild September breeze.

'You got everything you need?' Peter asked Tilly as he started the car.

She nodded stiffly and they drove back to the office.

When Tilly woke the next morning, she singed her toast, drank her tea so fast that she burnt her tongue and hurried out the door. She flew down the stairs and along the footpath to the newsagent on Macleay Street and flipped open the newspaper to see her story. It was still a thrill. Peter's photographs had perfectly captured the joy Tilly had seen in the faces of those welcoming their boys home. How could she have possibly conveyed to them how lucky they were? She read each paragraph of her story and at the end, there was a teaser to page six: 'Full list of returned troops'. She flicked hurriedly to the page to see all the names of those who'd flown in the day before on the Catalinas. Each and every one of the men was from the AIF's 8th Division, who had all been prisoners of war since Singapore had fallen in February 1942.

A middle-aged man with a newspaper open in his hands bumped into Tilly and quickly apologised, proffering the paper to her as if to explain. 'Sorry, love. It's my nephew. His name's right here in the paper. He's home.'

'Congratulations,' Tilly said and a great wave of grief threatened to knock her off her feet. 'You must be over the moon.'

'I am. Most definitely. I'm taking this home to show the wife. Have a good day.'

Tilly knew that readers all over Sydney would be poring over that same list to study each name, from NX76242, COLLIS. Captain. CH, to SX10422, DOWNER. Gunner. AR.

A pain in Tilly's chest cut hard and fast. Her grief was like a knife: sometimes a stab, other times a slash.

She closed the paper and lifted her gaze to the distance. 'Perhaps tomorrow,' she murmured to herself and tried not to be overcome by the terror that with every passing day there was less and less hope.

Chapter Nine

Tilly's fingers hovered over the stiff keys of her typewriter. She'd lost the thread of her sentence and was trying to snatch it back but it had gone. It had been happening more and more lately, this forgetfulness. The mystery of not knowing about Archie seemed to be eating her up from the inside, feeding on her waking hours as well as her sleeping ones, gnawing away at her capacity to take one step and then another. Some days, even when the sky was clear and blue and warm, she felt as if she existed in a Sydney winter fog.

She sat back, lit a cigarette and found a distraction in the windows overlooking Pitt Street. The rain had begun just after she'd arrived at work and hadn't let up, a great bucketing spring downpour that had filled gutters in a flash, flooded city street corners and rendered umbrellas useless. The windows' dirty faces were streaked, like faces with running mascara.

Tilly felt alone and increasingly isolated from all the celebrations happening around her. She hadn't had her happy reunion or miraculous story of survival, nor could she think about funerals and memorials. Mary's news about Bert's imminent return had created a perceptible distance between the two friends. Neither had acknowledged it, of course, but it was in every conversation and look they exchanged. There was a lightness to Mary now that made Tilly grieve even more for her own circumstances. And worst of all, she could not give voice to her envy, her sadness, her grief, because her friend was so happy. How selfish was it to bring Mary back down with her, to that dark place, when Mary had just been freed from her captivity.

Tilly dropped her head into her hands and tried to breathe. Her world was so close to being unbearable she didn't know how she could hang on for one more day.

The creeping loneliness was what hurt the most. She was inside her own head most of the time and the thoughts whirring around in it were things she could never say to anyone. A woman who worked with words was censoring herself with every sentence, every conversation and every interaction with the people around her. She had lied for years, saying, 'Yes, I'm fine, thank you. No news as yet but I'm keeping up hope. His last letter said the Japanese were treating him well so I expect he'll come back with a suntan. No, I'm not worried. Archie is strong and courageous.'

Who needed a censor's pen when one could so easily censor oneself?

Tilly had been away from the newsroom reporting on the closure of the Bathurst Arms Factory. It had supplied machine guns, Bren lights and Vickers, during the war but it had just been announced that it would be closing by the end of 1945. The one hundred and four women who'd gone to work there every day had been given a week's notice that they were now redundant. Men were employed there too but they were being kept on and would be gradually let go by the end of the year.

Tilly had arranged with the authorities to be there in the factory when the women were told they were being discharged. They'd been called together in the lunch room and when it had sunk in, they'd gathered around the piano and sung 'Pack Up Your Troubles' and cried and hugged each other.

There was a rumour that the factory might soon be transformed from wartime production to making peacetime consumer goods—refrigerators, handcuffs and golf club heads—which caused a great deal of laughter and questions from the women about how many golf heads Australia would ever need, but that gossip lasted as long as the plates of sandwiches. By the end of the next week, every woman there would be clocking off for the final time, released into a world that had changed for them forever. They hadn't said it but Tilly recognised that particular combination of joy and sadness in their forlorn smiles and their tears because she was feeling it, too. These women had had a taste of independence, of the freedom of their own pay packet and of the kind of camaraderie that comes with growing to know the people you work alongside. They'd shared cakes on birthdays, contributed a knitted blanket or a hat or booties (in yellow to play it safe) to layettes for the impending arrival of a child. They'd come together for birthdays and hastily arranged weddings to soldiers who were unexpectedly on leave for just a week, and yes, they'd grieved for each other at funerals, too. What would all those women do now for work and for money and for friends?

Tilly read the slug line she'd typed at the top of her page, the few words that gave an editor an idea of the story.

Bathurst munitions plant to close.

It was crisp. To the point. George Cooper would have approved of that economy. But reading it over, she realised it only told part of the story. She lifted her fingers to the keys and typed.

Women no longer needed.

She flicked the carriage return lever to a fresh line.

Women free to return home to domestic life.

And then, another line.

Women now unemployed in Bathurst.

Tilly yanked out the copy paper and screwed it up into a ball.

'Tilly!' Dear Agatha walked towards her, her face white. 'Take a look at this.' It was that afternoon's *Sun*, which had just hit the newsstands. The rival paper often got the scoop on stories if they happened late overnight or early morning, after the *Daily Herald* had already gone to press. 'I can't believe it, can you?' She poked page three and before Tilly could make any sense of the story, Dear Agatha read the headline out loud.

'"Massacre of Nurses on Banka Beach."'

'Which nurses?' From her desk across the room, Kitty Darling lifted her head. Her red lipstick was perfectly applied on her cupid's bow mouth, which was pinched together at hearing the news. She stood and walked over to Tilly's desk.

'From the *Vyner Brooke*,' Tilly said. Tilly, Dear Agatha and Kitty leant in close to read the story. Tilly's pulse began to race as she absorbed the harrowing details. 'It's been kept secret all this time,' she whispered, hardly able to believe it herself. 'The nurses who survived the sinking in February '42 were shot on Banka beach.'

Dear Agatha gasped. 'I thought the survivors were found in South Sumatra? It was in the paper last week.'

'Were they?' There had been so much bad news that Tilly had to work hard to remember the good.

'"Twenty of them were shot by the Japanese",' Kitty read out loud. 'The Japanese lined them up on the beach and shot them all. One survived. Sister Vivian Bullwinkel. And then she was captured too. Everyone's kept it secret until now. Her story has only been revealed because the war is over. She was told that if word got out that she'd survived, she'd be executed too. "Of the fifty-three AIF nurses rescued from the *Vyner Brooke*, twenty-one were murdered on the beach and eight others died in the prison camps."'

'That is just dreadful,' Tilly whispered.

'"It's been one of the most carefully guarded secrets of the prison camps,"' Kitty continued. '"The cold-blooded murder of helpless, stranded girls, who had already given themselves up, seemed like …"' She stopped, unable to continue and went back to her desk. Dear Agatha seemed unable to move.

Tilly squeezed her eyes closed.

If the Japanese could kill nurses in cold blood, what might they have done to Archie? Was it too much to ask to just want him home?

Chapter Ten

'Colour! Colour! Colour! That's what I'm expecting now the war is over, Mrs Galloway. If I never see khaki again in my life it won't be too soon.'

Tilly glanced around the long and narrow dress shop on Pitt Street, situated on the ground floor of a sandstone building filled with bustling offices upstairs, and wondered for the tenth time why on earth was she here instead of Kitty Darling. That had been the exact question she'd asked the women's editor Mrs Freeman that very morning when she'd been assigned the story.

'She has a stomach flu, Tilly, and I need someone to fill in.'

Tilly had never worked under the direction of Mrs Freeman, nor written stories for the women's pages, and wasn't about to start. Tilly belonged in general news. Serious news. Kitty Darling and Dear Agatha and Vera were the women's pages reporters and Tilly knew she had to stand her ground, because one story would lead to another and then another and her newspaper career would come grinding to a halt in a miasma of charity lunches and fashion parades.

She'd girded her loins. 'While I have sympathy for Kitty, Mrs Freeman, I don't believe it's my role to cover fashion for the newspaper.'

Mrs Freeman's petite frame had been almost lost behind her enormous oak desk but Tilly couldn't miss the intent of her stare over the top of her typewriter. 'Mrs Galloway, you are a reporter, are you not?'

'Yes.' Tilly sensed where this was going and immediately began formulating a line of defence in her head.

'And being a reporter involves reporting on newsworthy events, does it not?'

'Of course,' Tilly had replied, suddenly wondering if Mrs Freeman had been a lawyer in a past career. 'I just don't happen to believe that this is a newsworthy event.'

Mrs Freeman had slumped behind her desk, her shoulders lowered in what suddenly looked like defeat.

'Tilly. I can't say I disagree with you. But I need help at the moment and you're all I've got. I've been asking and asking for more staff, as you may well remember from your years working for Rex, so we can improve our coverage and do more important stories. The *Weekly*'s doing it so I can't see why we can't. But every single extra pound has gone to sending the men overseas to cover the war. So, please, humour me just this once? I'll owe you.'

The dress shop proprietress, Mrs Delia Swanston, looked Tilly over. 'Can I tempt you with something while you're here, Mrs Galloway? I have a delightful shirt-style dress in navy and white stripes with a buttoned waist that would suit you. I may have your size. And it's a bargain, I might add. Only twenty-nine shillings eleven pence. With thirty coupons.'

'Thank you, but no. I'm not here to purchase anything, Mrs Swanston. It's strictly reporting duty for me today.' Tilly glanced around the shop and found herself agreeing with Mrs Swanston about the lack of colour. The items did seem rather wan: pale yellows and pinks and baby blues. Winter frocks on the sale rack in the back of the store were in drab navy and maroon crepe, and tweed suits featured patterns of brown and white, and light and dark blue.

Mrs Swanston's own jacket and skirt were a royal purple and her shirt the whitest of white silk. An oval diamante brooch that shone like real diamonds was pinned to her lapel and her shoes were black velvet courts. A measuring tape hung from her neck like a doctor's stethoscope and a pin cushion at her left wrist was studded with pins, as if a small echidna had fastened itself to her wristwatch. Having failed in her first attempt to sell a new frock to Tilly, she was clearly making no effort to hide her scrupulous inspection of Tilly's outfit.

Tilly's mother had told Tilly the green-and-white tweed fabric of her suit matched her pale skin and her brown hair. Elsie had always believed there to be a hint of auburn in her first-born's hair, but Tilly had never seen it. 'That's the Irish coming out in you,' Elsie had said proudly, having lost the red in her own hair to white-grey decades before.

Tilly's mother had expertly whipped the fabric into a two-piece skirt suit that had served Tilly well during the war. But at that moment, she looked at it through Mrs Swanston's eyes. The jacket hung loose now and there was a small ink stain at approximately the left thigh area of her skirt, which Tilly had convinced herself could only be seen upon very close inspection. The round necked fine knit she wore underneath the jacket had been white once but now, no matter how determinedly Tilly soaked it in Lux soap flakes, had transformed into the colour of wartime tea. Everything Tilly owned was old, worn, patched. She had grown out of the habit of desiring new things, believing it to be frivolous and wasteful. She had absorbed the make-do-and-mend ethos of the war, which encouraged women to get the last possible ounce of wear out of clothes and household items. Women had become obsessed with preserving their garments, learning to darn and patch, and changing out of work clothes the minute they walked in the door to preserve them as long as possible. Women had become scrubbers, menders, darners, knitters and purveyors of methods to remove grease stains with an iron and blotting paper and, most seriously, to fight the war against the moth menace. Once each month, women were advised to beat, brush and shake out their clothes, particularly woollen items, and especially over winter into spring, when the grubs were hatching. When rubber was so scarce, a corset had become one of a woman's prized possessions and women had been advised to never let them get too dirty, to wash them frequently and that it was best, if you possibly could, to have at least two, so they could be worn alternately. Tilly had warmed most of all to the advice about dishes: that they should be left on the draining board to dry naturally so as to avoid wear on tea towels. Tilly had been all for avoiding wear on tea towels.

'Now, Mrs Swanston,' Tilly asked, attempting to divert the proprietress's attention from the ink stain on her skirt to more serious matters. 'I take it then that you're very pleased that Mr Chifley's government has lifted the styling restrictions on clothing manufacture?'

'Oh, my goodness, yes. It's all been rather drab since 1942. There have been too many uniforms out on the streets and this fashion for the austerity styles? I couldn't do it myself. Where's the style in an army or airforce auxiliary uniform, I ask you?'

'They were practical,' Tilly offered. 'For all those women who were working in factories and offices and the like.'

Mrs Swanston sighed. 'Yes, I suppose they were. And here,' she jabbed at Tilly's notepad. 'It's not just women who'll be rejoicing. My husband is a tailor and he can't wait to put pocket flaps back on men's suits. And double cuffs! But I'm not sure he can do double-breasted suits and jackets just yet and, of course, there are still restrictions on the number of buttons one may use, which is a terrible pity. But this is a wonderful step in the right direction. We'll be back to pre-war business in no time.'

'But there's no indication as yet that clothing rationing will be removed until the worldwide cotton shortage is over. What's your view on that?'

'I expect a certain level of frustration among mothers, having to continue patching sheets and postponing buying a particular dress they may have long coveted.' Mrs Swanston glanced around at her racks, making no secret of her profound regret that her frocks might have to wait a little longer to find their perfect owner. 'But I suppose we should be thankful the war is over and that we haven't experienced half the hardships that our cousins in England have had to endure. I'm sure that with a little care, mothers and their children will still look neat. Even if they aren't wearing the latest fashions.'

Tilly bit her tongue. 'I'm sure that with winter approaching in the northern hemisphere, all those millions of people who are struggling for their basic necessities, such as food to put on the table and a warm place to live, might need cotton more than we do right now.'

A flush rose in Mrs Swanston's cheeks. 'Of course.'

Tilly's pencil flew over the page of her notebook. 'Mr Chifley said the clothing, textile and knitted goods trades made a greater contribution to victory than is possibly realised. What do you say to that?'

Mrs Swanston puffed out her peacock bosom. 'I'm very proud of all we've done and all that the women of Australia have done. Yes, it was hard at times but people took the austerity restrictions to heart, for the most part, without complaint.' Mrs Swanston leant close and lowered her voice. 'And it hasn't been announced yet but I've heard that we'll get lace from England by the end of the year. We haven't had baby lace since the beginning of the war. And wool for knitting and crocheting!'

Tilly's mother would definitely be pleased by that news. 'Will Sydney ladies be wearing a wider range of styles by summertime, do you think?'

'Oh, yes, most definitely. Skirts will be flowing and they'll be longer, too. I can't wait to see cap sleeves for spring and summer, with all the delightful trimmings we've gone so long without. Ruffles and dirndl skirts and coat styles. All that fabric, Mrs Galloway! We'll embrace the feminine again.' She paused, lowered her voice. 'We'll soon have some new nightwear and lingerie. Now women can get back to the feminine things in life. Looking pretty for their husbands, for instance.'

Tilly didn't take the bait. 'Well, thank you, Mrs Swanston. I do sincerely appreciate your time.'

'I'm just so glad it's all over, aren't you?'

The change in tone in Mrs Swanston's voice caught Tilly off guard. She paused and then asked softly, 'Is someone in your family serving?'

Mrs Swanston tugged a pin from the pincushion on her wrist and pushed it back in, over and over. 'My son-in-law. He lost a leg in Malaya. He's been back twelve months now. He and my daughter have two little boys. They were so scared to see him after so long away. I had to hem all the left legs in his trousers.' Her voice drifted off and she found a stoic smile. 'But we got on. At least he came home. What about you, Mrs Galloway?'

'No.' The word slipped out of Tilly's mouth before she could stop it. She couldn't bear to have another conversation about Archie, and her lie was another attempt at self-preservation. 'My husband's in a reserved occupation. Shipping.' Oh, how the lie continued, so easy, so seamlessly, and she felt such a rumble of shame in her heart.

'You're lucky, then.'

'Yes, we are. But my dearest friend Mary's husband is about to come home. He was a prisoner in Changi, in Singapore.'

'That's a blessing from God right there. Wish her all the very best.'

'I certainly will.'

Tilly stepped onto the footpath and lit up a cigarette. Her cheeks flamed with shame. It hadn't been the first time she'd pretended to a stranger that Archie didn't exist. It had become easier than the truth. So many times since April 1941 she had tried to forget him as a way of holding herself up, a way of not tumbling into that rabbit hole of grief that she feared would subsume her. Other times, she imagined that he'd walked onto the ship and simply disappeared into thin air. In that version, he'd never been captured. He'd walked up the gangplank and had become a missionary in deepest, darkest Africa. Or perhaps he was in a monastery in Tibet, having vowed to be silent forever. And it was all so foolish, she knew, but did it make any more sense than thinking about what might really have happened to him?

All those letters she'd written to him—faithfully, cheerily—every week for four bloody years, in which she'd lied, too, pretending that she was fine and dandy. She'd filled those pages with useless, utterly frivolous rubbish to stop herself from writing the truth. Had he received anything she'd sent to the Red Cross for him? The fruit cake every Christmas her mother had helped her bake? The new handkerchiefs she'd embroidered with his initials? The mints? The clippings from the *Daily Herald* featuring her stories? Had any of those things stopped him from going mad?

As each day passed, the newspapers and the radio broadcasts had revealed new and horrific revelations from liberated prisoner camps and she'd read them and listened with a growing sense of dread. Of course our boys had been courageous and brave. Their pride had never faltered and their unquenchable spirit had carried them through the ugliest tortures men had ever known. Tilly believed the reports of sickness and starvation among the POWs because she'd seen it in the faces and the ill-fitting uniforms of the men who'd arrived at Rose Bay on the Catalinas. It was beri-beri and malaria and other tropical diseases whose names she'd forgotten, but she suspected it was more than that, something that had taken the light from their eyes.

Every day, another house she passed had been decorated almost overnight with Australian flags and the Union Jack and coloured bunting, with welcome home banners strung from verandah posts and balconies, and the scent of freshly baked biscuits wafting through open windows as she passed by. Another family was preparing a welcome celebration and she wanted to hate them for it.

Every night, families were keeping vigils at the wireless, listening to the ABC broadcasting from Singapore with names of released POWs. And every night, another family was able to hear the voice of a loved one, the voice they might have forgotten except for in their dreams over the past five years, and they would rejoice.

If only she was able to share in the tremendous relief of those thousands of next of kin.

She crossed Pitt Street and when she stepped out of the lift on the second floor, she found herself in the midst of another celebration and she faltered. Cookery editor Vera Maxwell was sobbing in the arms of Dear Agatha, and Maggie and Frances were hovering, with smiles and tears. They must have heard the lift bell because each woman turned towards Tilly. She registered shock and joy in their faces.

Tilly looked at each of them in turn. 'What is it?'

Archie. Archie. Archie. It was all she could think. Did they have news? Had they seen the list of names that was going to appear in tomorrow's paper? A surge of adrenaline sent her head throbbing.

Maggie motioned for Tilly to join them. 'It's good news, Tilly, although you might not think it, looking at us.'

And suddenly her friends were not looking at her but at Vera.

It wasn't Archie. The good news wasn't for her.

Tilly set her handbag and notebook on her desk and quickly went to Vera, who looked up with more than relief in her eyes.

'He's alive, Tilly. He was found on an island in New Guinea. I don't even know the name of it.'

'Rodney? But ...' Tilly struggled to make sense of the news. 'But he was listed as missing. All this time he's been alive?'

All Vera could do was nod and shake her head in a confused rhythm of disbelief and joy. 'Yes. That's all I know. Oh, Tilly.' The two women held each other and the others stepped back. They knew that Vera and Tilly shared something they could never understand but when Tilly's tears flowed, Kitty and Dear Agatha swooped in too.

Chapter Eleven

Across the road from their apartment building, Mary and Tilly sighed wistfully and pressed their noses up against the curved windows of the French perfumerie.

'Do you think I should?' Mary asked.

It was Saturday morning and the two women were on their weekly window shopping expedition. Over the years, they'd developed a comforting routine of activities to fill their days and help take their minds off the war and their missing husbands. On Monday nights they knitted. Elsie always seemed to have found a moth-eaten old jumper that she unravelled and turned into balls of wool ready for reimagining into something else for someone, an orphan perhaps or a widow's child, a returned soldier with no wife or mother to knit for him. On Tuesday evening they had wrapped bandages for the Red Cross, although that work had recently come to an end. On Wednesday night they often saw a picture, usually something of the action-adventure variety and absolutely positively nothing war related. On Thursday nights they liked listening to *Mr and Mrs North*—Jerry and Pam, the laughing sleuths—who were billed on 2GB as radio's gayest, most adventurous pair. Each week, they wise-cracked their way through blood-chilling drama and Tilly and Mary loved their riotous adventures in crime. Who didn't need a laugh during the war? On Friday nights after work they walked to Repin's on George Street for a treat of Vienna-style coffee with whipped cream on top. It was so much fancier than a regular brewed coffee or the tea they could make themselves at home, and it always felt like a wonderful way to cap off a working week.

On Saturdays they walked into the city to moan in good humour about the meagre window displays in David Jones and Foy's. They couldn't remember the last time there had been new fashions to swoon over or new hats to covet. Sometimes they tried on shoes they didn't ever plan to buy or slipped new handbags over the crooks of their elbows to admire the way they looked on each other.

It was all a game of make-believe and they were like two young girls playing with clothes from a treasure box. They had been young when the war had begun, on the brink of starting families of their own, but all that had been put aside, tucked away in their own treasure boxes, preserved for the day their husbands came home and their interrupted lives could begin again.

On Sundays, Mary went to church and Tilly slept in before having lunch at her parents' house with her sister, Martha, and Martha's three boys. If there was a watersider out of work, or a widow in need of a meal and friendship, they would find a place around the kitchen table at Argyle Place too.

And then on Monday, the working week began all over again.

It had been best to keep busy. Tilly had found it had been the only way to stop her thinking about Archie every waking minute. There had to be some respite from the fear and the gut-wrenching dread, and by keeping busy and draining her energy dry she might, just might, fall asleep as soon as her head hit the pillow each night. Because the alternative—lying awake all night, heart pounding, thoughts racing about where Archie was and what had happened to him—had been no way to survive the war with her sanity intact. She had learnt early on in his captivity that letting those thoughts get the better of her was a clear route to going mad with grief.

Tilly still found herself waking slowly, asleep and then awake with each blink, and in that restful half-slumber, she would forget for just a moment. After all the years of waiting, it was the same every day. With her pillow soft under her cheek and the air already warm with the promise of a sunny Sydney day, the world was right again and she would find herself reaching an arm out behind her to feel for Archie. They were the best of days and the worst.

The glass bottles on display in the perfumerie window caught the light and seemed to glitter.

'I don't know,' Mary dithered. 'You know that every spare penny I have goes straight into the bank for a home of our own. And Bert's pay, of course. It's a nice little nest egg now.' She sighed. 'If one day, by some miracle, there are any homes to actually buy.'

'Don't even hesitate,' Tilly said adamantly and jabbed her friend with an elbow as if to shock her out of her malaise. 'Bert's coming home. What better reason do you need to splash out a little? Think of all the times you've gone without during the war. Treat yourself. Not that I think you'll need a fancy eau de cologne when it comes to Bert. You could smell like Bon Ami and I'm sure he won't be able to keep his hands off you.'

Mary laughed. 'Do you think they're really French?'

Tilly narrowed her eyes and studied the labels. There might be room for a little scepticism when it came to the advertising in the shop. She had wondered, more than once, how on earth this little place in Potts Point had managed to come across authentic French perfume during the war when couture houses had been closed for the duration. 'Perhaps not.'

'"Jean Didier". That sounds French, doesn't it?' Mary peered close through the rounded curve of glass at the corner. 'Look. There are sixteen different bouquets.'

An elegant display of larger bottles sparkled on glass shelves, artfully arranged next to framed photographs of sophisticated models with impossibly long necks and Veronica Lake hair. 'Which one shall I choose? Red Rose? Gardenia? Five O'Clock? Soir de Chene? Oh, it's two and six per dram and you have to bring your own bottle. I still have something or other in mine. It seems a pity to waste that, don't you think?'

Tilly pointed. 'I think you should go for Temptation.'

Mary tugged Tilly's arm and burst out laughing.

'If only there was Long Time No See.' Tilly laughed. 'Wouldn't that be perfect?'

Tilly and Mary walked along Orwell Street and then Victoria, ambling past frock shops, dressmakers, dry cleaners and dyers. Tilly had had a pale yellow cotton frock

dyed navy blue the year before and it had done well enough
to see her through another season. The streets were busy in
the sunshine and the women of the city were on parade in
wide-brimmed straw hats with white gloves, in floral dresses
that seemed to announce that spring had finally arrived and
new sandals for the warmer weather.

'You know, Tilly,' Mary started. 'I think I'm going to
chuck in the Classified Advertisements department.'

Of course Mary would. The war was over. Her husband
was coming home. She could start the life she'd been waiting
for. But the news, entirely expected after all, caught Tilly off
guard and she tried hard to hide the disappointment she felt
at the idea that any day now she would lose her dear friend.
When she'd felt confident that Archie would come back,
she had never gone that next step and imagined quitting
her job. She loved being a reporter and her unconventional
rise to the reporting ranks made her appreciate it even more.
Just like tens of thousands of Australian women, the war
had created opportunities for Tilly that she would never in
a million years have had and didn't want to let go. There
would always be news, she knew, and as long as there was
news the papers would need someone to write it.

But Mary had different dreams and who was Tilly to
say they weren't equally as important or as meaningful as
her own?

'Are you thinking you'll have children right away?' Tilly
tried to keep her voice bright and hopeful.

'Goodness, yes. The minute he gets back, if I have my
way. And I want to be Bert's wife. I mean, a real wife. I want
to cook him dinner every night from some of Vera Maxwell's
recipes in the paper. I want to learn how to sew—properly,

I mean—and make curtains for the windows in our new kitchen. We always had chooks when I was growing up on the farm. There's nothing like a sponge made with real eggs. Don't get me started on those powdered eggs we've had to endure.' Mary grimaced. 'I want to teach Sunday school. I want to do all the things my mother did when I was growing up. As a matter of fact, all the things she still does now. That's the kind of wife I want to be, Tilly. That's the kind of wife I've always wanted to be. And that's what Bert wants, too. We talked about it before he left, what kind of life we'd make together when he came home. It may not be that exciting to some people, but we never had big dreams. Not like you, Tilly. Being a war correspondent and flying off everywhere.'

Tilly realised how it must have looked to Mary. Tilly had always felt herself confined by the small role she'd been allowed to play in the newspaper's war reporting, at being relegated to Australia and being pigeon-holed into writing stories about the role other women played in supporting the war effort. But to others, of course it seemed adventurous, like something out of a movie: donning a war correspondent's uniform and hopping on a plane.

Tilly's first instinct had been to say that she hadn't really been a war reporter at all, not really, but in the warm glow of Mary's regard, she let herself feel just a little bit proud of herself. She'd been the *Daily Herald*'s first female war correspondent, a badge and an honour no one could ever take from her.

'It was fun, actually. Who would have thought …' Her voice drifted off, lost in the memories she couldn't seem to bury lately, although she'd been trying so hard to, of tropical humidity and lush palms and dancing with a man who wasn't her husband. She tried to gulp away the guilt that rose in her throat but it stuck there like a half-swallowed pill.

'Did I ever tell you,' Mary began, 'that when Bert and I got married, we couldn't even afford a honeymoon. We spent one night at the fanciest hotel we could find the money for and then we both went right back to work the next Monday.'

'Same,' Tilly replied. 'Married on Saturday. Work on Monday. We spent our wedding night at our flat in Bondi. Sleeping on an old straw-filled mattress on the floor.'

They had been blissful days but Tilly was finding it hard to hang on to the memory of them now. They were becoming as difficult to hold on to as a dream upon waking.

'As much as I have loved being your roommate—'

'And I yours,' Tilly added.

'I can't wait to have a home of my own. I don't care where it is as long as there's enough room in the backyard for a chook shed and some fruit trees.' She paused and turned to Tilly with concern etched on her face. 'What if I'm too old to have children, Tilly? I'm already thirty years old. If it doesn't happen soon it could be too late. My aunt Josephine married when she was thirty-five, to a widower with four children, and she tried and tried and never had a baby.'

Tilly scoffed. 'You will have plenty of time, I'm sure. Thirty isn't ancient, Mary.' Although it certainly felt like it sometimes. Martha was a full two years younger than Tilly and she already had three boys in short pants.

'Well, that's reassuring, I suppose. I'll keep that thought close. And I'll keep praying. That's all I can do. What about you, Tilly? Don't you want to be a real wife again?'

Tilly barely remembered what that meant. 'I don't know, Mary. Until I know about Archie, I can't make any plans about what I'll do next. I like my job. I love it, actually. And anyway, what is a proper wife these days?'

A car horn sounded and two young women scuttled across the street, their hands on their hats to stop them flying off into the gutter.

'It shouldn't be long now. I know it's seemed dreadfully slow, but new lists of names are still coming through every day,' Mary said. 'Don't give up hope.'

'There are still nearly five thousand POWs missing. That's all I can think about. "Fate unknown" is the official term for it. It's been fate unknown for four years.'

The Japanese had provided little information about who they'd been holding, about the numbers of prisoners they'd transferred between different camps and countries or about the numbers of deaths. George Cooper had promised Tilly that he would keep looking for Archie and she knew he would be good for it, but she hadn't heard any more from him since his phone call in August the day after VP Day. He was still in Singapore, reporting on the repatriation efforts and the Allies' preparations for the War Crimes Tribunals that were due to begin early the next year.

Mary gasped. 'There you are, Tilly. That's nearly five thousand boys who might be alive.'

Or five thousand who were dead.

'Never lose hope, Tilly,' Mary implored and pulled her close. 'It's all we have.'

Chapter Twelve

The next morning while Mary was at church, Tilly answered a knock at the door from a scrawny man in a brand-new and stiff-looking army uniform. A kit bag hung over his shoulder and he lifted his slouch hat in a friendly greeting, revealing shadowed cheekbones and a shaved head.

It took her a moment.

'Bert?'

'You must be Tilly.'

'Yes, of course I am!'

'How do you do.'

And even though they'd never met, Tilly lunged forward and threw her arms around Mary's husband as if she'd known him for years.

'Oh, Bert,' she cried. 'Welcome home.' And she immediately released her grip on him, trying not to let him see her shock at what she'd felt: the hard bones of his shoulders, his thin frame in her arms. She created a smile to cover her dismay and then, in the shock of the moment, threw a million questions at him.

'Come in. Mary's not here. I can't believe it. She's at church. But of course you would know that, being Sunday morning. She didn't know you were coming home today. What are you doing home today?' Peppering people with questions was her bread and butter and she couldn't quell the natural instinct to find out everything all at once. 'What's happened? Why have you been discharged early? How did you get here?'

Cooper would no doubt be shaking his head at her if he were there. She wasn't listening to Bert at all.

Bert's eyebrows lifted into the creases of his tanned forehead. 'Mary's not here? I didn't think. Yes, it's Sunday. Of course.'

'Oh my, are you going to give her a surprise.' Tilly clapped her hands together with glee. 'Bring your things in.'

Bert stepped inside and lowered his kit bag to the floor. He looked the place over. If only it had been fancier for his return to the real world. The settee was worn and two of the cushions were patched and darned where the fabric had worn through. The old floral curtains, once hidden under Elsie's blackout curtains, had hung at the window since well before the war. Only the wireless in the corner was relatively new, a wedding gift from Archie's parents when he and Tilly had married. It had been a fortuitous gift, serving as her lifeline to a frightening world that had seemed alternately a million miles away and then right on their doorstep. Each night at ten pm, Tilly and Mary had perched on the edge of their seats, their hearts in their mouths, listening to the Japanese war broadcast that aired on the radio. They hated it and yearned for it equally and cruelly, because its star, Tokyo Rose, taunted Americans and Australians with news and messages from all the boys who were a long way from home. Tilly and Mary had been silent, hope in their hearts that maybe that night Tokyo Rose might read a message from Bert or Archie while 'There's No Place Like Home' played traitorously in the background. It was only a half-hour broadcast but they were routinely crying two minutes in, desperate to turn the dial to something else but absolutely compelled to keep listening.

Bert's inspection stalled when he saw his own photograph on the mantelpiece. He tentatively walked over, lifted the frame and took a good long look at his likeness. Tilly watched him and his younger self looking back at him, as if he were looking in a fun-house mirror that had distorted and shrunken his reflection.

Did he know that Mary had kissed his photo every night? Would he ever know that Mary had cried herself to sleep over him?

'Mary shouldn't be much longer.' Tilly checked the time on the carriage clock next to the photograph. 'Perhaps half an hour.' She waved Bert to the settee. 'Why don't you sit down? Or perhaps you want to put your bag in Mary's room? It's your room now too, of course. It's just through the hallway and first on the left.'

'Thank you, Tilly. I'll do that.'

Tilly waited anxiously in the living room, her heart aching for Mary. Bert was here and she was probably on her knees in church right that very second praying for him and all the children they would have. Poor Mary. She'd had so many plans for Bert's proper arrival home. The banner on which she'd written, in her neatest hand, *Welcome Home Bert from your loving wife Mary* and decorated with pencil sketches of waving flags was in the kitchen on the dresser, still folded. The bunting she'd found in a shop in Kings

Cross was still in a brown paper bag alongside it, as was the Union Jack they had planned to wave from the window.

Bert returned to the living room and cleared his throat to catch Tilly's attention. 'This is a beaut little place you've got here.'

'Yes. It's small but we like it.'

Tilly was having trouble reconciling this Bert with the man in the photograph. The Bert on the mantelpiece was round-cheeked, smiling-eyed and young, his long nose perhaps not quite so prominent as it was in person. His cheekbones were now as angular as a sail on a yacht, and when he smiled Tilly saw a dark space in his mouth where one of his top front teeth was missing. His clothes hung on him, his shoulders like a coathanger, the fabric of his obviously new uniform as voluminous as a priest's robes on his thin frame. Two men could have fitted in the space between his flat stomach and the buttons on the front of the jacket.

'Mary told me about moving here. How much she likes you. That was back in '41. September. I didn't get many letters, you see. Those I did get, I must have read them a thousand times. I know them word for word.'

Tilly smiled. 'She wrote to you every week, Bert. I swear it. Right in the kitchen on the table. Every Sunday she would go to church and then write her letter to you and then do her washing. That was her day. She's been absolutely diligent about it.'

Bert shook his head. 'I don't doubt that. I know my Mary. The Japs weren't the best postmasters, it's fair enough to say.'

'I hear. Now, let me see. Are you hungry? Can I make you a sandwich or something else to eat? A boiled egg? I'd love to offer you coffee but all we've been able to get is that horrid chicory essence and after real coffee at Repin's, I can't bring myself to drink anything else. Can you imagine? They roast their own beans. So, perhaps not a coffee. What about a cup of tea?'

If Tilly had been in the privacy of her own bedroom, she would have kicked herself. She was fully aware that she was prattling on like a nervous ninny but couldn't seem to stop.

'No thanks, Tilly. Not tea. Those nurses in Singapore made sure we got buckets of it. With the milk, it helped fatten us up a bit, you see, before we came home.'

'Of course.' What had Bert looked like before the fattening up?

Bert slipped a finger inside the collar of his jacket and tugged at it. 'I'll just wait for Mary, if that's all right with you.'

'Of course. Please, make yourself at home.'

Bert opened his mouth to speak, hesitated. 'I do want to say one thing to you while I'm waiting for my wife. I owe you a debt of gratitude for looking after my Mary while I've been away. I know you've been a good friend to her.'

Tilly swallowed her sudden tears. 'You don't owe me anything, Bert. If anything, she looked after me. We've managed to muddle through the war, she and I. Two wives waiting for their boys to come home.'

Bert stilled. 'And your husband?'

'Still waiting for news, I'm afraid.'

'Where was he serving?'

'The 8th Division, AIF. Lark Force. He was taken prisoner in Rabaul in '41 and it's been very difficult to get word from him since then. The Japanese, you know.'

'Yes. I know.' Bert cleared his throat. 'I look forward to meeting your Archie when he's home. Maybe we can have a beer together. What did he do before the war?'

'He worked for an insurance firm on Elizabeth Street. He was a clerk. And Mary tells me you were a watchmaker?'

Bert nodded. 'That's right.' He lifted his wrist and exposed the place a watch might have sat a long time ago. 'Haven't worn much of anything for the past four years, let alone a watch.'

They exchanged polite smiles and Tilly bit down on the urge to fire a thousand questions at Bert, about his captivity, about the Japanese, about how he'd managed to hold on to hope after all these months and years, about how it felt to be free. The need for answers almost overwhelmed her and she felt the beginnings of a headache at the back of her skull, radiating upwards. Would any answer revive her ever-diminishing hope that Archie might be free too one day soon?

She shook away her desperate desire for answers. 'Bert. I do apologise, I seem to have forgotten. Was that a no to the offer of a sandwich?'

'Don't trouble yourself, Tilly. You go about what you were doing. I'll just wait for my wife. I can't believe I'll get to hold her again.' His gaze was off in the distance and Tilly swallowed the lump in her throat, of happiness and envy all wrapped up together.

Tilly returned to the sink and to the scrubbing of a large saucepan that had been soaking overnight. She'd made a rabbit stew the night before and had left it too long. What a glamorous homecoming for a soldier, she thought. The smell of Bon Ami and burnt stew.

If more proof was ever needed that life went on, that would be it.

An hour later, Tilly had prepared a tuna casserole for supper, and had scrubbed every surface in the kitchen until the room sparkled. She'd climbed up on the sink and cleaned the windows overlooking Orwell Street with a page of the *Daily Herald* and a splash of methylated spirits before refreshing the water in Mary's little vases on the sill. She had left Bert alone in the living room and he must have turned on the wireless because she heard the soft background noise of voices. She hadn't wanted to crowd or overwhelm Bert, who was still a stranger to her, and she to him. The last thing he needed on his first day of discharge was the curious stares of a stranger, or worse, a barrage of questions. That was all she wanted to do, though. To ask him: what do you know? What was it like?

But what use would that be? He wouldn't be able to answer her most pressing one: where is Archie?

When Tilly heard the click of a key in the front lock, she stilled, the latest *Women's Weekly* open on the kitchen table before her. The lock. Bert clearing his throat. And then Mary shrieking and bawling. If there were confessions or declarations or expressions of love and longing, they were whispered, kept private between husband and wife, which was as it should be. Tilly tried not to listen. They deserved this private moment.

She rested her head in her hands and fresh tears dripped onto a colourful Ovaltine advertisement, right on the blond curls of the baby in a high chair, rosy-cheeked, blue eyes, wearing a blue knitted jumper, full lips smiling and clutching a spoon full of the malt milk powder. It surely wouldn't be long before Mary and Bert had a cherub of their own, one who was sure to inherit Mary's blonde curls and round cheeks, her sunny optimism and her caring, generous nature.

Tilly swallowed the envy that traitorously flared again and forced more tears to flow. Mary's future was bright now, laid out before her like the first chapter in a book, filled with so much promise. From the deepest depths of Tilly's own despair, the words *it's not fair* echoed in her mind.

'Tilly!'

She hurriedly wiped her face and turned in her chair. Mary and Bert stood arm in arm in the doorway, both beaming, both full of joy. How on earth could she begrudge them this moment?

'I ... I don't ... oh, Tilly. He's home!' Mary pressed her palms to Bert's face and stood on tiptoes to give him a passionate kiss. She broke away and laughed more gaily than Tilly had ever heard her laugh. 'You've met my dearest friend, I see?'

Bert pressed his lips to the curls at Mary's forehead and Mary's eyes fluttered closed as a blush reddened her décolletage and crept up her neck.

'I have to admit, she wasn't the welcoming committee I was expecting.'

Mary's fizzing excitement was like sherbet. 'What do you think of the flat, Bert? I know it's small, but it'll do until we find a place of our own. Tilly said to take as long as we need, didn't you, Tilly?' Mary slipped an arm through the crook of Bert's elbow and leant into him. He folded an arm around her and pulled her close.

'It's beaut, love,' he said and reached for his wife's hand, kissing the back of it. He couldn't stop looking at Mary, taking in every detail of her face. He adored her, it was clear as a bell. Fresh tears of joy welled in Tilly's eyes.

'We've been happy here, haven't we, Tilly? I mean, it's not much and there's damp in the bathroom, but it's been fine for two single girls.' Mary covered her mouth. 'Oh, no. That's not what I meant. I meant two girls on their own. Two girls with husbands away.'

Tilly started. 'And it's close to the newspaper. We walk even when it's raining.'

'The buses and trams have been so crowded it hasn't been worth the bother of squeezing in like sardines with every other soul in Sydney. We've walked everywhere, haven't we, Tilly? Shank's pony and all that.'

Bert looked from Mary to Tilly. 'All the Americans here, I suppose? Making the buses and trams so crowded?'

'Not, not particularly, although we've had a lot of them around since you—' Mary stopped. 'For the past few years. You'll be able to see them for yourself, all lined up outside The Roosevelt Club on Friday and Saturday nights. It's just across the road here. It's quite the place, apparently, very swanky, although I've never been inside.' Mary's nervous chatter came to a sudden halt and her red flush continued its creep to her cheeks.

'Neither have I,' Tilly added, sensing the need for a conversational diversion. Poor Mary and Bert. He was a rabbit in a spotlight and she was as jittery as a bride on a wedding night, both of which made Tilly feel like an absolute gooseberry. 'The Americans are all over the Cross, but it's the petrol rationing, Bert. If anyone had a car in the first place, it's been almost impossible to get enough petrol to go anywhere.'

'There's petrol rationing?' Bert glanced from Tilly to Mary and back.

Mary looked to Tilly, wide-eyed. 'Yes … for the um …'

'Every spare gallon was reserved for the war and supporting our boys,' Tilly said. 'Diggers like you, Bert.'

'And Archie, too,' Mary added.

Sweet Mary. 'Yes, and Archie, too. You know, Bert, everyone's calling you the Invincible 8th, you boys from the 8th Division. On account of the fact that you were all POWs for such a long time and fighting on, coming home like you have. That's marvellous, isn't it?'

Bert smoothed a hand over his shaved head. 'Sure beats The Lost Division. That's what they called us for three-and-a-half years, I hear. So one of the doctors at the hospital told us.'

'Do you remember what I told you, Bert? Tilly's a reporter at the paper. She always knows what's going on, usually before the rest of Sydney does.'

Bert smiled generously at her. 'I don't know if I remember that.'

Mary's face fell. 'I told you that, I'm sure. In one of my letters.'

Bert kissed her cheek. 'I bet you did. Letters were pretty few and far between in Changi, love. You'll have to fill me in on everything I've missed.'

Mary looked up at her husband, and Tilly swore she glowed with love and relief and sheer joy. 'We have all the time in the world now, dearest Bert.'

'That we do.' He turned to Tilly. 'I hope you won't go asking me any questions about the war.' His smile faltered then disappeared entirely and his expression was blank. 'I didn't see much of it myself.'

'Of course you did,' Tilly replied. 'I wouldn't want to intrude. But, you saw the war.'

Bert stiffened. 'Changi wasn't war. It was captivity.'

Mary's face betrayed her confusion.

And Tilly took that as a cue to leave the reunited lovers alone. She untied her apron and hung it on the back of the kitchen door. 'Welcome home again, Bert. It's so lovely to finally meet you. I'm off to see my parents for Sunday lunch. I bet that's something you've missed, too.'

Chapter Thirteen

'It's the least I can do, Mum.'

Tilly pushed the hessian bag of groceries across the kitchen table towards her mother. When Elsie pushed it right back, it toppled and a plump red apple rolled onto the floor.

'You don't need to be feeding your parents,' Elsie said with a frustrated huff. 'I can't believe you'd think such a thing.'

Tilly stared at her mother hard but lovingly. She realised how alike they must look: their arms crossed in the exact same way, the same narrowed hazel eyes and determined mouth. Anyone looking on would have no doubt they were mother and daughter, each as obstinate as the other.

Tilly retrieved the fruit, checked it for bruises and set it on the table. 'Stop being so stubborn, Mum. With the strikes still on, I know there's no rent coming in. For goodness sake. It's a few slices of corned beef, a loaf of bread, two apples and a few potatoes. And three bananas. Did I mention I found bananas? Martha's boys will eat them if you won't.'

Elsie turned away from the bounty. 'Take it away. I'm not taking charity from my own daughter, for pity's sake.'

Tilly spread her hands on the table and stared down her mother. 'How many times have you fed everyone in Argyle Place when there haven't been any ships in for a week? Who did the washing for the McCartneys when Mrs McCartney was sick after having another baby? Who always sees to the men at the Coal Lumpers' Hall across the way when they're skint? Yes, Mum, you. If you're accusing me of having a generous nature, I plead guilty as charged, your honour. And I wonder where I learnt that? All I'm doing is sharing what I have and doing what I can.'

Elsie went to the stove, still mumbling her protest, and put the kettle on.

'Where's Dad? I'm sure he'd like an apple.' Tilly took it from the table and tossed it from hand to hand like a juggler missing a ball or two.

'He's having a rest before the meeting starts. You know how het-up he gets. It's worse now and all with the strikes going on so long.'

'Why is the meeting here? Why isn't it at the union office?'

Elsie didn't reply and couldn't look at her daughter. Tilly's pulse quickened. 'Mum? Is he all right?'

Elsie gripped the counter and dipped her head. The bun that sat at her collar looked unusually frayed.

Tilly felt a surge of guilt that she'd fought with her mother when so much more was going on in this house than the need for an apple and some potatoes. 'Is it his back again? Or his hernia?'

'These past few days he's barely been able to get out of bed. You should hear him moan, Tilly. I've had to put his shoes on and do up the buttons on his shirts. The doctor says there's something wrong with his heart. He's fifty years old but he's got the ticker of a seventy-year-old. The only thing that's helping him at the moment, would you believe it, is the strike.'

'Oh, Mum. Why didn't you tell me?'

'You've got enough on your mind.'

'Never too much that I can't hear news about Dad.'

'And while I'm at it, don't tell your sister, either. Your father doesn't want either of you to worry.'

'Why ever not? Martha will want to know if Dad's poorly.'

Elsie clasped her hands together. 'She's already got enough on her plate with the boys and working as many hours as she does and Colin still at sea and no word yet on when he'll be back.'

The war had stretched every person's capacity for worry and fear and grief and forbearance. What was one more thing to add to the scales when they had been overbalanced for so long?

'I promise,' Tilly said, knowing full well that it was a commitment she would break the moment she saw her sister.

A broken-down watersider—and a union man at that—was in a world of trouble. The men, like a flock of seagulls waiting for food scraps in the form of a pointed and beckoning finger, only had the strength of their bodies to recommend them. The stevedoring companies wanted the strongest and fittest men who were able to cope with the work, who wouldn't break down or quit when the work got

too heavy or too hard. Not men who would cause trouble.
But the day Stan had handed over his dues to the Waterside
Workers' Federation and joined the fight for shorter shifts
and washrooms and canteens down at the wharves, he'd
quickly been branded a socialist troublemaker and he'd
only got work when there was a desperate need for men.
The war had created that desperate need and there was more
work than there had been in generations. The wharves at
the northern end of Cockle Bay along the western shores
of Millers Point became the engine room of Australian
shipping to supply the war effort, with watersiders the cogs
in that machine.

When she'd been a teenager helping her mother with
the boarders, Tilly had taken food to her father as he'd
waited in the crowd of desperate men along the Hungry
Mile. Carrying his sandwiches and fruit cake wrapped in a
tea towel, Tilly had scurried along High Street to the High
Steps, which she'd taken as gingerly as she could because
they were narrow and so, so steep and she was a tall girl with
a tall girl's large feet, and then hurried down to Hickson
Road to find her father among the crowds of men.

They had been fierce and desperate times on the
waterfront. The hungry men looking for work, some with
famished families at home, numbered three or four hundred
at a time, yet there was only work for forty of them. The one
in ten chosen for the day's shift would eat the next day, while
the rest walked pitifully away. There had been nothing more
miserable to Tilly's eyes than the agony she'd seen in the
slumped shoulders of men who wore their failure as heavily
as their old coats, their begging having come to naught. Her
father and his comrades always talked with derision about

the decision of Australia's Arbitration Court, back in 1931, to reduce the basic wage for workers by ten per cent.

Tilly knew her father's thoughts about that as well as she knew her own name. 'It was supposed to get things moving again, give the bosses more money to bring on more people, but all it did was lead to more poverty for people like us, Tilly.'

For the Bells and for other waterside families, their lives didn't really improve until the war, when the demand for labour gave them a collective power they hadn't had in decades. For the first time, Stan Bell had regular work, but it arrived at the same time as his body was starting to betray him. His last few good years were slipping away from him as sure as one of the ships he helped load would disappear across the ocean to distant lands.

In those lean times, Elsie's labours had kept the family afloat. The second floor of the terrace, below the attic and above the family's bedrooms, had for many years been let to men who worked the wharves, coal lumpers or watersiders or seamen, men who needed to be close to the Hungry Mile. Tilly had met men from all over Sydney and even a few Norwegians who'd come to work the ships back when she was younger. It had never seemed out of the ordinary to Tilly to have strangers in the house, nor to be asked to serve them their dinner in the evenings after school or wash up a household's dishes. She'd earnt her keep from a very young age.

When the kettle whistled, Tilly filled the teapot and then set it on the trivet on the table. She went to her mother, slipped a comforting arm around Elsie's shoulders.

'We're family.' Tilly kissed the top of Elsie 's head. 'You sit for a while. I'll take Dad a cup of tea.' Tilly loaded a tray with two cups and some fruit cake and made her way up the narrow staircase to the next floor.

'And don't you think I'm taking those damn bananas home.'

Tilly's parents' bedroom was on the ground level of their terrace—above the kitchen on the lower floor—and its window overlooked Argyle Place. In the mornings it was flooded with light but once the sun was overhead it was dim and in winter, cold as charity. It had always been plain and nothing had changed. It still smelt as it always had, of shoe polish and Velvet soap. There was a two-door wardrobe. A dresser with a lace doily Tilly's grandmother had sewn as a wedding gift for Stan and Elsie, a hand mirror, a brush and a wooden box, which held Elsie's hair nets and pins. Tilly knew that in the first drawer on the dresser on the left side there was a green velvet box with a string of pearls and matching clip-on earrings. Tilly knew because she and Martha used to slip the necklace on when they were convinced their mother was too distracted in the kitchen to notice them playing dress-ups in her bedroom. It was easy when their father worked twenty-four-hour shifts and Elsie was busy with the house and the boarders. The bed was the same, the curved bedhead rising in the middle like the Harbour Bridge, and two tables on either side. A mirror hung by a silver chain above the fireplace.

Her father was lying on his side on top of the blanket, drowsy but not asleep, and Tilly's heart clenched at the sight of him. All his strength had slowly seeped out of him over the years and it still broke her heart to see it.

'Dad?' she said quietly as she approached. The cups tinkled against the saucers like a chime.

Stan stirred and moved to sit up. 'Hello, Tilly girl.'

'Don't get up.' Tilly set the tray on the bed by his socked feet. 'Let me fix your pillows so you can stay right where you are and drink your tea. There's fruit cake, too.'

Stan smiled sleepily at his daughter.

'You're a sight for sore eyes, Florence Nightingale.' His face was pale, even in the dim light, and his breathing rasped.

Tilly smiled. 'Me? I would have made a terrible nurse. I feel nauseous at the sight of blood, you know that. Remember when Tommy McCartney—or was it Roger—came off his billycart outside number 32? We were still all together at school, I think. There was blood all over our front step. I almost fainted.'

Stan chuckled. 'That's not how I remember it. You bolted inside and told your mother and me all about it. Left the poor kid bleeding all over the place.'

'I did?'

'Oh, yes. How Tommy—or was it Roger—had dropped dead right outside our front door. And that his little sister screamed blue murder and his mother tanned his hide as she dragged him off the cart, which I reckon was in pieces by that stage.' That her father had remembered that particular five minutes from twenty years ago touched Tilly in a way she couldn't express.

'I did have a flair for exaggeration. Perhaps I should throw it in at the *Daily Herald* and go and work at *Truth*.'

'Those *Truth* racing pages are pretty top notch.'

'And that's not all that's racy about it.' Tilly rolled her eyes.

Stan sipped his tea. 'Just what your old man needs, this.'

'Mum tells me you've been at the doctor's again.'

He tsked good-naturedly. 'I s'pose there's nothing secret between a mother and her daughter, is there?'

Tilly shook her head and took a bite of cake. 'No, there isn't. Not when it comes to you. I suppose he's given you orders to stay right here in bed?'

'You going to boss me around too?'

'Yes, of course I am,' Tilly replied. 'And tell me you're going to listen to him this time. Please.'

'From where I sit, I can't see I've got much choice, Tilly girl. Your mother will have my guts for garters if I don't. Since we're all out, it seems like as good a time as any to get crook. I'm not paid for lying in bed when I'm at work, and I'm not paid when I'm on strike, so it's much of a muchness.'

She spoke as she ate more cake. 'Mum tells me the men from the union are coming here for your meeting.'

'That's right,' Stan said, giving nothing else away. He had grown used to her habit of probing and he had developed his own way of dealing with it, usually by not saying much of anything at all.

'Can you tell me what the strike's really about, Dad?'

Stan narrowed his eyes at his daughter. 'This isn't for the paper, is it?'

'No. Maybe.' Then she shook her head. 'The industrial reporter might have something to say about it if a woman reporter started invading his patch.'

'What does it matter what I say? They'll never run the truth about what we're fighting for. The *Daily Herald*, and come to think of it, almost every paper except *The Worker*, has had it in for us as long as I can remember. Before I was born, even. They've always been on the side of the bosses and the big shipping companies. None of them will be happy until we work for nothing.'

Before Tilly could reply, her mother appeared at the doorway. 'You all right, love?'

'Just giving Tilly a history lesson.'

'A lecture more like it.' Elsie winked at her daughter. 'They're all here.'

Tilly followed her parents down the stairs to the kitchen where the union men were waiting, making sure to grip her father's elbow as he took slow and tentative steps.

This was a familiar scene. She'd spent many nights as a child eavesdropping on meetings like this, sitting out of sight at the top of the stairs when she was supposed to be long past asleep.

'Comrades.' Stan wheezed and coughed, the exertion of the stairs taking its toll, and Tilly ushered him to a chair.

The three men were organisers with the Waterside Workers' Federation. Arthur Black was a bull of a man, as tall as her father, with neat, white-grey hair and a large red nose. Bob Bailey was half bald and stocky as a boxer dog with a twinkle in his sea-blue eyes, and Walter Rose still had a head of curly carrot-red hair, which he attempted to smooth into position with brilliantine.

Walter stepped forward. 'Your mother's just told us all about Archie. We hope he's home soon, love.'

'Thank you, Mr Rose. That's very kind of you to say. I hope so too.'

Tilly moved to the sink. Elsie was slicing a loaf of bread and together she and her mother made a plate of sandwiches for the men, who were smoking and strategising.

'We're up to thirty thousand workers out now,' Arthur announced. 'That's watersiders, miners, ironworkers, those blokes in electricity up at Bunnerong, meat workers and the printers.'

A silence fell. Tilly glanced over her shoulder, aiming for nonchalance, to discover her father and the three union men looking at her through narrowed eyes.

Stan coughed. 'Might be best if you leave, Tilly. What with you working for the paper. This is union business. And men's business.'

Tilly took the plate of sandwiches to the table. 'Here you are, gentlemen.'

'It's a feast fit for a king, sister.' Arthur nodded his appreciation to Elsie.

'Don't get too excited, boys,' Elsie replied. 'It's only devon.' Then she looked at her daughter and whispered under her breath, 'I'm saving the corned beef for tomorrow.'

Tilly leant in, her palms flat on the table. She eyed them one by one. 'Do any of you understand the idea of what we reporters call off the record and protecting a source?'

'Something about not spilling your guts if you're told something other people don't want you to know.' Arthur crossed his arms and scrutinised Tilly. She knew she was battling on two fronts here: as a woman and as a reporter.

'I couldn't have put it better myself, Mr Black. Whatever I hear today is off the record. Okay?'

Bob poked Arthur. 'No offence, Stan, but I don't know if I can trust your daughter, working for the capitalist press as she does.'

Tilly sighed and held up a hand before her father could defend her. 'Mr Black. Mr Bailey, Mr Rose. Do you know what some of the blokes at the newspaper call me? The commie's daughter. And here, you think I'm a tool of the capitalists. I can't win, can I?'

'It's a proud day when you're called a commie's daughter,' Arthur laughed, winking at Tilly. She couldn't help but laugh in response. Arthur turned to Stan. 'Might be good to get our side of things in the paper for a change. What we're fighting for. An eight-hour day and a five-day week. No more twenty-four-hour shifts on the wharves where you can't even get a feed and a place to wash yourself after you've spent all day and night covered in muck.'

Bob exhaled and shook his head. 'We've never got a fair run in the press, Stan. It's always the bosses' side. You should read what they're printing about the strikes. That those workers at Bunnerong are greedy bas—' He paused and apologised to Elsie and Tilly. 'Greedy so-and-sos for wanting to be paid extra for working shifts. They're calling us "perverted" for standing by the Indonesians against the Dutch Government. Why wouldn't we stand on the side of freedom for the Indonesians against their colonial masters? We'll do it proudly, just like we refused to load pig iron back in '38 when Menzies wanted to ship it to Japan. What a bloody joke that was. Send them iron so they can turn it into guns and tanks to use against our diggers? And they have the bloody gall to have a go at Chifley, too, for standing with the workers against the waterfront scabs.'

Bob's stump speech set Walter off. 'And they print a photo of the deserted wharves, back-to-back ships and not a bloke to be seen, just to have a go, but then there's barely a word about the fact that our members still loaded the HMS *Reaper* to carry supplies to those POWs in Hong Kong.'

Stan added, slowly, 'Is it too much to ask, do you think, not to have to work yourself to the bone to live a good life in this country? For a fair day's pay and a fair day's rest? For a living wage? The working class has to fight now, and not later, for the world we fought for, for the things that were promised so easily during the war. If we let ourselves be fobbed off now, we'll be headed for another depression.'

Elsie spoke up from the sink. 'And who wants that?'

Walter had become so animated his copper hair began to curl. 'You know what I saw in the paper the other day? An advertisement for one of those refrigerators. A Frigidaire, it was called. And you know how much it cost?'

'How much?' Elsie called from the sink.

He leant in conspiratorially. 'Ninety-one bloody pounds! Tell me who can afford something like that when the average wage is five pounds a week. And what's the point of having a fancy Frigidaire when you can barely afford to buy the food to put in it?'

Tilly looked over at her mother and immediately knew that Elsie was thinking about that ninety-one bloody pound refrigerator. The ice man still came to the Bells and everyone else in the street. Imagine no more daily trips to the butcher or the corner shop. No more dripping water from the icebox. No more sour milk. It seemed like a luxury from another life.

'I don't know who they think is going to be able to afford to shell out for one of those contraptions,' Walter said. 'Only the bosses, for their wives, I expect. How can a working man afford it when he doesn't get a pay rise and the government and the bosses are doing all they can to cut the wages of workers now the war is over? It's a disgrace,' he huffed.

Before Tilly could stop herself, she stepped forward. 'Not all of your members are fighting the good fight. I was at Central Court last week. Two wharf labourers at Walsh Bay were sent down for thieving. One got four months for helping himself to a roll of fifty yards of cotton cloth. And his mate got two for stealing fourteen pairs of silk stockings.'

Walter cocked his head, as if he was proud of the men. 'Sounds like they were trying to impress their wives, if you ask me.'

Bob guffawed. 'Or girlfriends, judging by the silk stockings.'

Stan raised a hand. 'Now, boys. That's not on and you know it. They probably weren't even our members, Tilly. Scabs, I bet.'

'And what do you say to those who take the side of the troops? All the boys who fought the war are being discharged and they'll be fighting for jobs too. Hundreds of thousands of them. And yet the men who have jobs won't do them. Won't that just make it harder for them to keep their jobs in the long run?'

'Tilly.' Her father started but she wasn't a young girl any longer. He didn't need to wear any embarrassment at her questions, for she wasn't embarrassed. Wasn't her job to ask the tough ones, to hear both sides of a story and present them so a reader could make up his or her own mind?

'It's what some people are saying. So what's the answer?'

Arthur raised a hand to settle Stan. 'It's the only power workers have, Tilly, to withdraw their labour. Without the right to walk off the job, you're nothing but a slave.'

Her father coughed roughly but was determined to make his own point.

'Archie went to war to protect our freedoms, Tilly. You were probably too young to remember but back in '33, Herr Hitler banned unions in Germany,' Stan began. 'He sent in the coppers to arrest every union official and then he banned strikes, too. That's how it starts. Bit by bit, they take away a worker's power. One little thing on its own might not seem like much. But we know from bitter experience that it's never just the one thing. It's one condition and then it's a wage cut and then you load something else on top of that and all of a sudden you're going backward as a working man. That's what the four of us here and every bloke is fighting for, Tilly. Blokes like your Archie fought for freedom from the Nazis and the Japs and Mussolini and all the other fascists. We're fighting for freedom, too.'

Arthur loaded his plate with sandwiches. 'You know what's happened during the war. Workers have been hard at it six days a week, like … all those young ladies in the munitions factories and people doing those government office jobs. They've all put in extra time, hours and hours every week, for no extra pay, just to make sure our side won the war. They didn't think twice about doing their bit for the diggers. But the war's over. And you know what the bosses are doing to girls like you? Unions fought hard to make sure you're paid three-quarters of what men are paid for doing the same work. That seems fair. And the bosses aren't having a bar of it. They're taking it to the High Court, can you believe that? They're going to ask those judges to cut your pay.'

'I work just as hard as any bloke at the paper. And I'm better than most of them,' Tilly added, because it was true.

Stan puffed up with pride. 'I bet you are. We put this all to one side during the war. Now it's time to do something for the workers. The war might be over, but our battle has just begun.'

Chapter Fourteen

'It's nice to see you, Tilly.' Martha passed a pack of cigarettes to her sister and Tilly slipped one out and lit it.

She took a deep drag and exhaled slowly. 'I was at Mum and Dad's. You're on the way home. And I haven't seen the boys in ages. I swear they're grown six inches each.'

The sisters sat on two old wicker chairs on the front verandah of Martha's narrow brick cottage in The Rocks. Martha had slipped off her shoes and lifted the hem of her floral dress above her knees so most of her bare legs were stretched out before her in the warming sun.

'I think your legs are looking a little pink,' Tilly said.

'Good,' Martha replied with a laugh. 'A tan will be better than rubbing coffee grounds on them. Did you know I tried painting them with gravy once?'

Tilly snorted. 'Gravy?'

Martha laughed. 'All it did was bring every dog in the street panting after me on the walk to work.'

'That would have made a wonderful story. "Rocks Woman Licked to Death by Dogs".'

The sisters laughed and Tilly remembered for a moment how good it felt to relax and enjoy a joke. They sat back, basking in the warmth of the sun, watching Martha's three boys playing cricket out on the street with a ragtag collection of other children who'd come running when word spread there was a game on. International and interstate cricket had been suspended during the war and Martha's boys weren't the only ones waiting for the competition to resume in earnest.

Back in May, when the war in Europe had been won, the whole of Australia had been glued to the radio broadcast of the Victory Test match between Australia and England. It had been an important sign that despite the terrible chaos and disruption of the war, the most important traditions of empire would endure. Germany had only surrendered two weeks before the five-match series started but in everyone's eyes, it had been a much-needed sign that life would continue as it had before the war; that the traditions Australians held so dear would endure.

Tilly remembered the details of that series so clearly. The real hero of the Combined Services Australian side had been South Australian Flying Officer Graham Williams. The poor man had been released from a German prisoner of war camp only days earlier. He'd been weakened from four years in captivity, and he played sixty-eight pounds lighter than when he'd been captured. When he'd walked out into the middle of Lords, the crowd had stood as one in heartfelt applause. He'd scored fifty-three runs and helped lead Australia to victory.

Tilly and Mary had sat glued to the wireless with endless cups of tea during those cold and blustery evenings back in May and June, listening to Alan McGilvray describe each ball and every run. Tilly had never heard of Graham

Williams before that Test, but his bravery and courage had given her the hope she'd so desperately needed that perhaps Archie might survive. Here was a man who had endured the unthinkable, who had spent his captivity helping others and who had enough courage to play cricket at the end of it all.

In the scratch game unfolding on the street, Martha's boys were assuming the roles of their heroes.

'I'm Tiger O'Reilly,' Martha's eldest son Bernard called out, spinning the ball in his ten-year-old hands.

'And I'm Bradman,' nine-year-old Brian announced, waving his makeshift bat in the air. It bore a striking resemblance to a picket fence paling, down to the carving at one end, no doubt purloined from somewhere close by.

Eight-year-old Terry had drawn the short straw and was keeping wicket with his bare hands. 'I don't know who I want to be,' he shouted and Tilly and Martha laughed heartily.

Martha lived with the boys a short clip from her parents but had missed Sunday lunch at Argyle Place that day as she'd taken her sons to see their other grandmother in Newtown for her birthday.

'You're asking *me* what's really going on with Dad?' Martha slowly exhaled the smoke from her cigarette. 'You know more than I do.'

Martha was a pert bottle blonde who'd inherited their mother's height and spirit. She'd followed in Tilly's footsteps and learnt shorthand and typing at Fort Street High School, highly desirable skills for young women at the time. Office skills would keep them out of factory work or jobs as domestics and Tilly and Martha hadn't argued when their teachers had veered them down that path. They were good and decent jobs for bright working-class girls who didn't aspire to teaching or nursing and, anyway, they had seen the damage wrought on their father from a lifetime of physical work. If that could be avoided, all the better.

In the years since she'd left high school, however, Martha's path had diverged markedly from Tilly's. She'd had her first child at eighteen, to her husband of six months, Colin. He'd had been a house carpenter when they'd met and married but, like so many others, he had answered the call and had enlisted in the navy. Able Seaman Colin Winslow had served three years on the HMAS *Australia*, during which time he'd seen action in the Coral Sea and during the New Guinea campaign. He'd missed out on so much of his boys' lives and Tilly wasn't sure that Martha would have coped during his absence without Elsie's help. Each week day, the boys gambolled straight to Argyle Place after school where there was always something freshly baked for them to devour. Elsie knew the way to her grandsons' hearts.

Tilly lit a cigarette and blew smoke into the air, watching it rise to the sounds of the cricket match in the street. 'You see Mum and Dad every day. How long's he been this bad?'

Martha shrugged. 'He's been going downhill for so long I can't say I've noticed. You know what he's been like the past few years. He was the same age for ever and ever and then overnight he seemed to get old, just like that.' She clicked her fingers. 'Just like so many men around here.'

From the street, Bernard called out, 'How's that!' and every child in the street turned their gaze to Martha. She murmured under her breath, 'I wasn't paying attention.' Then she cupped her hand to her mouth and shouted, 'Not out.'

'But Bernard's knocked the crate over, Mum.' Terry, keeping wicket, pointed to the toppled fruit crate lying on its side.

'It was a no ball,' she replied with a wink at her sister.

'You're not even watching!' Brian shouted huffily and strode back to his bowler's mark, a line in the dirt etched with his bare foot.

'Yes, I am watching, as a matter of fact. And so is Aunty Tilly.' Martha propped her feet on the wire fence and sat back in her chair. She smiled at her sister. 'Bernard wants to play for Australia one day. All he talks about is Tiger O'Reilly. It's Tiger this and Tiger that. Why can't he talk about Keith Miller for a change? He's a handsome devil that one. And a fighter pilot.' Martha sighed. 'Colin had better come home soon, that's all I'm saying.'

Tilly and Martha watched the scratch teams play as if it were the Ashes. Skinny little boys and girls battling it out against each other, counting the runs from fruit crate to a line from a stone in the gutter marking the crease at the other end. Their father had been gone three years. How many cricket games had he missed? Tilly wondered how much of him they would remember.

'Bernard said something in passing last week about Grandad being asleep when the boys got there after school,' Martha said. 'I asked Mum about it and she brushed it off, told me it was nothing, which I expect meant it was something that she didn't want to worry us about.'

'Why didn't you tell me about it?' Tilly asked.

Martha tsked at her older sister. 'Honestly, Tilly. I'm working every hour god sends. Half the girls in the office are away because their boys are back and those three rascals are a handful. I barely have time to scratch myself.'

Tilly tried not to hear the implicit criticism. She hadn't been the best aunt to her three nephews, she could admit that. While she'd been happy for her sister and her brother-in-law when their children had arrived, in quick succession like shots from a spud gun, they'd always been a little too much for Tilly. They'd seemed to grow into boys all at once and overnight and she didn't know what to do with them. The idea of having children was one thing but coping with someone else's was another thing altogether.

'Have you heard from Colin? When's he being discharged?'

'I haven't heard from him since before VP Day. Soon, I hope.' Martha's voice grew brittle, resentful even. 'I'm tired, Tilly.' Martha wiped sudden tears away with the hem of her old frock. 'I'm tired of doing this on my own. Mum and Dad help me, don't get me wrong, but the boys are exhausting. I want to sleep in just one day. Is that too much to ask? And I want my husband back.'

Martha didn't ask Tilly about Archie and Tilly didn't make anything of it. Tilly would have said if there was news and her family had long ago, in silent agreement, vowed not to keep asking her. Curiosity on their part had given way to fear and then the gravest concern for Tilly. They knew she would tell them when she knew. If she ever knew.

She offered Tilly another cigarette and they sat, watching the skinny-legged kids of The Rocks play their game, smoking in a heavy silence.

Chapter Fifteen

The *Daily Herald*'s editor Rex Sinclair leant back in the worn leather chair behind his desk and studied Tilly. She became immediately suspicious. When the creases in the corners of his eyes grew longer and deeper, when he tugged at the belt that straddled his Father Christmas belly, he was on the verge of delivering news he was sure the recipient was not going to welcome.

Across from him, Tilly crossed one leg over the other and linked her fingers in her lap.

Her boss cleared his throat and met her gaze. 'Tilly, I'm going to come right out and say it. I'm sending you to the women's pages.'

He knew her too, and he held up a hand to quiet her before she'd even said a word. 'Just wait. Bob Arnold is back from London next week. Joe Charlton too. Roger Cleary's on the next plane out of New Guinea and George Cooper's on his way back from Singapore. And we've got five young blokes starting as cadets in January.'

The news about Cooper's return distracted her for half a moment but she zeroed in on the rest. 'What does their return—and five new cadets—have to do with me being demoted?'

'Who said anything about being demoted? You won't lose any pay, if that's what's worrying you.'

'Thanks to my union, women are paid the same as men in this business, as long as they're on the same grading. Pity that doesn't apply to every working woman in the world,' Tilly muttered to herself. 'Except, you know as well as I do, Mr Sinclair, that all the men at the paper are mysteriously clustered in the senior grades. I wonder how that happens?'

Mr Sinclair blew out an exasperated sigh. 'Not that again. The thing is, Tilly, now the war's over, things around here will go back to the way they were before. They've been through a hell of a war, those fellows. And Cleary's wife's expecting twins and he could do with a pay rise.'

Tilly's heart pounded fast and furious. 'You're giving Cleary a pay rise because he's about to become a father?'

Mr Sinclair seemed perplexed. 'Of course. Having a baby comes with all sorts of extra costs,' he began, and she'd never seen him so flustered. 'Push chairs and bottles and … you know.'

'No, I don't know. I don't have children myself.'

'Tilly, you know you were only a wartime stop-gap measure. You were never a permanent fixture in general news.'

'Really? Because that's news to me. Pardon the pun.' Her jaw ached suddenly.

His face was a picture of grandfatherly concern. 'You'll find plenty to write about on the women's pages, Tilly. Good stories. Interesting stories.'

'Interesting stories?' she gasped. 'If they're that interesting why are they sent to the back of the paper? When was the last time a woman's story made the front page?'

Mr Sinclair was suddenly speechless.

'You're telling me I won't be covering anything in general news?'

'That's what the blokes will be doing.'

Tilly's heart thudded. 'I should have known something was up when Mrs Freeman sent me to cover that fashion story. Dresses for twenty-nine shillings eleven pence and thirty coupons.'

He reached for the pack of cigarettes next to the pile of newspapers on his desk and lit one. He took a drag and breathed out.

'You're a reporter, Tilly. Go find some women's stories. They've done it as hard as the blokes during the past six years, all the doing without and whatnot. Happy reunions. Weddings. New babies. How to cook the diggers' favourite meals on rations. How happy all those munitions girls are now to be at home again. Find out what all the Sydney socialites are up to now the war's over. Go have lunch with the ladies at the Australia Hotel. That's what our lady readers want to see. We've had the war on the front page for six years. People want hope that it wasn't all for nothing. That there's a brighter future around the corner for this country. Write about that.'

Mr Sinclair flicked his cigarette over the Bakelite ashtray on his desk. It used to be her job to clean it out, twice a day. She would have to wipe his desk down too, the parts that weren't covered with yesterday's paper, copy paper, telegrams or snapped and blunt pencils, because the arc of his flicking cigarette was always wider than the ashtray.

'But … but I was a war correspondent.'

He gently shook his head. 'The war's over, Tilly.'

For a moment, she imagined she was his secretary again. *Ring Mrs Sinclair. You have lunch with the chairman of the board in fifteen minutes. The father of chapel wants to see you. The premier's office is on the phone. You need to change your tie.* Nothing had changed in all the years since. In his eyes she was clearly still sixteen years old.

'Have you heard any news about your husband?'

Everyone in the newsroom knew each other's business. If reporters liked gossiping about prime ministers and premiers and society ladies and governors-general, they were even more interested in the lives of their colleagues. People's private lives became fodder for the rumour mill, were discussed at the pub over a beer and at the coffee shop over a toasted sandwich, in the kitchen at the office and at press conferences all over the city. As soon as it had become known that Archie had been taken prisoner, she became the one with the husband who was captured in Rabaul. Cookery editor Vera Maxwell was the one whose husband had been missing, presumed dead. Maggie was the spinster, always said with a nudge and a wink, and Kitty Darling was the one supposedly having an affair with an Important American.

'No news, I'm afraid,' Tilly replied tightly.

Mr Sinclair took a deep drag on his cigarette and she noticed his fingers shaking. 'It'll come. The top brass are finding diggers all over New Guinea. They'll find him and all the other Lark Force boys. You can bet on it.'

She stood on wobbly legs, her voice brittle and breaking. Tilly had had enough. What more did she have to do to prove herself? 'Have I let you down in some way?'

'Of course not, Tilly. You've made a fine newspaperman. You're one of the best girl reporters we've got.'

While she knew he meant it as the highest compliment a woman in a newsroom could receive, it suddenly infuriated her that it had made no difference at all. And she knew she wasn't just one of the best girl reporters. She was one of the best writers the paper had.

'Take a turn at making a home for Archie and raising a family. We need to find jobs for the men so they can have the satisfaction again of being the breadwinner in their families. Be realistic, Tilly. You're not young any more. You've missed out on so many years. Your prime ones.'

Her rage rose in her throat and almost choked her. 'It's a waste, you know, sending me there. To the women's pages.'

Mr Sinclair stubbed out his cigarette. It stood on its end in the ashtray, bent in the middle. A thin trail of smoke rose from it.

'Tilly … get things ready for Archie. When he comes home, you'll have a job to do in looking after him. He'll need you. There's been so much chaos. Go and settle down. See him back to normal, Tilly. That's what wives want to do, hey?'

When had she last felt like Archie's wife?

Mr Sinclair stood and rounded his desk. He reached out hesitantly and patted her gently on the arm.

'We've all been thinking about you and hoping for good news.' He spoke softly; his words were kind and that hurt her more than if he'd been gruff and dismissive. She hadn't admitted to anyone that her hope had been stretched as thin as strands of a spider's web. How had she survived on daydreams and memories so old they were as faded as the curtains in her kitchen?

'Tilly?'

Mr Sinclair was blurry for a moment but slowly came into focus. 'Yes?'

'Go home. Get some sleep. Maybe … get your hair done.' He cleared his throat and watched her go.

Tilly made her way through the newsroom. The air rattled with the pounding of typewriter keys and was opaque with clouds of cigarette smoke. She stepped over wads of copy paper, dead paragraphs scattered on the floor like cigarette butts on the footpaths of Sydney. She passed George Cooper's desk and her eyes were drawn to the space where his Remington portable typewriter normally sat among the detritus. An empty teacup and an overflowing ashtray were still in place. No one had disturbed these artefacts of the war correspondent, as if it would be bad luck to do so. He would clean up his own mess when he came home. She wished he were there so she could talk to him about what had just happened.

'Galloway.'

Tilly turned at the sound of her name but wasn't sure where it had emanated from. She glanced around. The room was filled with rows of desks behind which sat young men, ten years younger than her or more in most cases. She'd known every one of the male reporters before the war, knew their habits and their foibles and was familiar with the excuses they made to get a story or for not having got a story. Where were they now? These were boys who had been too young to fight or had had either luck or family connections on their side. The kind of boys who went to school with the sons of the chairman of the board and who had stepped right on into the reporting roles that women had been shut out of for so long, and were continuing to be excluded from. What made her most angry was that in all likelihood they were already being paid more than she was, these wet-behind-the-ears privileged pups.

No one seemed to be trying to get her attention, so she resumed walking. Then, a low whistle sounded from another direction and the cacophonous sounds of striking keys ceased like music fading at the end of a phonograph record.

'There goes the commie's daughter.' It was a voice she didn't recognise, one that sounded as if its owner hadn't quite made it through puberty.

'Or one of the sob sisters.'

'Or both!'

Once she would have fired back a retort but in that moment she was sideswiped by Mr Sinclair's news and found herself with nothing to say. This had never been her place, up here on the third floor with the newsmen of the *Daily Herald*. She was an interloper, like a woman in a shearing shed, the men as much as calling out 'ducks on the pond' as a warning to the other serious men doing serious work for tomorrow's edition. The newsroom was just like every front bar at every pub, just like the Journalists' Club of Sydney: they were places that barred women.

She was being relegated to the equivalent of the ladies' lounge. During the war she'd at least written about women's labours in the army, navy and airforce auxiliaries; of their service in the Land Army, in munitions factories and in potato chipping plants. They were important stories about women's contribution to the war. And all the while, the reporters of the women's pages had filled precious column inches of rationed newsprint with articles on how to use coffee grounds to create the illusion of tanned legs and offering step-by-step instructions on sewing an old army blanket into a children's dressing-gown.

Her problem was she'd had a taste of a different life and didn't want to give it up.

'Look at her. The reporterette. Off you go back downstairs, dear. She should know her place, that one.'

Tilly kept walking, her heels clicking like a metronome on the linoleum. When the door to the stairwell slammed behind her, she barely heard it. She stopped, took a breath and stared at her shoes. They weren't what they seemed, either. It was only polish that had held them together these past four years and it was only hope that had kept her going. But now, every piece of her life was speeding towards a conclusion she didn't want to face. She was alone. She'd lost the job she truly loved. Her father was sick and getting sicker and Archie was still gone.

Suddenly, every limb felt leaden and she gasped as a choking sob escaped her throat. Her knees buckled and she grabbed for the handrail, lowering herself backwards onto a step. She pulled her knees up and dropped her head into her folded elbows, a hard pillow on the tweed fabric of her skirt.

The war was over. She'd read it in her own newspaper.

So why did it feel as if hers would never end?

Chapter Sixteen

War correspondent George Cooper stood at Tilly's door wearing a brand-new suit, a charming smile and a tropical tan. She was so happy to see him she almost wept.

'Mrs Galloway.' He bowed dramatically before presenting her with a bottle of Gordon's gin. 'A gift for you from Singapore.'

'You're too generous. Thank you.' She took the bottle from his hands and absent-mindedly read the label, glad she was holding on to something to quell the irresistible urge to throw herself into his arms for a hug and a sob. The return of any man—soldier or war correspondent—was a reason to celebrate. 'Welcome home.'

'Why, thank you.'

'Sinclair told me you'd be back this week. Are you home to dry out?'

'A cruel retort. I don't know what you've heard but I deny everything.'

'How was your flight?'

He frowned. 'Bumpy.'

Tilly hesitated for a moment about inviting him in. Mary and Bert were eating dinner in the kitchen and the last thing she wanted to do was interrupt what seemed like a lively conversation between the two of them. There hadn't been too many of them since Bert had returned. He was making the transition back to normal life, to the wife he'd been apart from for so long, to routines that might have become unfamiliar, and it was taking some time. He was getting used to being home and being a husband once more.

Cooper peered over her shoulder into the empty living room. The wireless was playing quietly in the corner. She'd been on the settee reading a magazine when he'd knocked and now here he was, completely unexpected, clearly in the mood for company.

His blue eyes sparkled. 'Aren't you going to invite me in? That gin won't drink itself, you know.'

Tilly lowered her voice and moved in to whisper up at him. 'I normally would but—'

'Tilly?' Mary appeared in the doorway with oven mitts on both hands. 'I'm just taking the canary pudding out of the oven. I was wondering if you'd like a bowl. Oh.' She waved her gloved hands in the air. 'I hope I'm not interrupting.'

Tilly stepped back, opened the door wide and motioned for Cooper to come in. 'Mary, you remember George Cooper from the *Herald*. George, Mary Smith.'

Mary tugged off the mitts and crossed the room. 'Yes, of course. So nice to see you again, Mr Cooper.'

Cooper and Mary shook hands firmly. 'You work in classified ads, if I remember rightly.'

'Yes, that's right.'

George nodded respectfully. 'Your section pays for war correspondents like me to travel the globe. On behalf of us all, I thank you from the bottom of my heart. And my liver.'

Just then, Bert appeared by Mary's side. 'Mary?'

She slipped an arm through his. 'Bert. This is Mr George Cooper, the war correspondent. Mr Cooper, this is my husband, Bert. He's just come home from Singapore.'

If anyone else had noticed Bert's twitch, no one reacted. Bert disentangled himself from Mary and shook hands perfunctorily with Cooper.

'How do you do.'

'George Cooper. Good to meet you, Bert.'

Tilly sensed the tension radiating from Bert's stiff shoulders and quickly filled the sudden uncomfortable lull in the conversation. 'George has just been up in Singapore. Not fighting, obviously. He's a reporter for the paper.'

'Where did you serve, Bert?' Cooper enquired.

'Changi.' Bert jammed his fists into the pockets of his trousers and blew out a noisy breath. 'Not that you'd call that fighting.'

Mary and Tilly exchanged a quick glance.

'But he's back now. That's all that matters,' Mary trilled, her neck flushing. 'Come on, Bert. I don't want that pudding burning.'

Tilly made sure they were out of earshot before she turned to Cooper and said quietly, 'Probably not a good time for that drink.'

Cooper studied her face. 'Not here, anyway.' He cocked his head at the door. 'Let's go.'

'The Roosevelt?'

'That's what the name on the door says. I figured, let's make it easy. Let's walk out of your apartment building, turn left and then left again and voila, here we are.'

Since it had opened in 1943, Tilly had had to steel herself to the noise and commotion that drifted up to the flat:

slamming taxi doors, raucous laughter, American accents
imploring some local girl or other to come inside for a drink
and a dance, milling crowds and the occasional thuds of a
fistfight—but she hadn't ever been inside the nightclub. For
a place with such a reputation, it was unprepossessing from
the outside. On the front of the building there was a single
door and two curved and darkened windows. Its name was
etched in frosted glass and passers-by might miss it entirely
if they weren't looking for it, which made it all the more
glamorous in Tilly's eyes.

As they waited for the doorman to usher them in,
George quipped, 'I suppose you're here all the time.' His
eyebrows raised in a question.

'Me?' She shook her head adamantly.

George laughed. 'You're pulling my leg. You practically
live next door.' He pointed to her apartment building, which
loomed tall in the dark, as if she might have forgotten where
she'd lived for the past four years.

'Why should that be a surprise to you? No one's ever
asked me,' she replied a little defiantly. 'Until you.'

Cooper seemed genuinely taken aback. 'And you let that
stop you? Why didn't you and Mary burst through these
doors every night and get sloshed? God, I would have. Every
damn night.'

Why hadn't they? It was a good question and the answer
was a simple one. Tilly had danced once with a man who
wasn't her husband and she hadn't been able to let go of the
guilt since Darwin. She and Cooper had never discussed
what had happened that night. That he'd wanted to kiss her
and she'd realised it; that she'd turned away just as their lips
would have met. That he'd held her while she struggled with

missing her husband, her loneliness and her confused desire. It had been easier to pretend it had never happened so they could remain friends, because she needed him as a friend more than anything.

She searched for an answer and found one to make him laugh. 'Because Mary and I work for a living, Cooper. We're expected to turn up every day and do our job, better than the men do and then some.' She didn't want to think about her conversation with Mr Sinclair that day. She still hadn't completely figured out what it all meant for her.

'Touché,' he said and saluted her with a laugh.

Tilly couldn't deny the small thrill of pleasure it gave her to make him laugh. She had missed the company of a good man. She had missed him. And while there was nothing she enjoyed more than the camaraderie of her colleagues in the women's newsroom, and in particular Mary's company and friendship, being with Cooper was different. They were reporters and there were conversations she could only have with him.

No one in the crowd around them, milling and jostling and hustling for entry to the mysterious club behind the narrow doorway, knew that she was a married woman, that Cooper was only a colleague and a friend. Here they could be anonymous, even in a city where most everyone read their words in the newspaper every day. She could pretend to be someone else, someone who wasn't the wife of a prisoner of war. She could act however she pleased without worrying about the judgement and assessment of others about what the right amount of grieving looked like.

It didn't seem like a moment before Cooper reached for her elbow and they were being ushered through the door and on the other side of it she caught a glimpse of that other life and it thrilled her. They had stepped into a party. Crowded tables were lined up in tight rows on either side of the dance floor, decorated with bowls of flowers and glamorous people chatting and laughing. A bar stretched along one side of the room and there was a bandstand at the far end, on which a group of musicians wearing tuxedoes were belting out the latest American songs, and people were crammed into every available space, dancing, talking, flirting and laughing. They were having fun and the thrill of thinking that she might have some fun tonight too gave her a smile she couldn't quell.

Cooper guided Tilly through the crowd and he quickly found two seats next to each other at the end of a long table. Tilly set her handbag there while Cooper manoeuvred his way to the bar. She stood for a moment so she could take it all in. The room was crowded with men in American service uniforms—the owners of gleaming teeth, all-American smiles and wallets full of cash. With them, young Sydney women who had already retired their drab austerity fashions to re-emerge wearing crimsons and purples and reds in every hue. Strands of pearls gleamed at their necks and were perfect shining full moons in their ears. Those men who weren't in uniform wore dapper suits with wing-tipped collars and velvet bow ties and there was more than one corsage on show. The scent of perfumes mingled with the sweet smell of whisky, and the stage lights behind the five-piece band streaked through puffs of cigarette smoke like searchlights in a Sydney fog.

The walls were decorated with large caricatures of military men and above the bobbing heads on the dance floor Tilly tried to pick out who they were but she was too far away to properly see. Roosevelt, obviously. Eisenhower? She slipped off her woollen coat and hung it over the back of her chair, before smoothing down the skirt on her navy crepe day dress. She hadn't thought about changing as she'd had no idea Cooper would take her to so fancy a place. But it was dark and no one would notice. And if they did, she suddenly didn't care.

'Whisky for me. Gin and tonic for you.' Cooper slid in beside Tilly and lifted his glass to clink with hers. 'Cheers.' He upended the glass and swallowed the whole shot.

She eyed her gin and tonic, remembering the first time she'd ever been drunk. But she wasn't twenty years old any more. She sipped it. She liked it. She lifted the slice of lemon from her glass and sucked on it. Her mouth tingled.

'Is that a new suit?' she asked Cooper. The navy suited his blond hair and the cut of the snug-fitting collar with wide, square shoulders and two buttons looked modern.

He straightened his tie. 'It's fresh off the rack from Lowe's. Six pounds, three and six it cost me. Plus the obligatory thirty coupons. I even have new socks.'

He pinched the pleat down the front of his left leg and lifted the cuff. 'Cashmere. Feel them.'

She reached down to run her fingers along the fine weave. 'Fancy.'

'Tell me. Does it say weary and cynical war correspondent? Because that's the look I'm going for.'

'It says cashed-up war correspondent to me. It suits you, I suppose.' It did and he knew it so Tilly wondered why he needed her approval. The suit hung elegantly from his tall frame, and the colour deepened the tan on his face. His hair had been freshly cut too, and it was swept back from his forehead, sitting short around his ears. This hairdo looked better than some of those he'd sported in the past. Once, back in '41, he'd hopped off a military plane from New Guinea with his head completely shaved. 'Lice,' he'd explained. Tilly had shivered with dread and taken three steps away from him.

'Why, thank you very much.' He looked her over. 'You don't scrub up so badly yourself.'

'This old thing?'

And where she might have expected a wink and a grin at her joke, there was something different in his countenance. A soft sadness in his eyes had replaced the sceptical glint she was used to, and he dropped his gaze to his glass of Scotch for a long moment. It wasn't like Cooper to be sentimental or complimentary or speak without a newsman's cynicism shadowing every word. Perhaps it was the music or the end of the war or, more likely, that he hadn't been in the company of a woman for a long while. When his eyes lifted, he held her gaze and she suddenly felt self-conscious so she turned away, searching for distraction in the twirling couples on the dance floor.

Behind them, the band ended a tune with a cymbal crash and the crowd broke into wild applause. Cooper turned and lifted his hands to join in. His cigarette dangled from his mouth as he whooped out of the side of his lips. Not for the first time, Tilly wondered what he'd seen, what had gone unreported between the lines of the stories he'd sent back home. Details about the war and its consequences were emerging in more detail with every edition of the newspaper and the grim and appalling reality was only beginning to be told. Were people ready for the truth? Perhaps there would be a time for it, for the reckoning of the damage done and the damage caused, but it wasn't tonight and it wasn't here. There would be a price to pay for it all, a collective communal hangover. It was just a question of when.

Sydney still wasn't of a mind for that reckoning. The city and the entire country hadn't stopped dancing and celebrating since VP Day but Tilly felt as if it had all been happening on the other side of a window. She could see it, but couldn't touch it or feel it. She was still stuck somewhere between the middle of her war and the end of it.

'You glad to be home?' she shouted above the music.

'Sure. What's not to love about the old home town?' Cooper flicked his cigarette at the ashtray and rested an arm on the back of her chair. He didn't meet her eye but looked over to the dance floor.

'How long are you back for this time?'

He shrugged. 'I don't know. The bean counters have been on at Mr Sinclair who's therefore been on at me to take some leave. I've got months and months owing. So I thought the end of the war was as good a time as any to come back home and see what real life's like for a change.' He turned to her. 'It's been a while since I've seen my father and my nieces and nephews.'

'How many do you have now? Six?'

He looked up to the ceiling while he thought. 'Six. No, wait. I don't know if I've told you about number seven. Robert Allan Johnson was born two months ago to my oldest sister,'

'April?'

'Yes, April.' He counted them off on his fingers. 'So there's Ronald, Dennis, Raymond, Diane, Kathleen, Carol and Robert.'

'I suppose you've missed out on a lot with all the time you've been away.'

'Too true.' He lit a cigarette for Tilly who took it. They sat back, smoking languorously for a long while and watching the dancers move and sway.

'Tell me, Mrs Galloway. Do you have all the postcards I sent you?'

Cooper was probably on his tenth passport by now. Home in Sydney for a month, then Townsville or Darwin or New Guinea or Singapore. Earlier in the war, he'd spent twelve months in London and had been in Paris weeks before it fell in 1940. Tilly didn't even have a passport.

She lifted her chin to exhale into the air above them. 'Of course. I keep them as a reminder of all the places I wasn't allowed to go during the war.'

Cooper looked surprised at her jibe. 'You covered the war.'

Tilly scoffed. 'I never got to go where the real action was, like you did.'

There was a flash of darkness in his eyes. 'You shouldn't be envious of that.'

'Why not? I've worked hard to be a good reporter. I could have been a good war correspondent too. A real one. You told me that yourself.'

'When did I say that?' His deadpan look made her laugh.

'You don't remember?' She'd never forgotten how his praise had uplifted her. 'Three years ago when you were back from New Guinea that first time, and Mr Sinclair had just announced that Cleary was the *Daily Herald*'s new war correspondent.'

Cooper had started a slow clap and the men in the newsroom had joined in.

'You turned to me and said he'd only got the job because his father's on the board of directors.'

He conceded that point. 'Which happens to be true.'

'And you told me that I run rings around him and that I should have got the job.' How could he not remember something so important to her? She'd been both thrilled and furious all at once about his compliment and at the fact she hadn't been considered because she was a woman. The thought that he'd said it simply to humour her or tease her was mortifying.

'Did I say that? Was probably half cut at the time.'

'It was ten o'clock in the morning at the staff meeting!' Tilly exclaimed.

'My point exactly.'

Cooper had taught her everything she knew about being a reporter. Not only had he explained to her about the elegance of a crisp first paragraph and the best ways to tighten copy when it was too verbose, she had learnt from him that a story wasn't just the who, what, why, where, when and how of it. He'd encouraged her to put to full use the personal qualities that she had assumed would hold her back and he had never hectored or lectured her.

'You're curious,' he'd said. 'Smart. You're not afraid to ask a complete stranger a question. And that's what this job is, by and large. Asking people questions and putting those answers together in a way that interests other people. It's simple, really. People respond best when reporters like us talk to them as if they're actually fellow human beings. It's a conversation, Tilly. If you want to find out what really makes people tick, what their beef is, it helps to listen to them. Too many people in our line of work don't do that. They fill in the dots in a story they've already written in their heads. They're after a confirmation of the facts according to what they believe the story to be and that, Mrs Galloway, doesn't make them a reporter's rear end.'

The other worthy piece of advice he'd given had saved her bacon more than once.

'Be good to the copyboys,' he'd said. 'They're the lowest of the low around here, and they get a lot of crap thrown at them. I started at fifteen and spent a year being a dogsbody. I've never forgotten who was decent and who wasn't.'

Cooper had a lot of reporting years up on Tilly. At thirty-five years old, he'd notched up twenty years on the road. The day he'd looked at her, put his pencil on his desk and informed her she'd written a story he couldn't improve on was the day she knew she'd made it.

'You'll always be able to say that you were once a war correspondent, Mrs Galloway. You had the licence to prove it. I hope you've framed it and hung it somewhere.'

She huffed and sipped some more of her gin and tonic. '"Woman war correspondent". I still feel like a fraud calling myself that. You know, when I got my licence, I thought I'd be off to New Guinea or Malaya. Just like you boys.' She swallowed the anger that burnt anew, fired by her gin. 'The war changed everything, opened up so many places for women. Places we thought we'd never set foot in. Factories, offices, courtrooms.' She waved a hand in the air and felt a little woozy. Perhaps she needed to eat something. 'And a group of us women reporters thought we'd be allowed to cover the truth about what was going on.'

Cooper's expression was cynical and the laugh in his voice was harsh. 'You think war is about truth?'

Tilly had been slightly envious of the women she'd interviewed in Townsville. They were young—some nearly ten years younger than she was at the time—and they were uniformed and crisp in their navy suits and stiff blue shirts. They even saluted each other. The women had titles like Flight Officer and Wing Officer, and they did crucial work for the air force as radar operators and cypher assistants, sitting in top secret rooms while coding machines clattered away and meteorologists undertook weather observations.

'I didn't get to do what you did, Cooper. Not even close. And by the way,' she started, suddenly nervous to tell him. 'I have news.'

George stared at her for what seemed like forever. 'Is it—'

'No. Not Archie.' Her husband's name filled the space between them for a long moment.

'I've been demoted.' She hadn't wanted to tell anyone before she needed to, expecting that admitting it would make her feel like a failure. As it turned out, she should have trusted that instinct. She did feel like a failure.

'What the hell are you talking about?'

'I'm off general news. It's the women's pages for me from now on, where I'll no doubt spend the rest of my days covering weddings and flower shows and the chairman of the board's wife's latest charity fundraiser.' Tilly heard the bitterness and disappointment in her tone and didn't care. 'I need another gin, Cooper. Or perhaps three.'

When he returned with the fresh drink she'd requested and another for himself, a double she noted, she watched as he slammed it down and decided to try it herself. The bubbles in the tonic made her burp and she covered her mouth.

Cooper fired questions at her. His whisky breath was warm on her cheek. 'When?'

'Next Monday.'

'Who broke the news? Freeman or Sinclair?'

'Sinclair. He called me up to his office.'

'Why? Did he give you a reason that made any sense?'

Tilly gritted her teeth. 'He told me that since Arnold, Charlton, Cleary and you—' she poked him in the chest, 'are all back from the war, I'm surplus to requirements.' Just like the Land Army girls and the WAAAFs and the WRANS and the RAAFNS and the AWAS and the women all over the country being sacked from their jobs in munitions plants and canneries and factories. 'The boys are back, Cooper.' She took a steadying drag on her cigarette. 'And girls like me have to make way.'

Cooper shook his head in disbelief. 'That's a mistake.' He slammed his fist on the table. 'Damn it. I need another.' This time he waved down a waiter, passed him a handful of notes, and narrowed his eyes at Tilly. 'Did you just take this lying down or did you fight?'

'Of course I fought. I know I'm as good as any of the men up there. Take Arnold. He's a drunk. Did you know that he disappeared for a whole week a couple of months ago. One whole week! And when he finally reappeared, no one said a word. And Charlton? He's so lazy he can barely drink his own beer.'

George's eruption of laughter temporarily halted Tilly's tirade.

'I've run rings around them while you've been gallivanting all over the world being Ernest Hemingway.'

Cooper chuckled. 'If only.'

'And the other thing that really got my back up ...' Tilly breathed deep to calm down. 'Mr Sinclair told me the change would do me good, that I could spend my time better helping Archie settle in when he gets home.'

Cooper's gaze dropped to her lips for half a second and her mouth went dry. The gin hit with a whoosh and a warmth flooded her, making every limb feel loose.

The band struck up Glenn Miller's 'Pennsylvania 6500' and the Americans in the room began whooping. Men and women were dancing, happy, twirling, smiling, flirting, laughing. Tilly stood on wobbly legs. She couldn't talk about Archie any more. Not with Cooper. She held out a hand, her palm pointing to the ceiling in an invitation. 'Get me out on that damn dance floor, George Cooper.'

He was on his feet in a flash.

Chapter Seventeen

Tilly had always loved dancing with Archie. His parents were ballroom dancers in Taree and had provided expert tuition to their son. He knew every dance craze going around and had taught them all to Tilly, from the lindy hop and the cakewalk to the jive and the jitterbug and swing.

'Being in your arms is like dancing with Fred Astaire,' she'd told him and he'd kissed her quick and whirled her feet off the floor every single time she said it.

If Archie had been at the Roosevelt that night, the crowd would have parted, gasping in admiration and bursting into applause at how skilfully he moved Tilly, twirled her, pulled her close and then swung her out into the space. Every man would envy him and every woman would want to be the next one to dance with him.

George Cooper was definitely no Fred Astaire. It was abundantly clear that his considerable talent had been poured into words, not quick steps. However, what he lacked in talent, he made up for in half-drunk enthusiasm and Tilly forgot her anger and all her frustrations about work long enough to enjoy herself. When the band struck up a slow song, Cooper gently pulled her in close and tucked her head in the crook of his shoulder and she didn't fight the overwhelming urge to be held and comforted.

Tilly's eyes drifted closed as they swayed to a jazz ballad and she felt a warmth rise inside her chest. She let the heat and the movement lull her into some kind of peace. Cooper's breath was whisky-sweet and the lapels of his new suit jacket were infused with something pine and crisp. Her mind wandered and she imagined a forest, not a jungle; snow, not drenching rain; and her attention focussed on the alive, not the missing.

At ten o'clock, after a couple more drinks and more cigarettes, Tilly and Cooper walked out of the Roosevelt and, instead of crossing the road back to Tilly's apartment, they turned right towards Victoria Street and the water. The night was cool but still, and the nightlife sounds of Potts Point faded as they got closer to the wooden warehouses of the Fitzroy Stevedoring Company that lined the wharf. The waterfront might have been busy during the day and during the height of the war, but the buildings and wharves were silent now, hulking in the dark. The only sound was the water lapping at the wharf.

Tilly walked to the edge and peered into the murky depths below. Cooper grabbed her elbow and she wobbled.

'Not too close there, Mrs Galloway. Wouldn't want you ending up in the drink. Not after all that gin.'

She laughed at him. 'You don't think I can swim?'

'I'm sure you can. But damned if I'm diving in to rescue you.'

'I'm a Millers Point girl, Cooper. I'm a water rat from way back.' She sat and dangled her legs over the edge and breathed in the scent of oil and salt and sulphur. When she closed her eyes, she was ten years old and the sounds of her young life were as fresh in her mind as if they were being broadcast from a wireless somewhere nearby. The squeak and scratch of billycarts on the road, filled with wood for the fire in the mornings and then transformed into racing cars after school, thundering along Munn Street, all the way down to Dalgety's Wharf and into Sussex Street. The echoing shout and then the splash of diving into the harbour from the wharves on hot summer days. The symphony of ships' horns announcing their arrival into Australia's busiest port, the engine of industry and agriculture, employer and exploiter of men. And a sound so familiar to her it was one she would never forget: the silent shuffling footsteps of men along the Hungry Mile.

Cooper stood behind her, his hands loose at his sides, as if expecting at any moment to have to yank her back from the edge. She patted the spot next to her. 'Come sit with me. I promise I won't push you in.'

He grunted and the familiar, wry sound of it echoed in the spaces between the buildings. He manoeuvred his long legs over the side with a groan.

Tilly bumped her knee against his. 'You're sounding like an old man, Cooper.'

He sighed, reached inside his jacket for his cigarettes, thought about it, and then left them where they were. 'War injury, Mrs Galloway.'

'You were hurt? You didn't tell me. What—'

'Don't fret. I fell off a bar stool in an army mess in Singapore and bunged up my knee. I was blind drunk and it was all my fault. That's what happens when you get into a drinking game with a group of Scotsmen.' He fell silent for a moment. 'It hardly compares, does it?' His words hung in the silence between them. He didn't explain any further and didn't have to.

'How was Singapore really?' she finally asked in the quiet.

'Hot.'

'And?'

'Full of troops. Military brass. Nurses.'

'Nurses? I'm surprised you didn't bring one home with you.'

He glanced at her before looking back out across the water. 'Nurses aren't my type, Mrs Galloway. Too much of the Florence Nightingales about them.'

'As I recall, you haven't had a type for a long while.'

'You keeping notes?'

'I notice. I observe. I ask questions. You taught me that.'

'Remind me not to be such a good teacher, will you?' A seagull squawked above them in the dark, circling. 'How's Bert?'

'Doing well, I think. It's a big change to be home. It'll take time.'

'Changi was ... brutal.' Cooper swept a hand over his face and his knee, still pressed against hers, shook.

Tilly wrapped her arms around herself. 'You don't have to protect me. I've read the stories. We've been running them endlessly. I can hardly bear to read them but I can't bear the not-knowing, either. There's so much detail about what the Japanese did to our boys. Beatings, bayonets, starvation. The unbearable cruelty. And those nurses from Singapore on the *Vyner Brooke*.' Her voice fell to a whisper, belying her rage. 'Nurses, Cooper. They weren't even bearing arms.

They were there to tend to the sick and wounded and they were executed, too.'

'He's settling back in, do you think?'

She paused, feeling strange about what she was about to say, about sharing such a private story, but she needed to talk to someone about it and if anyone would understand, it would be Cooper. 'He sleeps on the floor beside Mary's bed. That's peculiar, isn't it?'

Cooper listened intently, his gaze focussed on her.

'He's barely ever home with his wife. So far he's spent most of his time out drinking with the boys he served with. I can't make sense of it. If you'd been away all those years, barely able to get a letter home, or receive any news yourself, wouldn't you want to spend every waking moment with the one you love and not the blokes you've been locked up with? Wouldn't you want to hold tight to your wife and never, ever let her go?' Tilly's heart thudded and she felt breathless and skittish. 'She's trying to put on a brave face, of course. I've given them as much privacy as I possibly can. I've seen every movie under the sun and I even tried ice skating at the Glaciarium to keep out of their hair. But more than once I've come home to find Mary all alone and sobbing in her room. I'm not sure what to do. I've felt utterly helpless.'

Cooper's voice was gruff. 'Don't judge him. You can't know what he's seen. Or done.'

Tilly turned to him. 'How much worse was it really? What did you write that didn't pass the censors' pen?'

It was a long while before George spoke. He seemed to be collecting memories in his head as if he were sorting photographs and deciding which ones to show her.

'It was completely and utterly terrible. A mess. Those men, the ones who survived, held their best mates in their arms while they died. Imagine what that does to a man?'

Tilly held her breath.

'In Singapore, I went from hospital to hospital, taking lists and lists of names and ranks. And I promise I looked out for Archie. I asked over and over if anyone knew him, but nothing.' Cooper sounded as defeated as Tilly felt. 'Who the hell knows where the diggers I interviewed found the energy to talk to me. I've never written so bloody fast in my life trying to get every single word down. The blokes … they were all bones. You know,' he paused, trying to find the words. 'Some of them had lost all their teeth and their hair from being starved for so long. I don't know how they even managed to stand up. They must have been days from death. Some of the poor bastards were liberated from the camps only to die in hospital in the weeks after. It was exceedingly cruel.' Cooper spoke slowly, deliberately. 'And the nurses, the ones who'd been POWs too.' He blew out a deep breath. 'They were the walking dead, Mrs Galloway.'

His face contorted in an expression of defeat, disgust, despair.

'But …' she started, willing what he'd said not to be true. For herself, for Archie. 'Not all of them, surely. I saw them with my own eyes. The first POWs from Singapore, when they came home on the Catalinas. They looked … they didn't look like that. Thin, yes, but not skeletal. Or dying. And Bert? Well, he's scrawny but not that bad.'

'And do you know why? The army carefully chose the healthiest ones to come home first. And even then, they'd already had weeks in hospital to get some meat on their bones. To get treated for what was ailing them. To find new uniforms to cover up what lies underneath. There's still not much more than skin and bone under all that khaki. That whole thing was a public relations exercise and the paper fell for it, we all fell for it, because that's what Australians want to see. We want to see our brave, victorious diggers. Don't you think every newspaper in the country has a thousand photographs of what those blokes really look like? Have you seen any in the press?'

'No.' There were suddenly tears in her eyes. 'And I don't know if I'd want to. Sometimes the truth is too hard to bear.'

'Amen to that,' Cooper said quietly. 'We reporters want the truth. We dig for it. Fight for it. We cross the globe to find it but I don't know if our readers do. Even if we print it, I don't know if they're reading it. There's been way too much truth these past six years. People want to think about Christmas and shopping and next year. And who can blame them?'

Tears pooled in Tilly's eyes and made her cheeks wet. She looked away. She didn't want Cooper to see her crying, didn't want to admit how painful it was to hear his stories. She hadn't thought about the possibility that even if Archie was found, he might die in hospital. It was too cruel to imagine.

Cooper turned his left wrist and angled it towards the moonlight. 'It's almost midnight. Shall I walk you home?'

'Not yet.' She listened to the water lapping, as softly as a cat at a saucer of milk. 'This is the place where troops embarked on ships to sail away to the Great War. Did you know that?'

'My mother's brother, Uncle Vance,' Cooper said. 'He died in Ypres in 1917.'

'My mother's brother, Herb. Gallipoli.'

All around the harbour, ships' lights blinked in time with Tilly's breathing.

'My mother never got over losing Vance. I've got his name, you know. George Vance Cooper. He was the only boy in her family. I was a child when he died. I didn't really understand death back then. All I knew was that my mother was sad for a long, long time.'

Till brought a hand to rest on his thigh. He lifted it, kissed the back of it. His lips were warm and soft and they lingered on her skin. She gripped his fingers, didn't let him release hers.

'I don't know what I'm going to do, Cooper.'

For once, the wordsmith had no words.

Chapter Eighteen

In the kitchen at Potts Point, Tilly was carefully spreading some of her rationed butter—a measly one pound a fortnight—on the black bread she'd bought in Kings Cross on her way home from work that evening. It was Friday night and she and Mary had planned a special meal for Bert: something they hoped he might not have seen before that might encourage his appetite. There was black bread and frankfurt sausages and cucumbers in vinegar called gherkins.

Tilly still hadn't really got to know Bert. He was rarely there in the evenings when she came home from the newspaper. In the mornings when she rose, he was usually asleep, and on the weekends he was out spending time with boys from the army.

Tilly had tiptoed around the subject with Mary, casually asking how he was, how Bert's job hunting was progressing, but Mary had brushed off her questions. 'He's wonderful, Tilly.' And she'd presented her best smiling face.

'No work then?' Getting the boys back to work was all anyone in authority talked about. It had become a national imperative to find jobs for the men who'd courageously saved Australia so they could once again provide for their families and help build Australia's future.

'Not yet,' Mary had replied with a happy shrug. 'We'll be fine. He's got his army pay and three months' holidays. We're talking about going to Melbourne to see his brothers.'

'That sounds wonderful. You might be there in time for the Cup. You'll have to buy a new hat.'

Where Mary's eyes might once have sparkled at the idea, they were flat. 'He's enjoying the fresh air and his freedom,' she said, answering the very question Tilly was too afraid to ask. 'That's why he's walking so much. It's nothing to worry about, Tilly. Truly.'

Tilly hadn't wanted to admit that she knew the exact opposite to be true. She'd heard their late-night arguments, during which Bert's drunken and angry words and accusations had come bleeding through the thin walls of the flat. It was a rare night when he wasn't up in the middle of it, the kitchen light blazing, the sound of his pacing footsteps like a metronome in Tilly's wide-awake ears. Tilly was torn between respecting Mary's desire for privacy in matters concerning her husband, and her concern for her dear friend. Mary and Bert had wanted to find a place of their own, but with so many men being demobbed competition was stiff, and the government's prediction of looming housing shortages was creating panic and the emergence of all sorts of underhand deals to secure whatever was available by whatever means necessary. The entire country's manufacturing effort during the past six years had been directed to the war and housing construction had stalled. All the signs were that the three of them were to be together in the Potts Point flat for a while longer.

At the sound of a knock at the door, Mary looked at Tilly, her eyes wide and hopeful. 'Bert must have forgotten his key,' she said with such an expression of happiness in her voice that Tilly felt a surge of hope for Bert and Mary, that they would get through this trying time. Bert was home from the war and Mary was doing such an ordinary thing, opening the door at the end of the day for her husband, welcoming him and ushering him inside their home and haven. That was all she had ever wanted. They were ordinary dreams rendered extraordinary after so much upheaval, to be able to share small talk about the day, the characters in the office, the push and shove on the tram to and from work. Whose birthday they'd celebrated and how that person had been overwhelmed by a cake and a rousing office rendition of 'Happy Birthday'. What they might listen to on the wireless that night and whether they had any plans for the weekend. Perhaps a picnic or a walk. Church or a horse race. Tilly ached with a traitorous envy that Mary and Bert had it and she didn't.

'Tilly,' Mary called. 'It's George Cooper.'

Tilly picked up the slice of black bread, wiped her free hand on the apron tied at her waist, and walked through to the living room with a smile.

'Hello. This is a surprise. Would you like a taste?' She smiled at him, waiting for a retort but the expression on his face made her slow, then stop. There it was, as easily seen as if it had been written on his face: defeat, disgust and despair. It was in his hooded eyes, in the grim line of his lips and in the clench of his jaw. The blood drained from her face and she felt cold. A chill up her spine made her shiver and then shake.

'Cooper?' Her breath jammed in her throat, choking her.

He held on to the brim of his hat and his lips fell open but he didn't utter a word for what felt like an hour.

'I have some news.'

Behind Cooper, Mary covered her mouth with her hands.

Tilly suddenly felt ice cold.

'Why don't you sit down?' Cooper crossed the room to her, held her elbow and urged her towards the settee. Mary quickly came around the coffee table and sat next to Tilly on the other side, clutching at her arm. Cooper sat on the coffee table, facing her.

Was she sitting? Tilly couldn't feel anything, hear anything, see anything. She looked down in her lap. The piece of bread she'd brought from the kitchen was crushed in her fist and butter oozed between her fingers. She lifted her eyes and met Cooper's dark stare.

This is it, she thought. He knows. And suddenly, despite all the years of desperate, despairing ignorance, she wanted to hold on to this moment just a few minutes longer, to this place in her head and her heart in which there might still be some miraculous possibility that Archie wasn't dead. In this moment, frozen in time, she could let herself believe that he'd staged a fantastic escape or had been rescued by missionaries. That he'd been hiding out on a remote tropical island somewhere in the Pacific. That he'd had amnesia and hadn't remembered who he was or who he'd married or who he'd loved. That he was alive, somewhere, somehow.

But she knew. It was finally over. 'Tell me.'

Cooper reached into the inside pocket of his jacket and pulled out a bundle of paper that she immediately recognised as a telex cable, the kind that spewed onto the floor in the newsroom from the machines that typed by themselves all day and night. He unfolded it, studied the type on it and cleared his throat. When he spoke, his voice was husky and quiet.

'It's the answer to the mystery of what happened to the majority of the garrison that was overwhelmed by the Japanese at Rabaul.' He stopped and studied her. 'The External Affairs Minister, Eddie Ward, told Federal Parliament this afternoon some news about those Australians who were in New Guinea in January 1942. Soldiers and civilians. We know that some escaped and made it back to Australia but there has since been no evidence for what happened to the majority of the garrison overwhelmed by the Japanese at Rabaul. Lark Force. Like Archie. I know you've tried, Tilly, and so have I.' He paused. 'More than once. There's been an inquiry, and investigations in Japan, and General MacArthur's people have confirmed the government's worst fears. They were all lost at sea.'

Cooper stopped and looked at her, clearly deciding whether to go on. 'It seems that those who were left in Rabaul were forced on to the Japanese ship *SS Montevideo Maru*. It sailed from Rabaul on the twenty-second of June, carrying eight hundred and forty-five prisoners of war and two hundred and eight civilians. One thousand and fifty-three people.'

Mary began to softly pray. 'Our Father, who art in heaven ...'

'Tell me,' Tilly said firmly. 'Everything.' For nothing could be as bad as the things she'd imagined or the nightmares that had tormented her all these years.

'The *Montevideo Maru* was torpedoed on 1 July near Luzon in the Philippines with the loss of all the prisoners of war and the internees who were aboard. The Japanese have a manifest of names and it's being translated now so next of kin can be notified.' Cooper's gaze dropped to the cable. '"The Commonwealth Government extends its deepest sympathy to the next of kin of all those who died in such a tragic manner".'

Tilly was aware of Mary next to her, her arm around her, but couldn't feel anything.

'I jumped in a taxi and came right here as soon as I saw the cable. I would have run here if I'd had to. No one wanted you to see it in the newspaper first.'

Tilly's heart beat so loud it hurt her eyes. 'You're telling me that Archie drowned at sea in July 1942?'

'The Americans have confirmed it. The Japanese are handing over the names.'

'That can't be right.' Tilly shook her head. 'Archie's last letter to me arrived in September 1942.' She shook off Mary's arm and bumped past Cooper's knees, almost tripping in her haste. She ran to her bedroom, threw open the case by her bedside table and flicked out the cardigan that held Archie's letters. They flew into the air and scattered onto the rug. She quickly snatched them up. The name on the envelope said Mrs Tilly Galloway. That's who she was. Archie's wife. Mrs Galloway.

'Look,' she yelled and she didn't recognise her voice. 'It's right here.' A moment later, Mary and Cooper were at her doorway. Tilly thrust the envelope at them and jabbed at the date and the censor's stamps.

'See? September. The twenty-third of September 1942.' And she laughed and cried. All this time she'd thought the worst and there'd been a mistake. The goddamn army had made a mistake. 'How can he possibly have died in July when this letter arrived in September? He's still alive, Cooper. Talk to the Americans. Find him. Talk to the army. Tell them this isn't true.' And when she looked down at the envelope in her hands, she saw it was shaking.

Then Mary came forward and before she could sweep Tilly into her arms, everything went black.

ACT TWO

1,000 lost on torpedoed prison ship

The Sydney Morning Herald, 6 October 1945

Chapter Nineteen

Tilly woke to the sound of voices in the flat. It was Archie and their children. A girl and a boy, the pigeon pair they'd always wanted. They had been christened Elizabeth and Donald, but as soon as they'd been brought home from hospital they were Betty and Don. Two years apart, as close as two siblings could be. Don adored Betty and Betty cared for her little brother as she might a new puppy. That wasn't to say she didn't grow impatient with him sometimes—when he cried, she would stomp about the house with her hands over her ears—but when he was happy, she could make him laugh like no one else could. Betty was a sweet-natured little miss with the prettiest blonde bob, and Tilly knew that first thing in the morning it would be unbrushed and unruly and, without the barrette pinning it away from Betty's eyes, falling in her face like a pretty wave. And she just knew Don would be spooning Weet-bix into his mouth with such great haste that he would have dribbled droplets of milk down his flannelette pyjamas that Archie's sister-in-law had sent as a Christmas present all the way from Myer in Melbourne. Don had been named after Bradman and he was already obsessed with the game, just like his three cousins who'd taught him how to wield a cricket stump for a bat the way the real Don had when he'd been a lad.

'Someday I'm going to play for Australia at the Sydney Cricket Ground, Dad,' Don had called to Archie one sunny Sunday afternoon as he'd waved his bat around in the street, answering Archie's deliveries with a belt right into the neighbour's front yard. And as for their oldest? When Tilly had asked Betty what she wanted to be when she was a grown-up, Betty had tilted her head and looked at her parents as if the answer was so obvious they should have known all along. 'Why, I'm going to be a lady reporter like Mum, of course.' And she and Archie had turned to each other and shared a look that only parents who look at their children with pride and wonder can understand.

The sound of her children giggling was one of the most precious things on earth to Tilly. If she could have bottled that sound, she would have, snatched it up in a pickling jar and lifted off the lid when they were grown just to be transported back to their childhoods for a moment, to remember their innocence, their laughter and their complete adoration of their mother and father.

As Tilly stretched in the comfort of her warm bed, she listened to the soundtrack of the early morning in their comfortable, light, airy house. Outside her bedroom window, birdsong chorused from the fruit trees in the backyard, already plump with peaches and nectarines. From the street, there were only footsteps because it was quiet and lined with jacarandas, a home for people and more birds and dogs walking their owners, and not the traffic of newly purchased automobiles. From the kitchen, the kettle whistled as it boiled on the stove. Archie would have poured himself a cup of tea, black with two sugars, while the children ate their breakfast.

And then, when Tilly could no longer bear missing out, when she was bursting to see her children and clutch them to her, to smell their soapy cleanliness and feel the tickle of their silky hair against her cheek, she put her feet on the floor and without even pulling on her dressing-gown, opened her bedroom door and walked down the long hallway to the kitchen, as if she were floating on clouds.

When she pushed open the door, there were four strange people sitting at the table staring wide-eyed at her.

It wasn't Archie and Betty and Don.

The northern sun streamed in through the window overlooking Orwell Street and Tilly blinked at the glare of it. Slowly, she found her focus. It was her mother, her father, Mary and George Cooper. They were staring at her as if she had a head wound or some other horror they could barely face, their mouths agape, their eyes hooded, their mouths pinched.

And then she remembered. Where she was. Who she was. What had happened and how it had happened. But she would never be able to answer why.

Her dear father, crumpled, wincing in pain, slowly stood, pressing one hand flat on the table to support himself. He held out an arm. 'Your friend here from the paper got a message to us this morning.'

When he beckoned her, she went to him and his strong arm around her was safe and familiar and she wished she didn't need it. Then her mother crushed her into her embrace and sobbed into Tilly's shoulder. Tilly was so sorry for them in that moment. They had lost a future, too. It should have been filled with a happy daughter and a son-in-law they loved and Betty and Don. Her grief was theirs now. Their hearts would harden and crack just a little, and they would look back on this day too and realise they had been a little bit broken by Archie's death, that they would always feel the pain and sorrow of their eldest daughter as if it were their own.

Tilly lifted her chin, held her mother closer in the crook of her neck, and looked over at Mary and Cooper. Mary's eyes were puffy and red, her shoulders were rounded and tired and she was still in yesterday's clothes. So was Cooper. He still had his tie on, although it looked as if he'd been yanking at it; it hung around his neck like a present's discarded ribbon.

Her parents slowly released her and Elsie reached up and smoothed her fingers down Tilly's cheek. Tilly could barely feel the contact. What had happened since they picked her up off the floor the night before?

'I gave you two of my sleeping pills, Tilly,' Mary said, as if she'd read the question on Tilly's mind. Or had Tilly actually asked it out loud? 'I wouldn't normally but they're from a doctor. A proper doctor, and I thought that with—' Mary stopped.

'We thought you needed to sleep,' Cooper said.

'Thank you.' Tilly's tongue felt thick and furry and her own voice sounded far away, an echo. She tried to lift the corners of her mouth to smile but she wasn't sure her lips had made the right shape.

Mary stood, pressing a crumpled handkerchief to her eyes. 'I'll get your dressing-gown. You must be cold. Why don't you sit next to your mother and we'll make a cup of tea?'

Every limb felt as thick as tree trunks and when Tilly stared down at her outstretched fingers, she saw fat pork sausages.

'Would you like a cup of tea, Tilly?' Elsie hovered behind her as if she feared she might fall out of her chair.

'What time is it?'

Mary reappeared and draped Tilly's pink chenille dressing-gown over her shoulders. Tilly lifted her arms and slid them through the sleeves and Mary leant in to tie the knot at her waist. Elsie pressed Tilly into a chair and Tilly looked at the things on the table, as still as in a photograph. There was an ashtray filled with ash and cigarette stubs, some stained with lipstick prints. A pack of cigarettes she recognised as Cooper's Woodbines. Cups and saucers. The crumbs from a fruit cake on a plate. A bone-handled knife with a smear of margarine on its serrated edge. A crust from the black bread she'd bought the day before. And in the middle of the table a newspaper was spread out. The words moved and spun and Tilly glanced across the table at Cooper. He turned it around towards her and pushed it closer. She read the headline. It was only a small story of eight paragraphs, on the top right-hand column, dwarfed by an advertisement for household goods next to it. As if the deaths of Archie and all those other people were less important than refrigerators and washing machines and electric home cleaners.

Cooper watched her read it.

'Did you write this?' she asked.

He shook his head. 'I haven't been back to the newsroom.'

And from the fog in her head the memory emerged anew of what she'd asked him the night before. *Tell me everything.* 'You're still here?'

He nodded.

'Are you hungry, love?' Elsie asked. Two warm hands gripped Tilly's shoulders. 'We have some cake. Or there's toast. You should eat something. It'll make you feel better.'

'Just tea, Mum.'

Elsie bustled to the stove. Tilly heard a match strike and a cupboard open and close.

Someone was missing.

'Where's Bert?'

'He's gone out,' Cooper said quickly and at the sink next to Elsie Mary's back stiffened. 'Do you remember what I told you yesterday? About Archie?'

Did she remember her own name? Who she was? Every injury she'd ever suffered came back to her in a lightning-fast catalogue: a burn on her forearm when she was ten and cooking porridge on the wood fire at Argyle Place. A skinned knee when she'd toppled over running down Hickson Road behind one of the McCartney boys on their billycart. The needle pricks on the pads of her fingers when she was learning to sew with her mother. The sprained ankle when she'd jumped off a tram too eagerly on Pitt Street in her new work court shoes and then the pain of hobbling into work. The day Archie left for the war. They all inflicted hurt in varying degrees. But this pain at knowing Archie's fate was numbness. A raw emptiness. It wasn't painful, at least not yet.

'I remember what you told me. About the *Montevideo Maru*. About Archie and Canberra.'

'I'm so sorry, Mrs Galloway.'

The dam had been breached and Tilly could hear it in her father's inhalation of breath. She knew then that they had been waiting until they could be sure she remembered that Archie was dead.

'It's a bloody crime what they did.' Stan slammed his big fist on the kitchen table and the cups and saucers and the ashtray and the empty cake plate shook and clattered. 'It was a prisoner ship. They torpedoed it. In cold blood. All this time … three bloody years it's taken them to get the Japs to tell the truth.' His giants fists clenched on the table like gnarled tree roots.

Stan's words hung in the air. His breathing, already laboured before his exhortations, rasped.

'I know,' Tilly said finally, and she reached for her father's hand, her small one on his, and she felt like a child again, marvelling at the giant of a man she was lucky enough to call her father. 'I know.'

Tilly tried to make sense of everything. Was there a relief in knowing the truth? She couldn't think about that yet. Archie was gone and there had been no funeral and there would never be a grave she could visit, nor anywhere to leave flowers, to sit and talk to him when she needed to bring him back to life.

What a futile waste. She'd been writing to a dead man for years. What had happened to all the letters? All the food parcels she'd sent through the Red Cross to Rabaul? What was she to do now with all the jumpers she'd knitted for Archie that were neatly folded in the camphorwood chest in her room, ready to wear and keep him warm when he'd returned home?

All the days that had been snatched from him. All the moments that make up a life. A summer breeze blowing puffs of wind into the sails of boats on the harbour. The waves at Bondi. The giddy licking of a dog on the walk home with an ice block in one hand and a fresh loaf of bread in the other. The first rose of spring. The first Ashes Test of the summer and every cricket game forever. The birth of a child. A baby's cry. Its first steps. The sun on his face. The soft touch of his wife's hand in the night.

And then there was tea and toast and silence and an unspoken understanding that Archie's death, and the loss of so many others, had been a tragedy and that no one, none more so than Tilly, would ever get over it.

Chapter Twenty

The previous Sunday, a letter had arrived for Tilly, delivered by one of the copyboys from the paper, who'd walked all the way from Pitt Street on his gangly legs.

Reggie had doffed his flat cap and said solemnly, 'A letter from Mr Sinclair, Mrs Galloway. And these.' He'd presented her with a bunch of pale white roses, as pretty as anything Mary had ever picked from the gardens of Potts Point, and Tilly had held them to her nose and inhaled their scent. She'd even managed a smile for the young lad. And then he'd added on his own behalf, because Tilly had always been the copyboys' favourite, 'We're all so very sorry to hear about your husband. Damn those Japs.'

And she'd thanked him and closed the door and put the blooms in a jam jar and set them on the kitchen table. She'd propped the letter against the jar and studied the looped handwriting. Right away she had been able to tell that it hadn't been written by Mr Sinclair—it was far too neat—and she'd supposed it was most likely scribed by Miss Northcott, the woman who'd taken on Tilly's job when Tilly had been promoted to reporter. Miss Northcott was a mature woman, bright and efficient, and apparently gave no quarter to the men in the newsroom, which Tilly had decided was an attribute worth celebrating.

Mrs Galloway.

The letter was still there on the kitchen table, a week later. It wasn't the kind of war souvenir she'd wanted to tuck away with Archie's letters and the telegrams from the army, so once she'd read it, she'd left it be, staring at it every morning as she'd sipped her first cup of tea of the day, studying the handwriting on it as the flowers slowly wilted, until Mary had thrown the stiff stems away and replaced the dead blooms with fresh ones.

Tilly set the kettle on the stove and went to the sink while she waited for it to boil. The aluminium was sparkling and she almost saw reflected in its shine the grieving hands of her mother, who believed in cleanliness almost as much as she believed in the power of a union. There was no godliness in her heart any longer, so she sent all that hope to another form of collective action. Tilly wondered if having a belief would have helped her get through the loss of her husband. Would it be easier if she believed in a higher power, a purpose, a plan? While the idea of being reunited in the afterlife was one that might provide comfort to a believer, Tilly thought it was an awfully long time to wait. She was thirty years old. She might live another fifty years. Four years had been hard enough to bear. What would another fifty do?

Outside, the sun had risen, as it had done every day since Archie had been killed, as it would go on doing every day. Mary would no doubt tell her that the sun shining down on Tilly was a sign from God, that he was sending her his love and guidance after her bereavement. For a moment Tilly wished herself a cat so she could curl up in it and sleep forever.

On the street below, life continued and Tilly watched over it from her eyrie as she'd done every day for the past week. Couples walked arm in arm along the footpath; children skipped gaily ahead of their parents, pigtails bobbing and skinny legs dancing; and cars slowed along Macleay Street looking for a park. She had grown to know the rhythm of the street since she'd lived there. Tomorrow, when the working week began, deliveries would be made to the butcher across the street, and sides of lamb would be lugged inside by men with shoulders as wide as the front doorway. Gentlemen in need of haircuts would come and go from the barber's shop in the bottom of the building and when they stood outside smoking, the smell of their tobacco and cigarettes would waft into the kitchen through its open windows. When the sun set, the Roosevelt would fill with people celebrating love, that evening's romance or the end of the war—perhaps all three at once.

And all over this city and the entire country, widows and grieving families would be waking, drinking tea and trying to make it through another day.

The boiling kettle shrieked and Tilly lifted it from the stove. While the tea brewed, she fetched her cigarettes and matches from her handbag beside her bed and tapped out a cigarette in the light of the window. She put it between her lips and went to strike a match but was distracted by the flapping wings of a magpie on the kitchen window ledge. She stilled. Its head bobbed and it looked through the window at her, its white beak opening in a song that trilled its way through the glass and right through her. She wondered what the birds in New Guinea were like. Had Archie longed for that peculiar Australian sound of the warbling magpie—the *oodle-ardle*, each bird trilling its different lifelong song? Were the birds in the jungle as exotic as she imagined, with plumes of deepest crimsons, iridescent emerald greens and glittering opaline blues? Had Archie been able to cast his eyes over such beautiful things in the jungle when he was held captive, or had all the birds fled with the fighting, as skittish of gunfire as a flock of pigeons in Hyde Park were of a handclap?

The magpie took flight. Tilly's match went out and she put the cigarette back in its pack. For the first time in four years, she'd lost the compulsion to smoke.

She sat and sipped her tea, finding the silence in the flat comforting. Since she'd found out about Archie, it had been full of so many people. She and Mary had spent so much time alone, just the two of them, passing time, wishing the days away until the war ended and now it had been full to bursting almost every day with the two of them, Bert, Bert's sister Irene from Newcastle who had caught the train down to see her brother and had stayed overnight Wednesday on the settee, and Tilly's parents who had stopped by three times in the past week. On Friday afternoon, the women reporters had stopped by with flowers and a basket of homemade jam and mustard pickle and a batch of scones baked just that morning by Vera Maxwell but the women hadn't stayed very long, which Tilly found to be somewhat of a relief.

No one had asked directly, but Tilly knew what they were all thinking: how on earth have you not been driven mad by the knowledge that your husband has been dead all this time?

She was a reporter after all and was fully aware that it was a very good question. If she'd had the answer, she would have told them. Was she going mad? She didn't think so, or at least, if she was, it had started so long ago and had been so incremental that she hadn't realised it.

She took one slow and comforting sip of tea at a time and stared at her name on the envelope on the table.

Mrs Galloway.

She'd been a widow longer than she'd been a wife. And she hadn't been anyone's since July 1942, when Archie had drowned in the hull of a torpedoed ship somewhere in the dangerous oceans off Luzon in the Philippines. Before Cooper told her where Luzon was, she'd never heard of it and now it would forever be her husband's watery grave.

How oddly strange to be addressed as one thing but to have been another entirely for so many years. Should she stop using that honorific? Was it fraudulent now to call herself someone's wife? Tilly knew widows. You couldn't grow up around Sydney's wharves and not know a woman whose husband had been crushed, drowned, poisoned or just plain worn out too early, not know the etiquette. Those women remained, sadly and proudly, honorifically Mrs their whole lives. Would it be different now, a generation on, and with so many husbands having been sacrificed to win the war? And if she didn't call herself Mrs Galloway any longer, was she dishonouring Archie and all he had meant to her?

Although gossamer threads of those questions had been in the back of her mind since his last letter, she still had no answers. And now, this letter, addressed to Mrs Galloway, Mr Galloway's widow. Letters had assumed such importance during the war, for everyone separated by it. Every day she had wondered would a letter arrive today? That thought had sustained her during what she'd assumed had been

Archie's captivity. And then, as time slowly passed, she'd begun to think of it in months. Would a letter arrive in July? Or perhaps August? And as those months stretched out to become years, she'd stopped hoping altogether.

She picked up the envelope and slipped out the letter. It was a single page with the newspaper's name printed in a staid dark blue across the top. She almost knew the words by heart now but she read it again, the words a murmur on her lips.

Dear Mrs Galloway. A line had been struck through her name and seeing it again made her breath catch in her throat. Then, above it, in a hand that she did recognise was her name: *Tilly.*

> *It was with the greatest sadness that I learnt the news of the loss of your husband, Archibald. Please accept my most sincere condolences at your loss and the commiserations of all at the newspaper. These have been trying years for so many, none more so than those who've lost someone so loved and precious. We don't expect you back at work for two weeks, when you will commence your new role, which I hope will go some way towards sustaining you in this time of such loss.*
>
> *With my utmost sympathy,*
> *Rex Sinclair*

Tilly set the letter on the table. She had accepted the offer of compassionate leave. She had known right away she would need it. How could she possibly be interested in the lives of other people when she couldn't even feign an interest in her own?

In the long hours of each night since Cooper had told her the news, she had wandered around the flat, her feet cold on the floorboards, thinking about June 1942. Archie's last days on this earth. By then he'd been away for more than twelve months but his regular letters had kept her hopeful that he was all right. He'd seemed buoyed by his enlistment and had often written during his training about how proud he was to be serving king and country. In his letters, he'd been as he always was: the happy-go-lucky, sweet-natured man she'd married. And who had she been then? A wife who still carried in her heart dreams for their future together.

Every hope and dream she'd had for them since June 1942 had been a mirage. The agony of that realisation was unbearable. Why hadn't she known? Why hadn't she felt it, somehow, that he was gone? Shouldn't she have if she'd loved him so? Such a cruel, cruel trick to play on someone, for their loved one to be dead and for them not to know.

Tilly folded the letter and slipped it into its envelope. The rest of her tea had gone as cold as her heart.

She went back to bed.

'Tilly?'

At the sound of the gentle and familiar knock on the door, Tilly roused from her drowsy half-sleep. She couldn't guess what time it might be. Her days and nights had begun to blur into each other and her sleep had developed the same pattern.

'Come in, Mary.'

The bedroom door opened hesitantly. Mary stepped quietly across the rug and found a perch on the end of Tilly's bed. Mary wore her Sunday best: a tweed suit with a spray of the tiniest white flowers pinned to one lapel. On her head she wore a pale blue velvet hat with a half-veil and a feather, and the gloves she held in one hand exactly matched the blue of her hat.

'You look lovely,' Tilly told her croakily, blinking against the light spilling into her bedroom.

'Thank you.'

Tilly propped herself up on her elbows, realising with a start that Mary was dressed for church which meant it must still be Sunday. How had a whole week passed since receiving the letter?

'I should get out of bed.'

Mary placed a firm hand on Tilly's leg and held it. 'Stay in bed. You need your sleep. I hope you don't think I was lying awake listening for it, but I heard you up and about during the night. Since a week has already passed since ... I thought your sleep might have settled a little by now.' Mary sighed and reached for Tilly's hand. 'Poor Tilly. I wish I knew what to do and what to say. If I knew I would do it, a thousand times over. You know that.'

Mary's eyes welled and Tilly said, 'I know you would.'

'There's a pot of tea in the kitchen. Shall I bring you a cup?'

'No, thank you. I really should get up.' Tilly knew Mary well enough not to have to stifle the yawn that overcame her. 'I suppose it must be past nine o'clock if you and Bert are heading out to church already.'

'It's just me. Bert's not coming,' Mary said, her voice brittle.

'Is Bert unwell?' Tilly asked.

Mary slipped on her gloves and avoided Tilly's eyes. 'Bert's in a dispute with God just now. And I must admit, he's not the only one. But while my answer is to pray harder, Bert's is to not pray at all.' Mary shrugged her shoulders and sniffed. 'The archbishop said last week that we can't expect all the men to rush back to the pews now they're home. They might have prayed on the battlefield to get out of nasty scrapes but that all disappears once they're home. I hope it's not forever.' Mary knitted her fingers together. 'We're all doing the best we can, aren't we, Tilly? The best we can with what God has handed us. He has his reasons for everything and I need to keep praying until he gives me the answers I'm looking for.'

'I wouldn't mind some answers myself. Say one for me, will you?'

'I always do,' Mary said as she stood. 'I'm doing a roast lamb for lunch with all the trimmings. And a rhubarb crumble for dessert. I even managed to find some cream.' Mary paused, her lower lip trembling. 'If you feel like eating, that is.'

Such simple kindness. Tilly wondered how she would ever thank her friend.

'I'll be up and spiffy in no time. I might have even peeled the potatoes by the time you get back. Tell me you found some potatoes?'

'I found some potatoes and they're already done,' Mary smiled. 'I'll see you after church.'

Tilly padded through the flat in her bare feet. She would have a shower and get properly dressed today. She would wash her hair and take some time with it, pin it into curls around her face so she might resemble the Tilly she used to be. She would massage cold cream into her tired face, so crumpled from all the tears, and brush on some mascara, even if she might not be able to stop it running down her face at some point during the day. And she would smile at lunch and eat roast lamb as if she were able to taste it and enjoy it. Because everyone had given her advice on how to cope with her loss and her grief and eating seemed to be at the heart of it.

Her mother's wisest words had been delivered with a warm embrace and a kiss on Tilly's cheek. 'Be brave, Til. That's what Archie would have wanted.'

Her father had held her to his chest and said through his own gruff tears, 'Those bloody Japs, Tilly. Those bloody Japs.'

Mary had been her rock and her advice had been something Tilly was desperate to make real. 'Life goes on, Tilly. You're going to get through this.'

She would have to dig down deep to find that strength from somewhere. She rubbed at her stinging eyes and hoped a good hot shower might be a start.

She stumbled into the hallway and pushed open the bathroom door before realising that Bert was bending over the sink brushing his teeth. But that's not all she saw.

Her ragged cry startled him and he shot to standing and spun around to face her in half a second, before she could even understand that he'd moved.

'Get out,' he screamed and the sheer force of it, like a hurricane gale in her face, stole the breath from Tilly's mouth. Bert waved his razor like a weapon and Tilly tried to move but her feet were numb so he gripped her by the shoulder, hard and tight, his fingers on her like a vice, spun her around and shoved her so hard into the hallway that she hit the wall on the opposite side of the door with a bone-jarring thud.

She stood there for a moment, dazed, feeling pain creep up her left elbow and cheek, trying to find her balance, trying to unsee what she'd just seen.

Chapter Twenty-one

The livid scars on Bert's back streaked in every direction, like gnarled threads of a damaged spider's web, welded together like strands of melted cheese. The savage crisscrosses of raised skin were shiny and twisted, pale scars meeting red and angry welts, and the soft skin along his spine in the middle of his back was the only place untouched, like an equator separating his two worlds of pain.

Everything Tilly had read and tried to forget about the Japanese and their treatment of prisoners of war blazed anew in her memory. Bert was one of those men who'd been beaten and brutalised. Who could think anything else, having been confronted with such clear and barbaric evidence? And it wasn't just the scars that had scared her. When they'd exchanged that glance at each other in the bathroom mirror, his face had contorted in a nightmare of pale white terror; his voice a primal growl, his teeth bared, his hand raised in threat.

And she hadn't been able to look away because every thought sprinted towards Archie and the scars he might have borne when he was murdered. Had he too been beaten? Had he suffered as terribly as Bert had? The agony of the not-knowing rose up in her belly all over again and she didn't try to fight the tears that welled and spilled, for Bert, for Mary, for herself and for her beloved Archie. What a terrible price they had all paid to have won the war.

'Tilly.'

Crouched on the floor in the hallway now, she opened her eyes. Bert was hovering over her, his arms above his head. Her own instinctively braced, and she pleaded in a supplicating, tiny voice she barely recognised as her own. 'Don't hit me, Bert.'

There was a gasp and she saw he had been hurriedly pulling a singlet over his head to cover himself. He swore and she heard retreating steps. 'Tilly, no. I'm so, so sorry. You don't have to be afraid. I won't hurt you. I promise.' His palms were raised as if he were urging her back and his pleading was pitiful.

He covered his face with his hands and jerkily fell to his knees. 'I'm so dreadfully sorry. Oh, crikey. Tilly. I'm so sorry.'

She struggled to her feet without his help. Her head pounded and her heart slammed against her ribcage, adrenaline coursing so hard in her veins she could only see in blurry black and white. She splayed a hand against the wall to steady herself. She could barely breathe. They were alone. Bert had almost attacked her, and when she realised the danger she was in she was overcome with tremors so strong it was as if she were standing in an earthquake.

'Oh, god. Oh, god. Oh, god.' Tears streamed down Bert's face. She walked away from him and went to the settee in the living room but he followed her. Her hip pinched as she sat. When she gasped, Bert tucked a pillow behind her and gently eased her backwards to rest against it. He sat next to her and covered his mouth with a hand to hold in his sobs. 'I didn't see you,' he croaked. 'Please, for the love of god, don't come up behind me like that ever again.'

Then he hunched so far over his knees that his face was hidden and Tilly's heart ached for this man, this broken stranger.

'I'll be okay, Bert,' she said quietly and lifted a hand to pat him on the back. She left it there, feeling his body tremor, for half an hour.

When Mary returned from church, Tilly was setting the table for lunch and Bert was putting the joint into the oven.

'Well,' Mary exclaimed, her face bright and as happy as Tilly had seen since Bert had come home. 'What's going on here?' She propped her hands on her hips and widened her eyes, as if she'd stumbled upon a lovely secret.

Bert closed the oven door and strode to his wife, kissing her long and lovingly on the cheek before wrapping his arms around her. Mary visibly glowed. 'Tilly and I thought we'd have everything done by the time you got home, love. I thought you and I might have a stroll before we eat. Get out into the sunshine for some fresh air. It's a lovely day out there, isn't it?'

Mary blushed with pleasure. 'That sounds marvellous. Let me put my hat and gloves away, Bert, and I'll be right with you.'

Mary shot Tilly a glance before leaving the room. When the sound of happy footsteps on the hallway floorboards filled the flat, Bert quickly moved to Tilly's side. She flinched.

He kept his voice low. 'Please, Tilly, I'm begging you. Don't say anything to Mary. I couldn't stand for her to know what happened.' He searched her face and he looked so genuinely forlorn and heartbroken that Tilly gave him the only answer she could.

'Of course,' she said in an immediate attempt to reassure Bert but the words had fallen from her lips before she could fully think through the implications of what it meant to keep this secret from Mary. Her mind whirred.

'Bert, I—' she started but Bert stepped in to her and cut her off.

'You're a good sort, Tilly. Mary's been telling me so and now I've seen it with my own eyes.' He patted her arm and hurried to his wife. A door opened and closed and then there was happy laughter for possibly only the second time since Bert had been home.

Tilly grasped for the kitchen table and sat. She dropped her head in her hands and breathed deep. Seeing Bert's scars had brought home the brutal reality of everything she'd heard in the newsroom and read in the paper. The senseless, sadistic and inhuman beatings, the decapitations, the shootings and starvation, the forced marches of Sandakan and the slave labour of the Thai–Burma railway. Of beri-beri and dysentery and dengue fever. Bert had clearly suffered so much and was still suffering and now she had made a promise, albeit reluctantly, to a man she barely knew to conceal his actions from his wife out of gratitude for his service, guilt that he'd suffered and the pretence for his wife that he was normal.

Tilly wondered, not for the first time, about what Bert had endured.

The newspaper had been running a column called 'Name Your War Criminal' for weeks, in which returned soldiers named their tormentors. It was one of the newspaper's most popular columns. George Cooper had been interviewing POWs with revenge on their minds, making regular visits to the soldiers' hospital at Concord to speak with those who were recuperating, and visiting those who were already back in the folds of their families at home. Tilly had developed a macabre morning ritual in which she read each name and the details of their crimes. It fed her insatiable and crippling curiosity about Archie as efficiently as manure on a vegetable crop, helping her fill in the gaps about what had happened in Rabaul between February and July 1942.

Lieutenant Fukuda of the Shimo Sonkrai Camp in Burma was accused of being directly responsible for thousands of deaths on the railway, forcing prisoners to walk one hundred and ninety-five miles in sixteen days without rest. Private Toyama at the same camp was described as a sadistic brute who was only happy when clubbing or bashing prisoners. Sergeant 'Monkey-Face' Hoiki, a guard at Changi, ordered any sick prisoners to be 'lollypopped' which was, Tilly had read with dread, a slang term for beheading. Many of the three thousand five hundred men who lost their lives on the railway died by his sword.

Archie's final letter to her had been a lie, she realised, and he'd lied to protect her because he'd loved her. He'd written that he was in excellent health and in good spirits and that the Japanese had been treating him well. If he'd told the truth in his letter it would have been censored anyway. So she'd believed for all those years that he was being cared for according to the protocols of the Geneva Convention, that he was being fed and provided with medication if he needed it, that he was receiving care packages from the Red Cross and all her letters.

None of it had been real.

The next day, Tilly met Cooper at Burt's Milk Bar on Darlinghurst Road, just across from the train station. She hadn't wanted to dress and make up her face and leave the flat, she hadn't wanted to see anyone, but Mary had urged her to get some fresh air and as soon as Cooper had promised more news about Archie and the *Montevideo Maru*, Tilly had agreed. Perhaps Cooper was the only person she knew who could understand what the mystery of Archie's death meant to her. He solved puzzles and deciphered riddles every day in his quest for the truth. And that's what she was after.

She'd arrived a little early and squeezed into the last available booth in front of the counter. She waved away a waitress, deciding to wait for Cooper to arrive before she ordered anything, and waited, alone in the crowded cafe, wondering how it was possible to feel so lonely in the midst of so many people. Booths all around her were filled with young women in twos and threes, their hair primped and curled, swept off their faces and tied with pretty ribbons. Young men gathered outside the curved window, looking inside at the young women and a ritual as old as time played out before her. A mating ritual, a peacock strut, a flip of the hair and a smile. She felt old suddenly. She envied them and the endless possibilities of their lives, stretched out before them now in peacetime. They were on the verge of an adulthood that she couldn't even imagine. Her life had been shaped by her parents' hard-scrabble lives and two wars and the Depression in between. By her marriage and all the years she'd lived, as if preserved in aspic. *Wait until the war's over. Wait until Archie gets leave. Wait until you get a letter. Wait until Archie comes home.* Wait. Wait. Wait. Wait.

Tilly played with the sugar bowl, lifting the lid and placing it back on the crystal bowl with a little *tink tink*. The brightly lit jukebox in the corner was playing Johnny Mercer, who was urging Tilly to 'Ac-cent-tchu-ate the Positive'.

She tried to take his exhortation to heart.

The uniformed waitress behind the counter, decked out like a nurse in pristine white with a cap pinned to her hair, expertly made milkshake after milkshake and Tilly watched her efficient one-woman production line. She slotted a metal container in its stand, frothed the milk with a flick of a switch, and then held it almost as high as her head and aimed the stream of milk into a glass held at hip height without spilling a drop. She was working two milk machines at once behind the counter and had served a dozen customers in five minutes, at least. How many milkshakes had she made for the Americans during the war, Tilly wondered. They'd crowded into the booths here and at The Clock down the road, where rumour had it that prostitutes had hidden in plain sight during the war years.

'Mrs Galloway.' Cooper slid into the booth opposite Tilly, simultaneously taking off his hat and waving a waitress over to take their order: two chocolate malt milkshakes.

'Hello,' she said.

Cooper crossed his arms on the table and studied her. It made her mouth dry and she felt immediately skittish. When she'd been waiting for him, she'd been anonymous, just another single woman in the crowded milk bar. But now, being the subject of his intense focus made her feel shaky and uncomfortable. Mount Vesuvius had erupted the March before, forcing the evacuation of San Sebastiano, whose villagers had already endured occupation and bombings. Scientists had kept a vigilant eye on it ever since and that's how Tilly felt. Like a disaster waiting to happen. Mary, her parents, Cooper and even Bert—when he was home—peered into her eyes and observed her, as if they were taking her emotional temperature, on edge in case she cracked. In one respect, it was only to be expected. She had erupted the day Cooper had told her about the *Montevideo Maru*.

'You look tired,' he said, and it wasn't a joke to make her laugh but a concerned observation.

'I am,' she replied and offered nothing else. What else was there to explain? He would know why.

'Hope you like milkshakes. I've moved into a flat just near here and this is my new local. My non-alcoholic local.' Cooper lit up a cigarette.

When he offered her one, she waved it off. 'You're just around the corner then.'

'It made sense to find somewhere a little more permanent. I'm sick of living out of a suitcase.' He offered her a vague smile but it didn't last long.

'You said you had something to tell me. About Archie.' She wasn't in the mood for small talk. He would understand why, but when she saw a flash of disappointment in his eyes, she felt guilty. He and Mary were clearly in some kind of cahoots to get her out of the flat and while she understood it, it didn't make her any more inclined to talk or see anyone or be watched for signs that she was about to fall apart.

He straightened and leant back in the booth. 'It's about the Japanese and the Red Cross.'

'Yes?' Tilly blurted, not immediately sure of their connection and what that had to do with Archie.

'The Japanese refused to have anything to do with these aid organisations, not even when it came to providing humanitarian aid during the war. They didn't pass over any nominal rolls to the Allies with the names of prisoners on them. They refused to pass on mail with any regularity. The eight thousand POWs in Europe, poor bastards, at least got parcels from the Red Cross and letters from home. I found out that the Portuguese government was the go-between, seeing as they remained neutral during the war.' Cooper shook his head, as if even he couldn't believe the convoluted ridiculousness of what he found himself relaying. 'But with the Japanese, it was complete radio silence. Thousands and thousands of men and women were never heard of at all, officially or unofficially. That's why people are turning up who were thought to have died. And the opposite, unfortunately.'

'Vera Maxwell,' Tilly said quietly.

Cooper furrowed his brow. 'Who?'

'The cookery editor at the paper. She hadn't heard anything about her husband. Missing, presumed dead, was all she was told. But he was found alive on an island in New Guinea. I can't remember the name of the place. Or maybe I've forgotten it already.'

'It's good to hear of a happy ending, isn't it?'

Tilly looked blankly at Cooper.

He continued.

'The Japanese government signed the Geneva Convention back in 1929, which was supposed to set out some civilised rules about how POWs should be treated if there was another war. But they never ratified it.' Cooper stubbed out his cigarette. 'Although Germany did, so what fucking point was there in having it anyway? I interviewed prisoners in Singapore and as you know I've been interviewing others at Concord, trying to get the full picture of what happened to them. They don't say much, or they laugh it off with a joke, until they think I'm not looking and I see their faces. They say there's something about the Japanese, about shame and disgrace and family honour. If you're Japanese and you've been captured, you don't want to go back home. You've disgraced your name. So that's how they treated our men and women.'

The hairs on the back of Tilly's neck prickled. She thought of Bert. His scars. The agony and fear she'd seen on his face.

'Are you making excuses for the beatings and the beheadings and the torture, Cooper? The starvation? The rapes? Because no one's said it, but I'm sure it happened, aren't you? Men are men, no matter where they're born. And war turns some men into beasts.' Her voice shook. She felt the cool sheen of sweat on her top lip.

Cooper reached across the table and took her hand. If she wasn't feeling so numb, it might have been comforting.

'You know that's not what I'm saying. Aren't we all simply trying to understand the whole thing? The Germans? The Japanese? And who knows what the hell our troops have been up to. We ask them to go to war and kill and then we act surprised when they do. All I'm trying to say, Mrs Galloway, is that the Japanese look at being a POW much differently than we do. We want them back. You've wanted Archie home all this time. You wouldn't think less of him for having been captured, would you? In their culture, being captured means you've disgraced your emperor and your family and humiliated yourself.'

A waitress set their milkshakes on the table, tall glasses with scoops of chocolate ice-cream bobbing in the frothy milk. Tilly pressed her lips around the straw and drank. Cooper lifted his glass and sipped. At the counter, the till closed with a metallic jangle and the milkshake blender screamed and rumbled. Bing Crosby was singing with the Andrews Sisters and the happy chatter all around them hit a crescendo as the door to the milk bar swung open and more laughing young women with painted faces and Brylcreemed young men with freshly erupted pimples and old sports coats arrived all at once.

Tilly pushed her glass towards the middle of the table. She suddenly felt sick. 'What was it all for?'

'The war?'

'Of course the war. I'm still having trouble remembering what it was all for. Millions dead, Cooper. Millions. I waved my husband goodbye one day and I never saw him again. What for? Will his death, or any of those millions and millions of others, mean there'll be no more wars? So the Japanese have some warped fear of being disgraced in the eyes of their families. I can tell you what is much, much worse than that fear they're worried about. And that's holding on to hope, day in, day out, year after year. That is the real hell.'

Cooper's face blurred in her vision and her voice rose, catching in her constricted throat. 'Right now, all I can think about is me and what I've lost. My heart's not big enough to be compassionate about the people who murdered my husband. Right now, I hate them. Every single one of them. I know that makes me sound cold-hearted and mean, but I can't help it. I've lost everything. My husband. My job. Somehow, from all of this, I have to make a new life and I have no idea where to start.'

Tilly slid out of the booth, grabbed her handbag and stood. When Cooper moved to follow her, she shook her head. 'Thanks for the milkshake. I'll see you.'

Chapter Twenty-two

One of the missing pieces of Tilly's puzzle was delivered in a telegram, small and pink and delicate and deadly.

When the boy from the post office handed it to Tilly on her doorstep, he cleared his throat and said her name aloud to check that she really was Mrs AH Galloway of Potts Point, to guard against the horrifying possibility that he might inadvertently present the worst imaginable news to someone else's wife.

'I'm she,' Tilly replied and felt a great wave of sorrow for the boy, for he really was a boy, barely out of short pants and certainly not yet in need of a razor. For every happy family, for every cry of jubilation and joy his telegrams received, just as many would have been thrust back at him in frantic refusal. How many doors had been slammed in this poor boy's face?

'Sincerest apologies, madam.' He nodded solemnly, tugged on his flat cap, and left Tilly right there in the hallway. He knew what pink meant. He didn't need to loiter. Her door was wide open behind her and a breeze from the stairwell swirled and caught the hem of her skirt and it fluttered about her calves.

She heard the shuffle of footsteps. Mr Kleinmann looked over at her and the telegram in her hands and lowered his head. He whispered something she couldn't hear or didn't understand and then gently he closed his front door behind him and retreated back inside.

Tilly went to her room and sat on her bed. Her name and address peeked through the clear window, typed on a typewriter most likely very similar to her own on her desk at the *Daily Herald*. She wondered about the people whose job it was to sit behind desks day after day and type up these death notices, stuff them into envelopes, making sure the name and address were set in just the right position to be seen through the clear window, and then pass them on to someone else who would pass them on to someone else who would give them to the telegram delivery boy. Did a little piece of death rub off on each of them as the information was passed down the line? What a burden the truth was to carry.

She steadied herself and carefully opened the envelope. She slipped out the folded pink paper. Such a jolly colour, almost watermelon, which before the war might have signalled something to celebrate instead of the worst news imaginable.

And there it was. Finally. Her truth. *We regret to inform you that L/CPL AH Galloway is now reported missing, believed deceased while POW on or after July 1, 1942.*

Reading the words there couldn't hurt Tilly any more. She had endured all the suffering and pain she was capable of in the years and months he'd been gone. These words on the pretty, pink, cruel paper, typed by a stranger who might have laughed and sipped tea while she worked to take her mind off the reality of the words she was typing, the sentences that could shatter someone's life, were water off a duck's back now. It was as if she had just read about the cliffhanger in a film she had already seen.

Tilly tucked away the telegram with the others, with Archie's letters, delivered after he was already a ghost, and closed her bedroom door quietly behind her.

Tilly walked the city point to point, from the flat to her parents' terrace. She bustled her way through crowds of shoppers, past schoolgirls in their straw hats and uniforms, past rubbish collectors and ferry commuters and office workers wearing smart suits and post-war hopefulness. She didn't saunter, she strode. The city pressed down on her, sucking the breath from her lungs, the buildings looming tall and menacing when she raised her eyes skyward. But she had to keep going. She had to keep moving, giving every building and monument only a few seconds of her attention and every passer-by the merest glance because she didn't want to connect with anyone or see or feel anything.

At Argyle Place, she couldn't bear her parents' silent grief. But the flat, which had always been her haven, her place of comfort for so long, was now a prison. The tension between Mary and Bert quivered unceasingly, like a violinist's bow, and she found herself swallowing her screams of rage at them, the words sitting fierce and unspoken on the tip of her tongue. 'Love each other,' she wanted to scream. 'Be thankful you're home, Bert. At least you have a husband, Mary.'

Tilly was struggling to recognise her dear friend. Where had her Pollyanna gone? In her place was a woman who walked on eggshells in her worn-out shoes, her voice reduced to a whisper when Bert was near. She'd become afraid of the night, for it meant an aching loneliness and a ratcheting anxiety about what state Bert would be in when he staggered through the door.

And what had happened to the man Mary loved? Or had loved once, a long time ago. He'd walked up the gangplank onto a troop ship and disappeared in Singapore. Someone else had returned home, wearing his skin as a shell, like a hermit crab.

The cruelty. The fighting. Bert would come home late at night, with a skinful under his belt, and then anger and grief raged in both of them. The walls in the flat afforded no privacy and Tilly heard everything.

'Where have you been, Bert?' It pained Tilly to hear Mary ask this same question night after night, that she had been reduced through her fears to this kind of woman. A fishwife, a nag, a harridan. Why were there no labels for the men who caused this pain and suspicion and fear?

Bert's answer would come, in a slur of words, bitterness in each syllable, and Tilly would cover her ears but still she heard it.

'None of your bloody business.'

'I'm your wife. Of course it's my business.'

'For god's sake, woman. None of the other bloke's wives nag like this. What happened to you when I was away? What happened to the girl I married? There's a knowledge in your eyes now, I can see it. I know exactly where it's come from.'

'I'm still that girl. I still love you. Come to bed now. Don't sleep on the floor tonight.'

'You think I want to get in that bed with you? Who else has been in it, hey? I hear the Americans were splashing round their fat wallets and their chocolates and their silk stockings to any girl who'd open their legs. Yes, they were very keen on themselves, I hear. That was you, Mary, wasn't it?'

'That's a horrible, horrible thing to say. I waited faithfully for you for four years. I didn't know if you were alive or dead and I waited and prayed for you, Bert. For us.'

Their endless arguments were variations on this theme, over and over, every night. Bert would shuffle home in his cups and Mary would beg him to join her in the newly purchased double bed in their room.

Why were they wasting such precious time when they still had each other? Didn't they know how lucky they were? After Bert's harsh accusations and Mary's sobbing rebuttals, she would retreat to the bathroom to wash her face and cry in private.

Tilly would go to Mary, put her arms around her and comfort her in a way that Bert was unable or unwilling to, and find some useless words to say.

'He's been through so much. Give him some more time, won't you?'

It was supposed to heal all wounds, wasn't it? To change everything? It flew, too, when you were having fun. But what if you weren't having fun? What if time was like warm toffee, stretching and teasing and enticing you to smell and taste and devour with a sweet promise, until it turned on you and set hard as a rock and all those memories and sadnesses and horrors were ensnared in its sticky grasp forever, like a fossil in amber? *Give him time.* The lie of Tilly's words stuck in her throat like a fishbone. Time changed nothing. Time brought nothing but pain.

'When I reach for him, he pulls away, as if I'm a stinging nettle. As if I'm poison.' Mary's shoulders fell in hunched defeat and her haunted eyes filled with tears.

'Oh, Mary.'

'What can I do?'

Tilly had no answers. All she could do was hold her friend, press her comforting arm tighter around her shoulders, listen to her, whisper words of understanding.

'I know you love Bert. I know you love him with all your heart. And he loves you.'

But I don't know anything about Bert, Tilly thought. *Except that he's not the man you thought he was. That he's a drunk. That he hurts you and it pains me.* But Tilly would not say those words out loud to her friend. What good would they do?

In Hyde Park Tilly lay on the grass, her eyes to the sky, counting the clouds that stretched like spun fairy floss on the bright blue day. She had always loved Sydney's big skies. Growing up at Millers Point, her outlook had always been sweeping: across the harbour from the arches of the bridge to the tops of ships in the distance; from the suburbs in the west, to somewhere in the distance the Blue Mountains. When she and Archie had lived at Bondi for those treasured months together, the sky had stretched out past the curve of the beach, beckoning them to places they imagined they might one day visit: Hawaii. Fiji. Tahiti. Now, the sky belonged to the faraway place that had taken Archie from her. It was the sky from which the Japanese had descended and bombed Rabaul and then the *Montevideo Maru* and robbed her husband of his life and a thousand others of their lives and her of her husband.

She closed her eyes against it, and lay, sprawled, one arm above her head, feeling boneless and broken as if she had plunged from one of the nearby buildings on Elizabeth Street, forming the outline of a body drawn in chalk on a footpath in a James Cagney movie. The damp from the grass was cool on her back and her legs and her hair.

Tilly heard a *tsk tsk*. 'Look at that woman. Probably in her cups.'

And then another spitting, judging voice. 'What these young people think they can get away with these days. It's a disgrace. The war is over. So should this excess be, this … immorality. Absolutely no decorum whatsoever. I blame the Americans, don't you? Lord knows what she got up to with them.'

Tilly opened her eyes and propped herself up on her elbows. Two matrons in floral spring frocks had their noses firmly turned up at her, white gloves hiding their talons and fascinators with sprays of white feathers hiding their gimlet eyes. They examined her as if she were a piece of litter in the gutter. Like an empty gin bottle or a soldier's condom.

'Have some self-respect, young lady,' Matron Large Bosom lectured. 'Get up off that grass.'

Tilly sat up and returned their supercilious gazes, a fire burning in her belly all of a sudden. 'My husband was killed in the war,' she said. 'That's what I was doing during the war. Waiting for him to come home and he never did. That's what I sacrificed. What did you? A few lunches at the Australia Hotel?'

Matron Large Bosom clutched at her collar. The other muttered, 'Well, I never,' and they huffed off towards Elizabeth Street.

Tilly got to her feet and walked south towards the Anzac Memorial. The pink stone rose up into the sky, monolithic, a temple to war and loss and sacrifice, and she took the steps to the entrance. Inside, it was cool and strangely silent, the sounds of Elizabeth and Liverpool Streets muted by the stone walls and the silent contemplation heavy in the air. In the domed sky above, thousands of gold stars twinkled in a constellation and it was only when she looked really hard that Tilly grasped how many of them there were, each one a representation of an Australian who'd died in the service of their country. Thousands and thousands and thousands of stars, thousands of men and women.

She gripped the cool rail under her palms and looked down to the sculpture on the level below and felt herself transfixed. It comprised a naked prostrate man, his belly hollow, his head lax, his eyes unseeing. He was lying on a sword under his shoulders, like the cross a man nearly two thousand years before had been nailed to. Under his back was a shield, symbolic of the Spartan legend that a soldier should honour his calling by coming home with his shield or dying on it. The hushed voices she'd heard a moment before became silent and all she could hear was her breathing and her heart beat, a *thud thud thud* inside her chest.

Underneath the dead soldier, bearing his burden, were a mother, a sister and a wife nursing an infant child.

Archie's mother was dead. He had no sister. He would never be father to a child. The only one left was his wife, bearing the weight of the burden alone. Tilly saw her life in that sculpture, in the darkest depths of the bronze, in the grief in the wife's expression. And that's when she let herself see the truth of how Archie had probably been in the months before he died. He would have been like the soldier, his protruding ribs harsh lines on his torso, taut tendons in his neck, his cheekbones gaunt. She couldn't pretend otherwise with all she had read and all she now knew, about Bert, about the returning prisoners of war, with everything Cooper had told her.

She had in reality been mourning Archie since his last letter to her in 1942. At least the warrior in bronze had returned. Her soldier warrior would never have a funeral or a grave. His death would never be commemorated with pomp and fanfare. He had drowned in the hull of a ship as it sank to its watery grave, torpedoed into jagged pieces.

She felt no glory about it, just the bitter truth that Archie was dead.

Chapter Twenty-three

Tilly woke with a shudder and bolted upright, jolted into consciousness by another dream of piercing screams and agonising shouts. Except now she was awake, and there was still screaming. She tried to get her bearings.

From the window, the light of the moon created a thin sliver between the curtains. Outside, a car turned down Orwell Street, its throaty chugging fading into the distance as it headed towards Victoria Street. Inside the flat, another shrieking, moaning nightmare.

Tilly swung her feet out of bed instinctively and waited. She listened for a moment, hoping the screams would stop, that Mary's soothing might urge Bert back to sleep. Sometimes he would settle, drift away from his hell into some kind of peace; other times there had been stomping footsteps through the flat, pleading, crying.

'Bert! Bert! Wake up, darling.' Mary's shouts sent shivers up Tilly's spine.

A roar, a cry of 'No, no'.

Then, running feet and Tilly's bedroom door swung open so hard it cracked against the wardrobe behind it.

In her nightgown Mary looked as white as a sheet. 'Tilly. Help me. Please. I can't wake him this time.'

The light was bright overhead in Mary and Bert's bedroom and Tilly paused at the doorway, wishing she didn't have to see this intimate scene, this devastating portrayal of what the war had done to Bert. He was naked on the floor, covered in sweat. His short hair was damp and spiked, his arms were flailing and thumping on the floor, and his face contorted in horror at a scene only he could see behind his closed eyes.

'Help me shake him.' Mary fell to her knees at his right side and Tilly took up position across from her. Mary cupped his head in her hands and Tilly grabbed a shoulder, shaking and jerking him, while Mary protected his head from smashing into the floor. A quick glance at Mary's practised care made Tilly wonder how often she had done this behind closed doors since Bert had returned.

'Wake up, Bert,' Tilly demanded.

Mary leant in close and whispered, 'Bert. It's Mary. You're having a nightmare. This isn't real. Open your eyes, my darling.'

And he did, for a moment, his eyes slowly focussing. And there was blessed quiet and Mary and Tilly were able to catch their breath. Tilly sat back, aware of his nakedness, feeling embarrassed for him that he would realise she had seen him that way.

But then Bert jerked and every limb flailed. An outstretched arm smacked Mary under the chin, a clenched fist clocking Tilly square on her left cheekbone. He roared to his feet, energy radiating from him, sweat shaking from him in droplets onto the floor, and bolted to the corner between the wardrobe and the dresser and hid there, wide-eyed, quaking.

Tilly pressed a hot hand to her eye, already throbbing with pain. She couldn't look at Mary. Her guilt at keeping Bert's secret bloomed faster than the bruise under her eye.

Mary began to sob. When Bert's breathing calmed, when he seemed to come back to his senses, he looked at his wife and Tilly and then Mary once more and whispered, 'Sweet Jesus. What have I done?'

The next morning, Tilly studied her swollen face in the bathroom mirror. Her lower eyelid was puffy and tender, and blood and purple bruising were pooling under the swollen skin. When she gingerly poked her cheekbone, it hurt. She'd read somewhere once, perhaps in her own paper, that the eyes were a mirror to the soul. She stared at her own and thought how true the adage was.

Her soul was bruised, black and blue, aching and tender. And while her left eye was worse, her other eye had dark circles underneath it too. She studied the hollows in her cheeks in the dim bathroom light. When had she got so thin?

After she'd left Bert and Mary to console each other the night before, she'd gone back to her bed but had slept restlessly and painfully, her heavy heart like a ball of lead in her chest and her head full of dreams she didn't want to remember. When she was woken by a shaft of morning light across her face, she heard shuffling footsteps and quiet voices in the flat and she lay still, trying not to listen, aching all over. Then, the front door closed and the flat seemed to be quiet.

Tilly had kept his secret but it was now out in the open and all three of them shared the shame and humiliation of it. She hadn't wanted to get in the middle of their marriage, of the secrets they'd wanted to keep about Bert, but she'd been dragged there against her will.

She held a flannel under the tap until it was sodden, squeezed it out, and pressed it to her eye. There were some powders in the kitchen cupboard and she decided to take two to help with the pain. With each step, it throbbed behind her eye and the beginnings of a headache made her feel dizzy.

She turned into the living room and froze. Through her squinting good eye, she could make out a tall man in a flowing overcoat standing by the mantelpiece holding Archie's photo. A surge of adrenaline and fear hit so fast that at first Tilly couldn't make a sound, but when she finally screamed, loud and piercing, she scared herself even more.

The coat turned. It was George Cooper. 'Bloody hell. It's only me.'

Tilly's heart galloped. 'What the hell are you doing here?'

Cooper's eyes widened and his lips fell open in a question he didn't have time to ask before he strode towards her, reached for her wrist and urged the flannel from her face. 'What the hell happened to you?' He leant down, peering close at the spreading bruise, and gently pressed two cool fingers to her eyelid.

'Ouch,' she grimaced, but it felt good.

His jaw clenched but he was restrained. 'What's with the shiner? You taken up boxing, Mrs Galloway?'

The tension in the flat had been so heavy for so long that it was a relief to hear a joke. Cooper had always been able to make her laugh. And how desperately she needed to. 'Perhaps I should, if my reaction to you just now is anything to go by. I see a strange man in my living room and all I can manage to do is scream like a schoolgirl. I should have grabbed a candlestick and clocked you over the head with it. How did you get in?'

'Very glad you didn't.' He made a show of glancing around the room. 'Do you even own a candlestick? I was coming when Mary was going. She said that you were in the bathroom and I should wait.'

There was a loud pounding at the door. 'Mrs Galloway. Is everything all right? Mrs Galloway?'

Tilly lowered her voice. 'It's Mr Kleinmann from next door. Coming,' she called and when she opened the front door, he gasped in shock. His white hair would have stood on end if he'd had more of it.

'Mrs Galloway!' he exclaimed. 'Should I make the police come?'

Tilly looked over her shoulder at the mise en scène. A tall man in an overcoat. A sad, thin woman with a black eye, holding a flannel to her face.

'Thank you, Mr Kleinmann, but there's no need to worry. I'll be perfectly fine.' If she was honest, she was still shaken from the events of the night and morning, from seeing Bert to finding Cooper in her living room, and from the pain radiating from her eye. Perfectly fine may have been overstating it, but there was nothing about this situation she wanted to share.

'But ... this man ... is he your husband from ze war?'

The husband you told me was already dead? She looked more closely at her neighbour. His left hand on his walking stick was shaking, giving him the appearance of someone holding a divining rod that had just discovered water.

'No. He's a colleague of mine from the newspaper.' And then she thought she may as well tell him. He might get a thrill out of having been right all this time. 'My husband died, Mr Kleinmann. Back in 1942, as it turns out. It's only just been discovered.'

The old man's face crumpled. He reached a wrinkled hand towards Tilly before pulling it back. 'I'm so very sorry,' he said. 'May you suffer no more.'

Tears glistened in his eyes and Tilly suddenly felt ashamed of herself for her ungracious thoughts about him. 'Thank you. That's very kind.'

'And may I wish you a long life.' He stepped back. 'Goodbye, Mrs Galloway.'

Tilly closed the door, and turned to Cooper, waiting until the sound of footsteps in the hallway stopped. 'He was our building's air warden during the war. He used to scold me for smoking during the blackouts.'

'That accent. Where's he from?'

Tilly wondered for a moment. 'I don't know. He's lived here a long time. Did he tell me once? Seven years or was it eight? I can't remember exactly. He's a violinist, or used to be. He would play for hours and hours.' She hadn't heard his music in a long time. She thought of his walking stick, his shaking hands.

Cooper took off his coat and tossed it on the settee. 'Now. Are you going to tell me what happened to your eye?'

There was no more humour in his voice. He stared darkly at her.

Tilly bit her lip to buy some time. However she said it, she knew it was going to sound awful and something other than it was. 'I'm going to tell you but I don't want you to overreact.'

Cooper listened, impatient, but he waited.

'It was Bert but—'

He gripped her shoulders and his blue eyes blazed with anger. 'You need to tell me everything, Mrs Galloway. Right now.'

'Please. I need to explain. It was the middle of the night. Last night. Bert was having a terrible nightmare. They've been getting worse and worse since he's been home. Mary was terrified when she couldn't wake him and she asked me to help. He lashed out in his sleep. When he was himself again, he was horrified, honestly he was. He didn't mean to hurt Mary. Or me.'

'But he did. What about Mary? Is she all right?'

'I haven't seen her this morning. You did, when you arrived. What did you think?'

'She looked a little out of sorts, I thought. She hurried past me and left.' His gaze shifted to her cheek, her bruise, her pale face. 'You're going to need more than this. Sit down.' He took the flannel from her and walked to the kitchen.

Tilly lowered herself on the settee and leant back. Her faint headache was now hammering in her temples. She lifted Cooper's coat and covered herself with it like a blanket. It smelt of his Woodbines. She heard the fridge door open and close. The *tink* of ice hitting the metal sink. Then Cooper was back and the ice-cold flannel stung as he held it gently to her eye.

'I couldn't find a steak,' he muttered.

'Not in this kitchen,' she replied.

She felt him sit next to her. He rearranged the coat so it covered her. A hand was on her knee. 'I need you to tell me the truth now. Do you think Bert is a danger to Mary or you?'

'No,' Tilly replied quickly. Too quickly perhaps. In the hours it had taken her to fall back to sleep the night before, she'd gone over and over the same thing. He may not have meant to hurt her but the evidence was that he had, twice now. The truth of it was that last night's episode had rocked her. That had been more than a drunk man lashing out. How could she be certain that he wasn't dangerous? Her trouble was that, even if she believed he was, what could she do about it? She loved Mary and Mary loved Bert so what choice did she have but to trust him?

'I don't believe you.'

'It's malaria, Cooper. The night sweats and the fevers. And the nightmares. That's what happened this morning. It's as if he's fighting someone. His dreams are torturing him.'

He lifted the flannel and checked her eye. 'His real life tortured him.'

'I can handle the nightmares. But they fight. And then he drinks. Mary is trying to believe that everything will be all right. She's down on her knees every night praying for Bert to get better. She talks to God more than she will to me.' Tilly opened her good eye and looked at him. 'I remember what you said about those soldiers you saw in Singapore. I saw his back, Cooper.'

His stricken expression revealed he knew what she was going to describe.

'The scars ... I didn't mean to. I opened the bathroom door, not knowing he was in there and he had his shirt off and he took one look at me and ... he came at me.'

'Are you telling me this is the second time he's hurt you?'

Tilly laid her hand on his and he dropped his gaze to the spot where they were skin to skin.

'I don't quite know how to explain it, but it's as if Bert's not there when this thing takes hold of him. His whole face changes, contorts, and his eyes are empty. And then, he snaps back and comes to, like he's woken from an anaesthetic. And he's so embarrassed and ashamed. The first time, he said it was because I'd snuck up on him. He looked at me like I was ... his enemy.'

'Like you were one of his Japanese guards,' Cooper said quietly.

'I've tried not to, but I've been reading that damn stupid Name Your War Criminal column of yours. You've been putting all the horrible details right there in the paper for everyone to see.'

'Not all of them,' Cooper added roughly.

'I think I need another powder for this headache.'

Cooper didn't move. Her hand was still on his and she didn't want to let go. She'd had to be so strong for so long that letting someone take care of her felt like shedding a weight, sharing a burden.

'I'll get one. Where are they?' But he didn't move. He sat by her side, his hand still under hers and she wondered what he would do if she linked her fingers in his.

'In a minute,' she said. 'The ice feels good.'

'You'll still get a bruise but the swelling won't hurt so much.'

She liked being cared for.

'I'm sorry, Cooper.'

'About what?'

'When we were at Burt's. I was angry.'

'You have every right to be. But I don't want you to hate because of what happened to Archie. That's what I was trying to tell you, I think. Somewhat clumsily. Your heart's too big and too kind to be filled with it.'

She didn't want to hate. It was exhausting. But it was stubborn and tenacious, this resentment and fury and rage.

He paused. 'What are we going to do about Bert?'

'I don't know.'

They sat in silence while Tilly pulled the words together so she could get it right. 'I'm sorry for walking out on you, at Burt's. It was petulant.'

She heard Cooper's soft chuckle. 'You've always liked a fight.'

She wouldn't tell him that she feared the fight had gone out of her for good.

The next morning Tilly ran into Mr Kleinmann in the hallway. She had just closed the front door when he appeared from his and called out her name. She turned, worried that she was late and hoping he wasn't after anything more than a brisk *hello* and *have a good day*.

'Mrs Galloway?'

She slipped her keys in her handbag. 'Good morning, Mr Kleinmann.'

He shuffled towards her, barely lifting his feet. 'Can you spare a moment?'

'I'm just on—' He'd been kind to her when he'd seen her with Cooper and noticed her black eye. 'Of course. What can I do for you?'

He nodded. 'If you wait here. I come back.'

'I'll follow you. How about that?'

'Please. Come,' he said and together they slowly walked the fifty feet to his door. She didn't cross the threshold, thought it most polite to wait, but that didn't stop her from looking across the living room. It was the same design as her flat so she knew its shape and flow immediately. On his mantelpiece there were two small silver frames with photographs she couldn't make out at this distance, and an unusual candelabra with room for nine candles. There was one armchair with a folded rug on it and, on a cabinet on the opposite wall, a violin case.

'Here,' Mr Kleinmann said. Tilly looked across to see him holding a cake plate in both hands and she knew immediately he didn't want to walk any further without his stick. Quickly she went to him.

The cake smelt of lemon and looked like the richest cream had been mixed with cheese and set.

'It's käsekuchen. A cheesecake, you say here. For your sad news, Mrs Galloway.'

'Mr Kleinmann,' Tilly whispered. 'You shouldn't have.'

His eyes glistened. 'What can comfort you in such a time? Food. That's all I can do. You take it.'

'I don't know what to say.' She took it from his hands. It was heavier than she'd imagined. The scent made her stomach rumble.

'You have lost a loved one. I too have lost. Your husband is dead a long way from here. My family, too.'

'Your family?'

He slumped against the door frame. 'My brothers and sisters. My nieces and nephews. Almost everyone I knew back in Vienna. They were sent to Mauthausen. The camp.'

A chill ran up her spine. 'I'm so terribly sorry, Mr Kleinmann.'

'I escaped in '38. I am lucky, I think.'

Tilly immediately understood why he'd been such a vigilant air-raid warden. All this time she'd misjudged him, belittled his officious over-concern. She had betrayed the first rule of her profession: to ask and, most importantly, to listen.

She hurriedly kissed his cheek. 'This is so lovely of you. Thank you.'

He smiled and his eyes shone with kindness. 'You go to work. Eat some cheesecake when you get home.'

As she left, she looked over her shoulder at this little old man and wondered about his huge story. 'Have a good day, Mr Kleinmann.'

Chapter Twenty-four

For the next week, Tilly's days passed in a blur of tears and tiredness. Sleep in the dark hours still came fitfully, as there always seemed to be activity in the flat through the night. Either it was Bert pacing or Mary placating, believing the darkness camouflaged their voices, and more than once all three of them had found themselves at the kitchen table in the dark, too tired to boil the kettle for tea but needing a cup desperately.

There had been no further discussion about the nightmare, the struggle, the black eye. It remained the elephant in the room. What good would words do when they understood implicitly that there was no solution but time? How could they blame Bert? The soldiers and camp guards at Changi were the real enemies; they had inflicted his war souvenirs, his physical and emotional wounds. The only acknowledgement of the altercation had been a surprise gift from Mary. She had wordlessly handed Tilly a paper-wrapped parcel one day when she'd returned home from work and inside was a new Helena Rubinstein foundation in Tilly's exact shade. Tilly understood it was for her bruises and thanked Mary with a nod of unspoken understanding.

The interrupted nights led Tilly to sleep in the late afternoons, and she had drifted into the habit of dozing on the settee as she listened to the *Women's Weekly* session on 2GB, but those snatches of sleep never seemed to be enough. The air in the flat had changed and no matter how much Tilly opened the windows to entice the harbour breeze in to whisk it away, it hung like stale cigarette smoke, a thick and cloying tension which set Tilly's teeth on edge. She realised she was still spending every waking minute on alert, as they had done during the darkest days of the war when the threat of air raids consumed every waking thought. She wished sleep would come, worried about trying to find the appetite that had deserted her, or constantly walked on eggshells around Mary and Bert.

The fights. Oh, the fights.

'I'm not an invalid so stop treating me like one. I'm allowed to go out for a beer with the boys. I can't spend all my time here cooped up with you in this bloody flat.'

Bert's words sliced like a knife and they cut deep. And before he slammed the door, he would hurl at Mary, 'Don't wait up for me. I'm not your son.'

Tilly's own distress at being forced to bear witness to the disintegration of their marriage flared in waves and was interspersed with a sense of numb invisibility that made every limb weak. When husband and wife were exchanging bitter retorts, she wanted to scream at them, to shout that they should be bloody grateful that Bert had come home at all. That Mary's god had answered her prayers. But that terrible rush of blood would always fade, after which she wanted to weep for what the war had done to both of them.

She grappled with the growing realisation that her own home was no longer the safe haven it had always been and she grieved for that almost as much as she grieved for Archie.

'Are you awake?'

Slumped in the armchair by the wireless, Tilly startled at the sound of Mary's voice. Since the incident with Bert, she had been keeping her distance from Tilly. Mary had created for herself a mask of reserve and calm dignity and wore it many long hours of the day. But the pain was evident in Mary's face each evening when she retired to bed, her face drawn, her mouth pinched with worry, her eyes downcast and dark at the idea that she'd passed another evening wishing in fervent hope that her husband might return and sit by her side and perhaps even take her in his arms. Mary's sorrow was palpable.

'I'm awake.' Tilly yawned and stretched her arms up to the ceiling. 'I think *Edwards' Gardening Talk* must have put me to sleep.' If Tilly made Mary smile, she might hold her attention and keep her close for just a moment. It had been so long since they'd talked and Tilly desperately wanted to.

Mary leant on the door jamb, folded her arms and sighed. 'I'm sad I missed it. I'm going to have a garden one day. When someone does something about the housing. I don't think one single house was built during the war.' She glanced around the flat. 'Or repaired.'

'You'll get your house.'

'I hope so.' Mary shook off her sentimental thoughts and suddenly scowled. 'You don't have a Bex powder, do you? I swear I bought some last week but I seem to have run out.'

Tilly sat up. 'Are you feeling unwell?'

Mary pressed a hand to her forehead and her eyes fluttered closed. 'A little. It was worse this morning but I can't seem to shake it. I've had a day of it and I think I just need to sleep it off.'

Tilly went to her friend's side. 'Mary?' Was there a way to be diplomatic about her question? 'You're not …?'

Mary seemed perplexed. 'I'm not what?'

Tilly's gaze drifted to Mary's slender waist. 'Expecting?'

Tilly waited for either realisation or confirmation but neither came. In the sudden silence of the living room, their eyes met and held and Mary covered her mouth with a hand. She stumbled to sit down and then covered her face with her hands as she began to weep, openly, raggedly, grief tearing at her throat as she sobbed.

Tilly was horrified. What had she said?

'There's no baby. It's not possible for there to be a baby.' Mary uncovered her face and her truth spilled out in a huge, unsuppressed rush. 'All this time I've waited for Bert to come home and … he won't touch me.' Mary's pleading eyes implored Tilly for an answer but Tilly had none.

'What's wrong with me?' Mary begged, desperate for an answer.

'There's nothing wrong with you. Absolutely nothing at all.' Tilly had never imagined their troubles ran this deep. 'Bert's been through a lot of strain, Mary. It's natural he'll have some nerves. His readjustment to civilian life, and to you, will take some time. He just needs time to settle, that's all.' Mr Sinclair's words of well-meaning advice to Tilly when she'd been demoted came back to her in that moment.

'You'll have a job to do in looking after him,' he'd said. 'He'll need you. There's been so much chaos. See him back to normal, Tilly. That's what wives want to do.'

Tilly wondered how many mothers and daughters and sisters and friends and neighbours and bosses and colleagues and doctors had expressed that same sentiment to soldiers' wives upon the return of their loved ones. Here you go. He's yours now to fix and cure and love and fear and hate and mourn. Hadn't Mary tried all the things expected of her? She had waited with the patience of a saint for her husband to return from the war. She had remained faithful. She had kept her hopes and dreams alive, even in the bleakest moments. She had prayed to her god day in, day out, for salvation. And yet she still was suffering so.

'Oh, dear Mary,' Tilly said and sat next to her, an arm around her shoulders.

'The nightmares, Tilly. He says he keeps seeing the execution of one of his mates. That his head was impaled on a post and left there for everyone to see.'

Tilly covered her mouth.

'He dreams he's being chased by a Japanese guard and that he's caught and he's kicked and punched to the ground. The agony—' Mary turned her face up to Tilly '—the agony of watching him go through this and not being able to do anything about it. It's killing me, Tilly.'

Tilly clasped Mary's hand and they held on tight to each other.

'It's been months now and we've ... not once. He won't even kiss me.' Mary's voice dropped to a devastated whisper. 'He still sleeps on the floor. He can't even bear to be next to me in bed.'

'He loves you, Mary. I know he does.'

'He did love me, once. I know that. But now.' Mary looked too exhausted by it all to even cry. 'Every night when he comes home I ask him where he's been, and he shouts at me and says it's none of my business. I know you've heard it, Tilly. I'm so sorry you've had to. I know where he goes. He meets up with boys from his battalion. He's just spent four years trapped in Changi with them and away from me and he chooses them over me.'

Tilly couldn't think of words of comfort for her friend so she said nothing.

'I want to be a mother. I want to have a baby of my own. Two. That's what got me through all these years, knowing I'd be a mother when Bert came back. Remember how I used to say, "When Bert comes home the first thing I want to do is have a baby"?'

Tilly remembered. She'd become too pessimistic to think it for herself with any conviction but Mary had never let that glass-half-empty attitude colour thoughts of her own future. Along with knitting socks for the troops and jumpers for their husbands, Mary had knitted booties and blankets and jackets for her dream babies, fashioning layettes of blush pink and baby blue and lemon yellow. They'd laughed and Tilly had played along, mostly to humour Mary. They'd chosen names for their dream babies—Mary favoured Jennifer and Gay for girls and Phillip and Robert for boys, while Tilly had toyed with Elizabeth and Joy for girls or Donald and Glenn for boys—and Mary invented a story that their children might one day fall in love with each other so Tilly and Mary could be bonded by marriage as well as their deep friendship and the war and their shared adversity.

'Bert used to want the same things as me. To be a father. It wasn't just me pushing for it. It was all we talked about before he went away. Before, he couldn't keep his hands off me. And now ... how on earth will I ever if we don't ...'

Tilly had no answer. She had never felt more powerless and useless. How could Bert not want to make love to his beautiful and adoring wife, who had prayed every day for his return, who truly believed that God had answered her prayers? Tilly had had her chance of resuming her normal marital relations snatched from her by a torpedo. Oh, how she had missed it. And to know that the person you had missed so much, whose skin you were desperate to feel pressed up against your own, whose hand your fingers itched to hold, whose lips you craved to be pressed against your own mouth, didn't want you? The devastation of that rejection was incomprehensible. Tilly missed that part of her own life with a desperation she had put away in a box, its lid snapped tightly shut. That part of her womanhood had lain dormant, preserved for Archie, and for what? She had suppressed it so long she feared it had withered and died inside it.

She pulled Mary tighter into her embrace. 'Have faith, Mary.'

Mary seemed to calm. 'I know I have so much to be thankful for. Especially when I think of what others have lost. You especially, Tilly.'

'It's not just me, is it?' Tilly replied, her resolve to stay calm teetering. 'How many millions of people go to bed these days with an empty space beside them and an empty space inside their heart. It's almost unfathomable, isn't it?'

'I can't think of them. I think of you and what you've lost.' Mary looked over at the photograph of Archie that still sat on the mantelpiece. Mary had moved Bert's when he'd complained he felt ridiculous staring at a photograph of himself, as if he was a movie star, but Tilly understood the real reason why. Seeing his visage from five years ago reminded him that he was no longer that man, in looks or in character. He missed his old self as much as Mary did.

'How could I begrudge you or anyone else their own happiness because mine was lost? Especially you. You're as much a sister to me as Martha is, you know that. We're family, Mary.'

'And you'll always be mine, too.'

'What if I give you and Bert more time alone together?' Tilly offered. 'When I'm back at work, I can make sure I'm out in the evenings too. We're all a little snug here, the three of us, aren't we? That can't have helped.'

Mary shook her head. 'This is your home too, Tilly. I couldn't ask that of you.'

'You can and you should. There has to be a silver lining in all this, somewhere. You have a chance to find your happiness again and I will do everything I can to see you get it.'

Chapter Twenty-five

'"Anarchy and lawlessness".' Tilly rolled her eyes at the story she was reading and looked over the top of her paper at Cooper, who had the opposition tabloid spread in his outstretched hands.

They were sitting on opposite sides of a wooden table decorated with a red-and-white chequered tablecloth, a *fiasco* chianti bottle with a drizzled candle sprouting from it and a wicker basket containing thick crumbly slices of *pane di casa*. The Mediterranean cafe in Darlinghurst had been Cooper's idea. 'I'll bring you up to speed on everything that's happened in the newsroom while you've been away,' he'd said when he'd phoned her the day before. Tilly had readily agreed to the idea of lunch. Her talk with Mary was still fresh and raw in Tilly's mind and she hoped that a romantic Saturday night on their own might be good for Mary and Bert. All Tilly had to do was stay out of the house all day and well into the evening.

'Honestly,' she continued. 'I can't believe what I read in our own paper sometimes.'

'Menzies again?' The cigarette pinched between Cooper's lips bobbed as he spoke.

'Who else?' Tilly dropped the *Daily Herald* to the table. 'My father will be apoplectic. Menzies wants to send all the strikers to jail.'

Cooper shrugged. 'She'll be right. I'll go with you to visit him. I'll even fashion a shiv out of an old comb. We can smuggle it in for him in a loaf of bread.'

Tilly threw her head back and laughed heartily.

Cooper smiled out of one corner of his mouth. 'Just don't let on that I'm keeping company with a jailbird's daughter.'

'I think people already know you're keeping company with a commie's daughter. Your reputation will be taking a battering.'

Cooper grinned. 'Lucky I don't have much of one left then, isn't it?'

It had been a tough few months for Tilly's father and his comrades on the waterfront. By the end of October thousands of other workers were on strike, not just on Sydney's waterfront but across New South Wales and the whole country. Strikes at the Port Kembla steelworks and by power workers at the Bunnerong power station were the tip of the iceberg: it seemed the whole country was riven by industrial action.

Tilly was sick and tired of reading the attacks in the newspaper, which went on day after day, headline after headline, week after week. Big business, the *Daily Herald* and the country's conservative newspapers claimed the communist-led militant unions were dragging the state through its gravest crisis since before the war. Workers insisted they were only digging in their heels for a prolonged fight because they deserved shorter hours and fairer pay. The end of the war hadn't meant the end of the battle. Opposition

Leader Robert Menzies had accused Prime Minister Chifley of yielding to anarchy and surrendering to lawlessness by giving in to the unions.

To some, these threats were only headlines on a page that would be put in a basket at the end of the day to take to the butcher's the next.

But it was all so much more personal to Tilly. Every time striking workers were attacked and impugned, Tilly's father and thousands of other fathers and husbands and wives and mothers, who wanted nothing more than to earn a decent wage for their labours and be treated fairly while they were doing it, were attacked too.

'I know what my mother would say,' she muttered under her breath.

'What's that?'

'Bloody Menzies.'

'Bloody Menzies,' Cooper repeated, shaking his head and tut-tutting in a dramatic fashion.

'And I can't say I disagree with her, even though as a reporter I'm not supposed to have an opinion, am I? How ridiculous,' she huffed. 'How can I not have an opinion on what's happening in the world? What sort of a person would it make me if I didn't care about injustice and cruelty and barbarism?'

Cooper butted out his cigarette.

'Now he's blaming the unions for standing by the Indonesians and putting black bans on all those ships. Imagine what it's been like for them? Colonised by the Dutch for three-hundred-and-fifty years and then invaded by the Japanese. And when the war's over we expect them to welcome back the Dutch with open arms?'

Judging by the smirk on his face, Cooper wasn't inclined to answer her.

'What?' she demanded with a smile.

'Nothing.'

'You think I'm wearing my heart on my sleeve, don't you?'

'No comment, Mrs Galloway.'

Tilly chuckled, and the freedom of wanting to laugh, finally, warmed her, as if that day's sunshine had seeped into her bones and lit a fire deep inside. And when her laughter caused Cooper's smile to widen into a grin, when he chuckled back at her, she felt even better.

How had he known? She needed this. Tilly was only beginning to realise that she'd not only shut herself away for the past few weeks, but for far longer than that. Slowly, as the months and years had gone on, she'd withdrawn from the world for fear of what it might force her to confront. And that sheltering, that hibernating, hadn't protected her heart or her husband. The world had happened anyway. All she'd done was pull her head in, like a turtle, and hide, but the world had still been waiting for her all along when she finally emerged from that shell.

Cooper had always been the one to knock on that shell to urge her out of it. With postcards, with phone calls, with a sandwich for lunch at Circular Quay, with a story every now and then. And he was doing the same thing today. When they'd sat down to order, they'd barely spent five minutes talking about their colleagues before lapsing into this comfortable togetherness. They were simply, and effortlessly, two colleagues with two newspapers whiling away a sunny Saturday. Two bowls of spaghetti bolognese with parmesan cheese and two glasses of chianti were on the way, as was a blossoming sense of equanimity in her. If all it took was a bowl of spaghetti and a glass of red wine, she wished she'd done it years ago. There was no doubt in her mind that the minute she was alone her grief would flood back again and drown her, but for now, for this moment, she could enjoy the sun and the company and the wine and not be consumed by the worst thing that had ever happened to her.

'He's positioning himself for the election, isn't he? Menzies.'

'Of course he is. He knows full well what happened to Churchill back in July. Winnie went into the general election thinking the war had won it for him.'

'And Labour won by a landslide and Clement Attlee is in Number Ten.'

'And guess who handed him that victory on a platter?'

'Who?' Tilly asked.

'Returned soldiers and their families. Attlee promised homes for heroes and the National Health Service and social security. Is it any wonder he won? Two million homes were destroyed during the Blitz and in the years after. People want to get on with their lives and how the hell can they do that if they haven't anywhere to live? Attlee got it right, I'd say.'

'They obviously trusted Churchill with the war but not with much else.'

Cooper dropped his paper onto the table. 'Menzies clearly thinks the same might happen here, that the wartime government will be ditched in favour of new blood. That's why he's going after the unions and the communists so hard.

Victoria Purman

284

He's the only one to preserve the new world order, and all that. Bloody cynical if you ask me.'

'Did you know that he's calling for unions to be forced to hand over lists of all their members? That'll mean he'll get my name and yours, Cooper, and that of every other member of the Australian Journalists Association.'

'So much for freedom of the press,' Cooper said.

'What are we becoming in this country? Didn't we just fight a war for our freedom? For freedom of the press, of association, of people to rise up against tyranny? Isn't this what Archie died for?' A lump closed Tilly's throat and swallowed half her words.

Cooper held her gaze. His expression of kind concern was so familiar now.

'Did you know Hitler banned trade unions? He managed to get people to think they were un-German. His thugs beat unionists to death, tortured them, sent them to Dachau. Thousands were murdered.'

If Cooper had been concentrating on the words on the page before him, he'd suddenly lost all interest. He was watching her, transfixed, as if she was breaking some momentous news that had frozen him to the spot, as if he was caught in the surprise of it before rushing to a telephone to hastily dictate a few paragraphs of copy for the late edition. Tilly felt a shot of energy surge from her feet to the hairs on her head. He rested one elbow on the table, the cigarette between his fingers burning, as if he'd forgotten he'd just lit it.

'Do you know what my father and all those other workers are striking for?' Her tone hardened as she grew more confident in her argument.

'Tell me.'

'The Trades and Labour Council is negotiating for power workers to have a forty-hour, five-day week on shiftwork, with a two shilling allowance for afternoon and night shifts, with no overall cut to the pay they earnt for working forty-four hours a week during the war.'

'Greedy bastards,' Cooper responded wryly.

'Every public servant worked long hours, five-and-a-half days a week and sometimes two evenings as well. Every second Saturday they worked all day. It was all for the king. And they didn't get an extra pound for it. In the munitions factories, those women worked twelve-hour shifts six days a week.'

'Not any more they don't.'

'That's right. They've all been let go. Don't you think they deserve something for putting in for all those years? It's a just reward for working all those extra hours during the war for no extra pay, don't you think? And you probably don't know what it's been like since you're flitting all over the globe all the time, with all your expenses covered by the paper, but the cost of living went through the roof during the war. No one's had a pay rise for years.'

Tilly felt her cheeks redden and was sure it was from her exhortations and not his penetrating gaze.

'There she is. The commie's daughter.'

'And what's wrong with that?'

Cooper chuckled. 'Nothing in the slightest from where I sit. I was thinking that you sound just like him.'

Tilly sat back, surprised at his observation. 'I do?'

'You can take the gal out of Millers Point—' he grinned '—but you can't take the Millers Point out of the gal.'

'Why would I want to? I'm proud of who I am and where I came from. I'm proud of my father and all the men like him who fight for what's fair and right, who fight for the right to be alive and healthy at the end of a working day. And I'm proud of women like my mother who hold those communities together on the smell of an oily rag and their own labours, day in, day out.'

Cooper sat back. Any trace of the wry, world-weary war correspondent had disappeared from his countenance. His shoulders rose and fell on a sigh and he lifted his cigarette from his lips to stub it out in the ashtray on the table.

'What?' she asked.

'It's good to see the fight back in you, Mrs Galloway.'

Chapter Twenty-six

The day before Tilly returned to work at the newspaper to begin her new job on the women's pages, the other shoe finally dropped.

Another pink telegram arrived and she accepted it with gracious thanks and a small tip. She went to her bedroom and sat on her bed. She stared at her name typed there. Then, she read it.

Regret to inform you that L/CPL AH Galloway became missing on July 1st 1942 and is now for official purposes presumed to be dead.

Accordingly, his payments from the army had ceased.

Tilly sat on her bed in the quiet of her room and read it ten times over before folding it neatly and slipping it back into its envelope. Then she put it with all Archie's letters from Melbourne and Bonegilla and then his last as a prisoner of war, sealed the old biscuit tin in which she kept them, and tucked it into her wooden chest. She had already accepted her husband was dead so this final piece of the puzzle couldn't make her feel sadder or more bereft. It only added to the weight of the burden she would bear for the remainder of her life, as permanent as a scar which might one day fade but would forever live on her skin.

She ended the final night of her bereavement leave on her own in the home she had only shared with Archie for two nights, when he'd come back up to Sydney in readiness to leave Australia. He had never been imprinted on it. She didn't have memories of him sitting on the settee reading or at the kitchen table eating toast for breakfast. She didn't remember him in her bed, his hair roughened by restless sleep, the sheets and blankets half tossed onto the floor. Those memories were from Bondi and a lifetime ago.

No matter how hard she searched now, she couldn't remember his voice. And that meant that his jokes and his stories and his words of love for her, the wedding vows which he stumbled over in church, the dreams he'd admitted to, of children and a long life together, were gone too. It was all just so tremendously sad. Her new life was beckoning her forward and she had no other choice but to take that leap. Not only had she bundled up Archie's clothes into parcels for donating to the Salvation Army, but she'd also packed away her dreams for a life that was now lost.

She would have to find new dreams to reach for. It was as simple and as complicated as that.

There were flowers on Tilly's desk when she returned to the newspaper in that last week of October. She saw them as soon as she opened the door from the stairwell to the women's newsroom. There were snow-white carnations, deep lipstick-red roses with verdant forest-green leaves and snipped thorns, and a tall bunch of calla lilies so top heavy they threatened to topple over under their own weight.

Her desk wasn't as she remembered it. The overflowing ashtray, which she wouldn't need any longer anyway, had disappeared. Her pile of notebooks filled with shorthand, blunt pencils and piles of newspapers and telex cables had been arranged into neat piles. To the left of her typewriter sat a stack of copy paper neatly interleaved with fresh carbons. And unless she was imagining things, a new maroon leather chair waited behind her desk.

The sight cheered her enough for a smile to tug at the corners of her mouth. She had wondered if she'd lost that muscle memory and realised how pleasant an emotion it was to smile and not worry that she would be judged for it. Her bereavement leave had passed slowly; the days had tugged at her like a child on her mother's coat, dragging her back, stopping that step forward to the next day and the next. Mary and Bert's problems were stifling and the only bright spot had been Cooper insisting she leave the house. Two days before, after they'd had lunch in Darlinghurst, he'd dragged her all over the city. They'd taken a ferry to Manly and licked vanilla ice-cream on the beach before dipping their toes into the warm water and commiserating with each other that neither of them had their swimsuits because the warm day would have been perfect for it. They'd come back into the city and after a bite to eat they'd playfully argued about which film they should see. In the end they'd compromised and sat through *National Velvet* with Elizabeth Taylor and Mickey Rooney at the St James on Elizabeth Street precisely because it wasn't about the war.

They'd taken a long time to walk home, talking all the way about the thrilling Grand National steeplechase scene at the end of the film and Cooper had kissed her on the cheek

at the door to her building before turning and whistling his
way home to his flat in Darlinghurst.

Cooper didn't talk to her about Archie, which was a
relief. At home, everything was a reminder of what she and
Mary had lost in their different ways. At Argyle Place, her
mother's tears and her father's stoic silence were unending.

Her work would have to be her new safe haven. She was
to make a life of her own now and she needed this. She'd
missed the clatter of keys and the always-brewing pot of tea
on Vera's desk, not to mention her cakes. She'd missed the
clouds from Maggie's Woodbines and Frances's precise way
of conducting a conversation, and surely Dear Agatha would
have some useful advice for the not-so-newly widowed.

Tilly set her handbag on her desk and bent to smell the
roses. If there was a scent, she couldn't detect it. Her senses
of smell and taste had deserted her since she'd heard about
Archie. The complicated mix of body and mind, survival
and grief, had stolen things from her, as if she no longer
needed those two pleasures in life because she was already
half dead.

'Tilly.'

She looked over her shoulder. Mrs Freeman, Vera,
Maggie, Frances, Dear Agatha and Kitty were standing as
one.

'Welcome back.' Vera stepped forward, proffering a
date loaf on a pretty china plate. The slices were perfectly
cylindrical, as golden as freshly dried fruit and spread with
thick pats of pale yellow.

'Oh, my,' Tilly gasped. 'Is that real butter?'

Vera sniffed and smiled. 'We each contributed some of
our rations.'

'Thank you all. It's very kind of you.'

One by one, her other colleagues came to her.

'I'm so sorry, Tilly,' Kitty Darling whispered in her ear as she hugged Tilly tight. 'The bloody war.'

Maggie shook Tilly's hand as her bottom lip trembled. 'You're brave, Tilly. Don't ever forget that.'

When Frances stepped up, Tilly opened her arms and held her tight. Frances had no words and Tilly respected her silence. What comfort were words anyway?

Mrs Freeman finally came forward. 'You've no doubt been through a very trying time. You have our most sincere condolences. We've been thinking about you every day.'

'I do appreciate that, Mrs Freeman. And thank you, everyone, for the flowers. They were lovely.'

Mrs Freeman reached for Tilly's hand and squeezed it warmly. 'We're so pleased to have you working on the women's pages, Tilly. You bring a great deal of talent to our ranks. And an extra staff member is never anything to be sneezed at, especially in these times. We'll have plenty for you to do.' Her editor lowered her voice. 'When you're ready, that is.'

Tilly nodded her understanding.

'We feel privileged to have a war correspondent officially working with us. The paper's first woman, no less. You've blazed a trail, Tilly, where we hope others will follow.'

Tilly struggled but found a smile. She wanted to be grateful that she still had a job to return to, that she had such understanding colleagues, but a new sense of failure bowled her over.

'Who's up for a cup of tea then?' Dear Agatha asked nervously.

Everyone waited for Tilly to respond.

She pondered if scenes just like this had been played out in offices and workplaces all over the country as news filtered through about the missing, the presumed dead, the injured and the returned. Was there cake in those offices too? Was there an etiquette about cake when it came to grief?

'I'm not fussed about the tea, but I'm dying to try a piece of your date slice, Vera.' There was an audible sigh of relief from her colleagues and she knew they were trying to determine how much of the old Tilly was back. She still wasn't sure, either.

An hour later, Mrs Freeman approached Tilly's desk. 'I know it's your first day back but I think the best way to deal with these things is to simply get you back in the saddle. What do you think?'

Tilly stood quickly, smoothed her hands over her tweed jacket, feeling a sudden urge to be prim. She had taken special care to ensure her freshly dry-cleaned suit was hung neatly, her shoes were polished and that her nails were carefully clipped and trim. She'd even slicked on a coat of the palest pink polish the night before. Her colleagues would be watching out of the corner of their eyes for any sign that she was letting herself go. If she became unkempt, if her hair wasn't styled exactly as she'd always worn it, if her lips weren't stained with lipstick, if her eyes weren't bright, if there was a run in a stocking or if her shirts weren't sparkling Lux white, they might think she was falling apart.

'I agree completely.' *Yes, please. Send me out into the world again to speak to someone who has no clue about what I've been through. I'll be able to pretend it never happened. Send me out into the world to write a story to help me forget my own.*

'Glad to hear it.' Mrs Freeman passed Tilly a piece of paper with a name and an address on it. 'This lady is going to be guest speaker on Wednesday night at a Red Cross function. She might be worth talking to.'

Mrs Daphne Teale was a tall, gaunt woman with short grey hair and a cameo brooch at her neck. If Tilly had met her on the street, she might have guessed her to be a librarian, with spectacles to aid her poor vision, a symptom of much reading, and the bearer of a quiet voice trained for hushing.

Tilly wondered if Mrs Teale had always looked so old. Sitting across from her in Sydney's Red Cross office, fresh scones on the table and a steaming cup of tea between them, she bore the same sunken cheeks and pale visage that Tilly recognised in Cooper. The war not only harms its victims, but its perpetrators and its witnesses too.

'Thank you for talking with me today, Mrs Teale.'

The woman nodded. 'I hope it helps. The Red Cross is still desperately trying to raise funds for refugees in Europe and in Asia, Mrs Galloway. It's estimated that in Europe alone there are millions. We need to do more and desperately quickly, and we're relying on Red Cross branches to continue their wartime fundraising effort. If your report is able to help in any way, it's what must be done.'

'I hope it does help.' Then she remembered and hoped Mrs Teale didn't mind her saying it. 'I knitted for the Red Cross during the war. My husband—' Tilly's words caught as they always did when she spoke of Archie, as if saying his name might summon his ghost and she should prepare herself. 'My husband served. I was always so very grateful for the work of the Red Cross because of him, you see. I sent so many letters and fruit cakes to him in New Guinea and I'd like to think he received at least some of them before he was killed.'

Mrs Teale's expression changed from one of polite reservation to implicit understanding. 'Please accept my sincere condolences. He served in New Guinea, you said?'

'Yes. Rabaul. He was taken prisoner when the Japanese took the town and was later drowned on a prisoner of war ship bound for Japan. The *Montevideo Maru*. It was sunk off the Philippines in July 1942 but it took the whole war to find out what really happened to him.'

Mrs Teale's face fell. 'I'm so dreadfully sorry.'

'Thank you.' Tilly took a deep breath and opened her notebook. It was brand new, with not a mark in it. She wrote the date across the top of the page: 22 October 1945.

'Mrs Teale, are you able to tell me a little about your recent work?'

The woman nodded. 'Of course. I was a relief worker with the British Red Cross in Europe. On 21 April this year I was among a contingent that was sent in to the Belsen concentration camp in Germany six days after it was liberated.' Her voice cracked a little and she became quiet.

'Our job was to begin rebuilding the minds and bodies of people that had been ... broken by the Germans.'

Tilly's pencil moved over the page. 'What did that work involve?'

'We staffed the hospital, coordinated all the fresh supplies into the camp, because there was absolutely nothing there for those poor souls, and we tended to the sick. Welfare officers took care of the children, the orphans, and some of us became cooks, establishing canteens to feed the inmates. It was such a simple thing but you can't imagine what difference a clean bed can make to new mothers and their dear, starving little babies. They were as small as birds. Barely alive.'

Reports from the Belsen war crimes trials had been in the newspapers every day, filled with harrowing, matter-of-fact testimonies. However, Tilly guessed that the worst of the evidence had never made it into the newspapers.

'It was a catastrophe, the proportions of such we couldn't even have imagined, Mrs Galloway. There were thirteen thousand unburied bodies and sixty thousand others, sick and starving.'

As Tilly filled the lines in her notebook, she wanted to ask this quiet, unassuming, kind woman how it was that she hadn't gone mad at being a witness to it all?

'What was it like when you arrived at Belsen, Mrs Teale? Do you think you were prepared for what you were to encounter?'

The colour slowly drained from her face. 'It's difficult to explain the absolute shock of it. Arriving there ... it was as if we had walked into another world. It was eerily quiet. I remember that so vividly. People didn't even have the energy to speak, nor the little children to cry. And bodies, the skin on those poor skeletons of people was stretched so thin you could almost see through them. The smell of typhus was ghastly.'

Tears welled in Mrs Teale's eyes. Tilly looked up from the curves and dots and loops of her shorthand, her own vision blurred by tears.

'There were lavatories but they weren't functional. There were buildings full of medical supplies but nothing had been given to those who were dying.'

Mrs Teale was staring over Tilly's shoulder, her expression blank and, as she continued to talk, she closed her eyes.

'I couldn't get over the fact that there were German doctors and nurses that had been complicit in that treatment. Doctors and nurses,' she repeated. 'And so many women. I had thought, perhaps naively, that those in the caring professions might be better than that, that the Hippocratic oath might outrank the evil philosophy of Nazism. But women wielded bayonets and set dogs upon prisoners, watching as they were savaged. One of the guards, Irma Grese, used to beat people with a riding whip. A mother was caught talking to her daughter in another compound and she beat the mother until her head and shoulders were covered with blood. When she fell to the ground, Grese continued to kick her. Women were sterilised, hung up by their legs for experiments in artificial insemination, injected with petrol. It was criminal barbarity on a scale that is unthinkable to any right-minded person. And yet they were ordinary people, weren't they, before the war?'

Tilly stared wide-eyed at Mrs Teale, with her librarian looks and her graceful demeanour. Allied forces had liberated more than three hundred concentration camps all over Europe. In the Pacific, they were doing the same. What fresh horrors were yet to be discovered?

It was a long moment before Mrs Teale met Tilly's gaze. 'I worked there until 21 May, when it was burnt down.' Her eyes hardened. 'It's a tragedy for you that your husband lost his life, Mrs Galloway. I hope it helps you to know that he did so to protect the rest of the world from that evil.'

Chapter Twenty-seven

Tilly surveyed the shorthand notes and crumpled cables and clumsily refolded newspapers that were strewn all over her desk, gathered like souvenirs from the stories she'd covered since she'd been back at work.

Suddenly, none of it made any sense. She looked around the women's newsroom and it was full of familiar faces: Mrs Freeman and her calm elegance, Dear Agatha spraying Tosca Eau de Cologne at her neck, police reporter Maggie Pritchard taking a break from hunching over her typewriter to light a fresh Woodbine from the tip of another, Frances Langly pushing her glasses up her nose as she pursed her lips and listened intently on the phone.

But Tilly saw them all as if she were on the other side of a pane of glass. There was a buzzing in her ears which blocked out every sound except the thud of her heart, so fast she thought it might break her ribs. She was still gripping the telephone receiver and as she stared at it for a moment, she felt herself begin to shake. She dropped it into the cradle with a Bakelite clunk and when she looked down at her hands she saw they were trembling. The tremor travelled up her shoulders and her teeth began to chatter at the same time as her stomach wrenched. She bit down the nausea and got to her shaky feet.

Tilly made her way in a daze upstairs to the men's newsroom and as she crossed the floor a shrieking wolf whistle split the air.

'The reporterette's back.'

Tilly turned to shoot Robinson a stone cold glare.

Her attention fired him up even more. 'No stories up here for you, love. Better head back downstairs,' he called out, which encouraged a round of hooting laughter and catcalls from the other male reporters.

'Stairs are that way.' It was a voice Tilly didn't recognise but one she would never forget. She kept her pace steady and her head held high, ignoring the jibes and the whistles and the disrespect that followed behind her like a waft of perfume, and went to Cooper's desk.

Cooper got to his feet, dipped his chin and pointed at Robinson with an accusing finger. 'Cut it out,' he growled, which only led to more wolf whistles and catcalls from across the newsroom. He pushed his hair back from his forehead with a quick, exasperated shove.

'Cooper,' Tilly said as she approached and his anger dissipated and quickly became concern as she came close.

'Mrs Galloway?' he asked quietly, reaching for her arm.

'It was us,' she murmured through trembling lips. Her knees felt as loose as rubber bands.

'What was?'

He urged her into his chair and swiped a spare from the desk next to his and came close to her. All around them, typing resumed, the striking of keys on butcher's paper creating an echoing *click strike click*.

'It was an Allied submarine that torpedoed the *Montevideo Maru*. The Japanese are finally telling the truth. At three am, sixty miles north-west of Luzon Island. The prisoners—Archie—were battened down in the hold. It sank with all hands on deck within a few minutes.'

The blood seemed to drain from Cooper's face. 'An Allied sub? Where did you get this from?'

'The army. I've been chasing it. I've been calling every day to find out about his letter and how the dates didn't match. They told me about Major Williams, who was sent to Japan to find everyone who was still missing. All those people from Rabaul, the soldiers of Lark Force, the civilians and the missionaries. He found a list of names from the *Montevideo Maru*. A nominal roll, but it was in Japanese and they had to translate it. Archie's name was on that list. That's how they know he's dead.'

'Jesus Christ.'

Tilly met Cooper's gaze. 'Someone, somewhere made a mistake, didn't they? How could we ... *we* ... torpedo a ship full of POWs? Of Australians?'

He kept his voice low. She could barely hear him. Perhaps she didn't want to. 'It wasn't a hospital ship to them, Mrs Galloway. It was a Japanese vessel.'

'We killed them,' she stammered, barely able to breathe.

Cooper squeezed her arm. 'War killed them, Mrs Galloway.'

The truth about the deaths of the prisoners on the *Montevideo Maru* only received a few paragraphs of coverage in the *Daily Herald*, on page eight of the 23 November edition. It seemed that a story about one thousand people being killed in 1942 was nothing but old news by 1945 and, anyway, they'd been missing so long didn't their families believe they were already dead? How could it possibly have been a shock to discover that the men of Lark Force and all the civilians had long ago met their maker? Australia had seen twenty-six thousand other soldiers killed in action and more than eight thousand prisoners of war had died in captivity. There was death and loss everywhere. The prisoners of that ship were nothing but more names and numbers to add to a long tally.

Tilly carefully cut out the story and set it neatly on Archie's letters and the telegrams in the box in which she kept her memories of him. When would she be able to put a lid on all the mysteries surrounding his death, the most perplexing of which was the arrival of his last letter months after he was already dead. Where had it been? Had it been misplaced by the Australian PMG in the Sydney Post Office? Had a bag of precious mail been lost off the back of a truck somewhere and lain undiscovered for months before being hurriedly sorted and delivered?

She had pursued an interview with Major Williams, calling the Australian Army Directorate of Prisoners of War in Melbourne every day for a week, but she couldn't get as much as a phone call to him in Tokyo. She would never know if it was because she was a woman, but a male reporter in Melbourne got the scoop. Williams said on the record that he'd discovered the Japanese had displayed utter ineptitude and indifference when it came to the mail of prisoners of war as well as information about POWs altogether. They hadn't kept complete or detailed records—unlike the Germans who were sadistically meticulous—of who they had captured and of those who had died in captivity. Withholding mail and parcels was another instrument of abuse against these tortured and starving prisoners, further isolating them from news of home and family. Bags of undelivered mail had been discovered abandoned in the Japanese Government's Prisoner of War Bureau—the Furyo Jôhôkyoku—in Tokyo. Is that where her letters to Archie were? The thought that her words of love, her funny little stories about her life at the newspaper and Mary and her parents and Martha and Bernard and Brian and Terry had been handled by the enemy, kept aside as a means to torture Archie, was a new and unbearable blow.

No one wanted to hear, after all that time, that the deaths on the *Montevideo Maru* were an accident. Because, really, what did it matter whose torpedo it was?

Cooper had been right. The war had killed Archie.

Chapter Twenty-eight

For the first month of Tilly's return to work, she kept busy by burying her head in stories during the day, doing all that was asked of her and more, so she could leave the office and her notebook behind, weary and spent, with as little time as possible between dinner and bed. It didn't pay to have too much time to think about anything else, she reckoned. Her mother had always said that idle hands were the devil's playground, mostly when she sensed her two daughters were bored and about to get into a scrap with each other, and her refrain usually presaged the handing over of some kitchen or household implement or other. A potato peeler. A broom. A mop. Tilly tried everything to fill her mind so thoughts of all she'd lost wouldn't find any purchase or succour. If she had time in the evenings, between a meal and sleep, she turned the wireless up loud, to listen to *Melody and Rhythm* on 2UE or *Amateur Hour* on 2CH, which sometimes made her laugh and forget.

For a couple of weeks, Cooper had been constant and diverting company. If it wasn't lunch at Circular Quay during the week in the sparkling Sydney spring sunshine, it was soup and a coffee after work before going to the pictures;

and one weekend they'd walked through the Botanic Gardens to Mrs Macquarie's Chair and waited their turn to sit on the stone steps so they could look out in the distance to the bridge and the sweep of the harbour still filled with ships, lined up like cigars in a box.

In the trees and shrubs and sky all around them, Cooper had pointed out the brown goshawks soaring overhead on their slightly upturned wings, the eastern spinebills hovering over lush blooms and the figbirds searching for fruit. There was a peace about that spot that Tilly had only come to appreciate sitting next to Cooper. He hadn't needed to spell it out for her to know what he was trying to help her understand. That there could be life and hope after the worst blow. That the sun rose every day on both tragedy and triumph equally. Fresh life would continue to be born anew all around them in nature's garden as it would again in hers. Buds and blossoms and blooms would burst from bare branches one might have thought were devoid of life and would reach for the sun and light and warmth as they had done for millions of years.

If anyone had questions about how much time she and Cooper were spending together—Mary, her mother, Martha—they had been silent on the issue. And Tilly wasn't sure what her answer would have been in any case. He was a dear friend and a wonderful distraction and a handsome companion. And that was it. In those moments when she'd forgotten who she was and what she'd gone through, when she'd looked into his eyes and seen something reflected back at her that she didn't want to see, she'd turned away, embarrassed. It had only been grief and loss playing havoc with her. She was sure of it.

Tilly had been to Angus and Robertson's on Castlereagh Street many times before, but Cooper's tour helped her see it with fresh eyes. She'd only ever lingered at the front of the store, glancing back along the brightly lit pendants which formed two perfect rows, their perspective narrowing until they might have met way down the back. Cooper led her through the crowds poring over the display tables that ran down each side of the store, filled with novels by Eleanor Dark and M Barnard Eldershaw and Kylie Tennant, past the Books for Boys and Girls shelves, to the section at the rear where he pulled from the shelves a copy of Miles Franklin's *My Brilliant Career*.

'I haven't read this one,' she'd told him, taking it from his hand and flipping open the inside cover to read the blurb on the dust jacket.

'You're pulling my leg.'

Playing at being offended, she said offhandedly, 'I was a little too busy being taught typing and shorthand and office skills at my high school to prepare me for a life as a secretary. What's it about?'

'Read it,' he'd said, and because it was Cooper, she'd gone home that night and devoured it, page by page, until she'd fallen asleep with the book cradled to her chest.

Tilly hadn't had the opportunity to discuss her many thoughts on Sybylla Melvyn or Harry Beecham with Cooper because the next day he'd flown off to the Dutch East Indies with his battered portable typewriter, landing in Batavia to report on the independence battle being waged by the Indonesians. There were still bans in place on Dutch ships in Australia and strikers at the Rose Bay flying boat base were doing their best to frustrate the Dutch suppression by voting not to service any Dutch aircraft at the base. Tilly was thankful of that because she imagined it would make Cooper safer.

Her father had been deeply immersed in union meetings as watersiders continued to be involved in the action against the Dutch too, not just in Sydney but in Newcastle, and in other cities and towns, where two thousand steel workers were still idle. Nearly one hundred printing firms were being boycotted because they'd sacked members of their workforce who had refused to toil more than a forty-hour week.

When an official statement was made on 2 November by the British that Hitler and his mistress Eva Braun had suicided after their marriage back on 30 April, two days before Berlin had fallen, Tilly found no sympathy in her heart for that murderer, nor his wife, and she wished she'd been there outside the German Chancellory to see their bodies burn and their bones smashed to shards.

They would never have the dignity of a grave and she was glad of it. Archie and thousands of others like him would never have graves either.

Hadn't the end of the war been supposed to herald a new era of peace and prosperity? Those lofty goals seemed a long way away in the lead-up to Christmas 1945. At home, Mary had come to a kind of weary resignation at Bert's odd behaviour, or at least it seemed that way to Tilly, and Mary coped by increasingly finding things to do that didn't involve her absent husband.

And through all this continuing turmoil and uncertainty, Tilly found herself writing stories about lives that looked nothing like hers or the lives of the women she knew. She covered prize-winning beach girls, telling readers how fortunate they were to have secured themselves good jobs such as models and receptionists after featuring in competitions—coincidentally sponsored by her own newspaper. She'd visited a kindergarten exhibition at the Sydney Town Hall and had crafted a story about how important kindergarten experts believed the earliest years were for the healthy growth and development needs of children, and wondered why that story was destined for relegation to the women's pages and not the main news pages at the front of the paper. She had written twenty paragraphs on the joys of spring cleaning and a list of ten gift ideas for the man in your life but her biggest story yet appeared in the first week of December.

Tilly had been assigned the task of investigating the high cost and low quality of women's post-war clothing. Mrs Freeman had directed her to the investigation one morning after Kitty Darling had regaled the women in the office with her tale of the cost of a two-piece wine-coloured linen suit she'd seen in a Pitt Street store: 'Six guineas, I tell you. And of the most inferior quality you can imagine.' Tilly had made it more than obvious that it had been quite a while since she'd shopped for much of anything and would barely know the difference between a bargain and a rip-off but Mrs Freeman wasn't for turning.

'Before you raise your eyebrows at me in protest, Tilly,' Mrs Freeman started with a wry grin.

'Oh, but I wasn't,' Tilly replied quickly. Mrs Freeman had clearly noticed the look of rising indignation on her face.

'Yes, you were. I saw them moving. This is a story that will catch our readers' attention and you know it.' She leant over Tilly's desk. 'Women have endured, Tilly. They've gone without. They've made do. And by god, they've mended. They've unpicked and knitted again and again. They've used the same old threadbare bath towels for the entire war until they're as absorbent as a piece of cardboard. They've remodelled and sewn until their fingers have bled.' Mrs Freeman inspected her own. 'Or at least I have. And now, finally clothing rationing is coming to an end and factories are gearing up production to cater for an enormous, Australia-wide pent-up demand for clothing, and what do women find? Expensive, second-rate tat.'

Tilly picked up her notebook and pencil and tucked them inside her handbag, which she looped over her shoulder.

'Head down to Castlereagh Street and to the shops further down Pitt and see what you can discover. And keep in mind our readers, women on average incomes. How are they supposed to afford these spiralling prices? Think of the women you grew up with in Millers Point, Tilly. Write this one for them.'

Mrs Freeman knew exactly where Tilly's soft spot was. Right alongside her bleeding heart. She inspected flimsy morning dresses for a pound—which she could have sworn were only eight shillings and eleven a few years before—and poor quality crepe dresses which looked like sacks if she was honest, and cost an exorbitant seventy-nine shillings and eleven. Browsing the racks, asking surreptitious questions of shop assistants who responded as if she wasn't the first woman to flinch when she spotted the price tickets, set Tilly thinking about her own wardrobe. Even before the war, before marrying Archie, Tilly hadn't been able to afford fancy outfits or new kid gloves every season or the latest summer hats. Not on a secretary's wage.

Archie's army pay had been deposited into a bank account to create a nest egg for a home loan deposit, so it was still sitting there untouched. What little money she had saved had been invested in war bonds. And anyway, it had seemed entirely frivolous and unpatriotic, actually, to crave new clothes and shoes and luxuries during the war. She had recycled everything she possibly could to leach the last possible ounce of wear out of every item she owned. Her mother had mended frayed collars and cuffs, added underarm patches to dresses whose seams had begun to fray from sweat and stretching, and darned more rips than Tilly could count. Tilly and Mary had assiduously washed their rayons in cold water—*never* hot—and removed their wedding rings when they'd soaked them so as not to catch anything and create a run. They'd ironed marocain when the fabric was damp and shantung when it was bone dry. And they'd never, ever soaked or boiled their woollens, nor rubbed or twisted them while rinsing. The rules had been exhausting.

And every day, Tilly had gone into the office to find Kitty Darling looking just as fresh and glamorous as could be. Tilly's suspicion was that Kitty's wardrobe had already been extensive before the war and that she'd managed to be creative throughout with her outfit rotation. Or how else was it that she never seemed to wear the same ensemble twice?

As she admired the clothes hanging on the racks in one of the big department stores in Pitt Street, Tilly let herself imagine, for a moment, what she might choose if she were in the market for something new. Would it be one of the short-sleeved two-piece linen suits? They would be perfect for summer, with bare legs on a hot and humid Sydney day, she reasoned, since the practice of eschewing stockings had become more common during the war. And if a society lady scoffed at her, did she really care? Or would it be a two-piece blue-and-red slack suit she'd admired or even a crepe afternoon dress that she might wear away from work, something new for the weekends?

She didn't fight the thought, for the first time, that she would like to wear something new, something Cooper hadn't seen her in already. Perhaps he might notice something different about her and maybe even comment about how lovely she looked. It would be quite nice to hear such a compliment from a man. It had been a long time since she'd felt really attractive to anyone. Of course there had been whistles in the street from young men being facetious and from soldiers and sailors and airmen roaming in groups looking for a woman to dance with and hold and kiss and more. But they whistled and called to any woman under forty, so she hadn't taken any of that seriously at all. She wanted to feel the way she used to feel when Archie looked at her, as if he couldn't bear not to be holding her, as if he was fighting an irresistible urge to kiss her. She wanted to feel loved and comforted and safe in someone's embrace. She wanted to feel desired and she wanted to feel desire herself.

When Archie had sailed away, she'd longed for him as any wife would but had had no choice but to sublimate those sexual feelings. What was the use of wanting him in that way when she reached for him and he wasn't there? She had thought of herself as a tree still in the grips of its winter dormancy. Her leaves had fallen, her seeds were a long way away from germinating, she was alive but not growing.

It was her survival mechanism too, to keep herself going until spring when new life might burst from her. But spring had never come and she was still in the stasis of her own enforced winter. She had conserved everything—her hopes, her future plans, her sexual desires—and for the first time in a long time, standing in a dress shop in Pitt Street, she felt the stirrings of wanting to be loved again; of that primal urge to be skin on skin with someone, to feel hands on her, a body on hers, lips on her mouth and her neck and her breasts, and to feel enveloped by someone.

She bought the two-piece wine linen suit, even though the quality was clearly not up to Kitty Darling's standards, went back to the newsroom and wrote her story.

When it appeared in the newspaper, she was proud to see her first by-line as a reporter for the women's pages. *BY TILLY GALLOWAY* it said, all in caps, under the main headline. She had officially arrived and tried not to feel hollow about the place she'd landed. The men upstairs would no doubt be having a good old laugh about it.

As the weeks flew by towards Christmas, Vera Maxwell continued to test the resolve of her colleagues with a constant array of delicious Christmas cakes. It was a point of pride with her that nothing ever appeared in her pages without her quality testing it herself, much to the delight and dismay of her colleagues.

'If I eat any more Christmas pudding I'll never fit into my corset again,' Dear Agatha had said with a satisfied moan. She'd been busy with a flood of letters from nervous mothers concerned that their flighty daughters were exhibiting far too much independence for their liking, from wives worried for their returned husbands' nerves, and from women who were having problems with their mothers-in-law now that their husbands were back.

In the first week of December, a telegram came from Cooper telling Tilly he would be back in Sydney in time for Christmas. She'd almost jumped on the spot with glee at hearing the news. She hadn't planned to, hadn't expected she would, but she had missed him terribly. When she read a headline about the latest fighting in Batavia or post-war reparations she wanted to discuss them with him. When she sat in a dark theatre eating sweets, she'd turned to the seat next to her expecting him to be there and jolted with sad surprise that he wasn't.

Mary and Bert continued to ride the waves of their daily turmoil, which rose and fell according to his moods. Tilly tried not to hear any of it—the rows, Bert's nightly midnight vomiting, the stomping and the sullen silences, loaded and heavy. What alternative did she have? Housing was in such short supply that newly married couples were sleeping on camp beds on verandahs behind canvas blinds in one or other of their family's homes, and returned prisoners were sharing bedrooms with their teenaged brothers. Every day, whatever accommodation was available was being snapped up almost before Mary could take the details for the classified advertisements section, and what was available became the object of under-the-counter bidding wars.

In that part of her life, at least, she was firmly stuck.

As Christmas week approached, all Tilly wanted this year, because this year meant so much, was a celebration with her loved ones, with those who had known Archie. It would be the end of a terrible year and a terrible war and perhaps, she allowed herself to feel a flicker of hope, the beginning of a new story in her life.

And everything was going according to her plan until Martha's husband Colin sent a letter announcing he was leaving her.

Chapter Twenty-nine

The news dropped like a bomb. Martha, Tilly and their mother Elsie sat at the kitchen table at the house on Argyle Place staring at the letter as if it might explode like a hand grenade.

In the backyard, Martha's three rambunctious boys were supposed to be collecting eggs from the chickens, shooshed outside quickly when Elsie had spotted the look of pale shock on her daughter's face, but were instead chasing them and throwing them into the air as if they were encouraging them to fly free.

'I can't believe it,' Tilly whispered.

'You and me both,' Elsie muttered.

Martha held the letter in her hands and it shook so violently Tilly could barely make out Colin's scrawled hand. She grabbed it from Martha.

Martha,
I am in Brisbane now, discharged from the navy. I'm sorry to tell you this way but I've met someone else and I wish to marry her. I'll not be coming back to Sydney. I hope you'll agree to a divorce so I can get on with things.
Colin

'He wants to get on with things?' Martha cried out. 'We've been waiting … I've been waiting all this time for that lousy sod and he ups and leaves me for a Brisbane girl?'

'And what about his sons?' Elsie asked, disgust dripping from every syllable. 'What are they going to do for a father now? I'm sorry, Martha, I know you married him, but in my mind, he's nothing but … a damn, no-good piece of … well, I won't say the rest out loud. The boys.'

At the mention of the boys, the three women looked out to the yard. Tilly and Martha had never played in it when they were children because the streets had been their playground, where there was always a billycart in need of a push or a hopscotch game underway or pirates in need of swashbuckling. The backyard was where the washing was done in the copper, where the ominous mangle threatened, where the chooks scratched and where vegetables stretched up tall to meet the afternoon sun setting in the west. On washing days—always Mondays—lines were strung from fence to fence and white sheets that had been boiled and soaked flapped in the breeze like sails until they were crisp. Stone walls separated them from their neighbours on either side, and there was a wooden fence at the rear with a gate into the back lane. Beyond the back fence and the laneway, terrace houses just like theirs loomed over their backyard, mirror images of each other, with slate-tiled roofs and squat chimneys with terracotta chimney pots on each. Tilly had taught Martha to count by peering over the back fence and up at those pots. *One, two, three, four.*

There was laughter and chickens squawking but Elsie was too shocked at the news about Colin to hop up and warn the boys to settle down and leave the chooks alone or they wouldn't lay and then what would they have for breakfast tomorrow. Her shoulders slumped.

Tilly read the letter over, still trying to grasp the enormity of the revelations contained in those four brief and pitiless sentences. Colin wanted to get on with things. How lucky for him that it seemed so easy.

Martha's nostrils flared and she spoke in a voice that Tilly barely recognised. 'How could he do this to me *again*?'

Tilly and her mother exchanged shocked glances. 'What are you talking about, Martha? You're saying he's done this before?' Tilly asked.

Martha tossed the letter at the table and strode to the window, which looked out and up over the steps to the street. The dim light caught her features in stark relief. She suddenly looked older than her twenty-eight years, worn, hollowed out.

'Of course he's done this before. He's a bloke, isn't he? He was always running after anything in a skirt. And he thought I hadn't twigged, or he just didn't give a fig.' She turned her tear-streaked cheeks to the boys, to check that they were still out of earshot. 'He's been a right skirt chaser since the day we married.'

Tilly was absolutely floored.

'You're surprised, Tilly?'

'I'm gobsmacked, actually. You never let on. You never said a thing. Did you know, Mum?'

'Of course I didn't.'

Martha scoffed angrily and wiped her eyes with the back of a hand. 'What good would have come from telling you, Tilly, or Mum? I married him. It was my problem. My burden to bear.'

'You could have left him,' Tilly said indignantly. 'Divorced him.'

'To go where and survive on what, fresh air? My measly wage doesn't even pay the rent much less put food in those boys' mouths.'

'I would have helped you,' Tilly insisted.

'Why should it be your job? A husband should support his family. I don't know what I'm going to do.' Martha broke off and gazed into the distance. 'I haven't seen any of his army pay for a month, either. He'd always send me some, minus what he didn't need for cigarettes and a drink.' Martha began to cry and hugged her arms around her waist. 'I thought there must have been some mix-up with the navy, being the end of the war and all. He's probably spent it on an engagement ring for whoever she is.'

'I'd ring his neck if he walked in the door right now—' Elsie broke off, shuddering. 'And your father would do worse.'

Tilly knew her father was in no fit state to do any harm to anybody.

'Damn him to hell,' Martha cried. 'And he's too gutless to even come home and face the music. This has never meant anything!' She thrust her left ring finger in the air as a new fiancée might display her new ring.

'Come and sit down, Martha,' Elsie implored. 'You mustn't let the boys see you upset.'

The boys were still teasing the chickens, playing happily and innocently. Colin had been gone so long, would they even remember him if he walked in the door? The war had taken him from them already so what had changed? They'd been forced to grow up without him anyway and, in that sense, their world would continue, with their mother at the centre of it, with their grandmother an orbiting moon, and an aunt who needed to do more for them. There were so many fatherless children now, so many children who were confronted with strangers in uniform whom everyone said was their father, so many who might one day wish their father hadn't come back from the war at all. It was another cruel twist that Brian, Bernard and Terry had a father who still lived but who didn't appear to want to father them.

Tilly's thoughts swirled and came to a sudden stop on something Martha had said. 'If you haven't seen any of Colin's pay for a month, how have you been paying the rent? How are you feeding the boys?'

'We pay ... I pay ... a month in advance, so I was good until today. Come Monday I'm in arrears and knowing my landlord he'll be knocking at the front door as soon as he realises I'm short. I'm sure he's got a queue of people waiting to take the place from under me, knowing how bad the housing is these days.' Martha looked at her sister with wide, scared eyes. 'I don't know what we're going to do.'

Tilly went to her and led her back to the table. How had two sisters who'd started the war with happy families and such high hopes ended up like this?

'What are you talking about?' Elsie huffed. 'You'll come home here. That's all there is to it. Take the two attic rooms and the beds. I know those boys of yours are growing like topsy but they'll have to make do with three in a bed. Top to tail should do it. They come to me after school anyway so nothing much will change. And if that husband of yours decides to show his face around here I'll knock his block off with my broom.'

And with a nod, and a choked sob from Martha, the house on Argyle Place was to once again open its arms to the lost.

When Archie had enlisted, Tilly had resisted her mother's urging to move back home. She hadn't wanted to return to a life she had left behind. She was going to be a reporter and her life was to be dictated by deadlines, not by the wharves that had dictated her father's—and therefore her family's—every waking moment since he'd turned thirteen years old and humped his first bag of wheat. Going home would have felt like going backwards and, besides that, she wanted to have a place of her own so that when Archie was home on leave they could have all the privacy that a married couple desired. Tilly had shared a room with her sister right up until she'd married Archie and had ever since that day become greedy and protective of that privacy.

She wondered how Martha felt about going back home. She would ask her later, when things had settled, when she wasn't so angry. That might take years.

A week later, Tilly arrived at Martha's house bright and early and they packed up the house. Colin's civvies were bundled off to the Salvation Army—Tilly had to work hard to convince Martha not to burn everything out in the street— and neighbours had loaned them suitcases for the boys to fill with their few possessions. Three watersiders from the union turned up with a truck and they loaded up the beds, the kitchen table and chairs, a sideboard that had been filled with photograph albums and a few pieces of good china and glassware, the settee and the wireless and headed home to Argyle Place.

Tilly wondered if the boys would grow to love the household routines that she and Martha had grown up with, routines that hadn't changed in all the years since then. Monday was still washing day and Elsie would spend all day feeding the fire under the copper in the backyard so it boiled their clothes until they were clean, before feeding every piece through the mangle that Tilly was still fearful of. When Stan wasn't working and was around to help with the household chores, he'd liked to feed the mangle himself, scaring Tilly by pretending that it had sucked his arm in between the rollers. No doubt the boys would be as perplexed as Tilly still was about Elsie's daily practice of sweeping the front steps precisely before ten o'clock each morning, or there would be trouble. And after the sweeping, she would have her second cup of tea and read the afternoon newspaper from the day before.

When Tilly had reminded her mother that yesterday's news belonged to yesterday, Elsie had shrugged and said, 'It's all still news to me and this way I can read yesterday's horoscope and see if it came true, can't I?'

So much had changed for the members of the family from Argyle Place, yet so much was now the same. Tilly and Martha had lost their husbands. Stan was still at war with the bosses.

And Elsie was still keeping her entire family together.

Chapter Thirty

'Hello, doctor. It's Dear Agatha here from the *Daily Herald*. I'm very well, thank you. Do you have a minute? I have a tricky one today. A lady has written seeking some advice about urination. Yes.'

At the desk next along, Tilly leant back in her chair and listened in as Dear Agatha murmured sympathetically, her pencil sweeping over her notebook.

Since she'd returned to work, Tilly had moved desks and was now in a cluster with Dear Agatha, Vera Maxwell and Kitty Darling. Police reporter Maggie Pritchard and courts reporter Frances Langley had moved their desks opposite each other at the other end of the newsroom. They found it useful to be closer so they could compare notes: someone Maggie wrote about on a Monday might be the subject of Frances's yarn on the Tuesday.

'Is that so?' Dear Agatha replied, her voice rising at the end of her question. 'She writes that the irritation arises when she urinates and that there's increased frequency. And there's some discharge as well.'

Tilly had always assumed that Dear Agatha simply invented the advice she provided to Sydney's lovelorn and itching and bereft. When she'd worked up in the main newsroom the men had read out the questions—and Dear Agatha's answers—for sport over morning tea. When the male reporters had invented their own creative and debauched solutions for what ailed female letter writers, Tilly had tuned it out with quick bursts of typing.

In the past week, she'd seen for herself just how much research it actually took. Dear Agatha had a contact book filled with the telephone numbers of doctors and nurses and even a psychiatrist, who regularly provided her with advice on how she might craft replies to the letters. Tilly hadn't until now understood the sheer volume of them, hundreds each week, delivered in boxes directly to Dear Agatha's desk by ambitious young copyboys.

Her skill was in distilling the professionals' knowledge into something that was easily understood by the letter writer and by other readers of the column.

'Oh, dear. Thank you, doctor. Talk soon.' Dear Agatha sighed before slipping fresh copy paper and carbons into her typewriter.

'Is it the clap?' Tilly asked.

Dear Agatha frowned at Tilly. 'Gonorrhoea, he says, with those symptoms. She needs a dose of penicillin and so does her husband.'

'Poor woman.'

'Poor woman indeed. I have to edit this part of her letter—we're a family newspaper after all—but she says here—' Dear Agatha reached for the letter. 'She says here she was faithful to her husband the whole war and she's only had the symptoms since he's come home. He was in the Middle East.' Dear Agatha raised her eyebrows. 'What do you think happened?'

'I'm supposing he brought something home with him that he didn't carry in his kit bag.'

'Yes. My pox doctor just now told me that in the First World War, there was an epidemic of it on the Western Front. Nearly fifty-thousand cases and it took six weeks in hospital back then to cure it. Thank god for penicillin.'

'Why didn't this woman go to the doctor instead of writing to you? It sounds incredibly painful.'

Dear Agatha sighed. 'Imagine what that's like, Tilly? Men don't get the blame for giving VD to their wives and girlfriends. The women are the guilty ones in these cases. And I don't know if this correspondent even has a husband, to tell the truth. But that hardly matters. If she's married she's suffering and if she's a single girl she's likely scared witless. If she did tell her doctor she'll likely get a stern lecture about her own moral cowardice. Or worse. She could be locked up.'

Tilly nearly fell backwards out of her chair. 'I don't believe you.'

'It's true.' Dear Agatha's eyes narrowed and her lips were a thin line. 'Back in '42 Canberra passed new laws. Wait a minute. I'll find the name.' Dear Agatha lifted a folder from her desk and flicked through pages and pages of news clippings. 'Ah, here it is. Listen to this. They're the National Security (Venereal Diseases and Contraception) Regulations and they gave health authorities the power to detain and medically examine people suspected of being carriers of VD.'

Tilly was flabbergasted. 'That's horrifying, Agatha.'

'Too right. And guess who they locked up?'

'No!'

'Oh yes. It gets worse.' Dear Agatha stabbed a page with her index finger. 'Our own health minister said, and I quote, "It is in the power of women to banish venereal disease by denying men the opportunity for irregular intercourse, and by refusing to allow their moral sense to be blunted by alcohol".'

'Oh, for goodness sake. What a lot of rot.'

'And that's not all, Tilly. The *Australian Medical Journal* said young women weren't exhibiting enough self-control and were giving in to illicit company, easy money and a good time, luring men into deviant practices and having babies out of wedlock. They were destroying the spiritual and moral values of the country.'

Tilly wondered how on earth they all had the time for all this society-destroying behaviour while raising children on their own, volunteering for the war, working six days a week in factories, heading off to the country to work in the Land Army or donning uniforms for positions in the defence forces.

'That's the most ridiculous thing I've ever heard,' Tilly huffed.

'And I suppose you weren't aware either that the 8th Special Hospital in Palestine was the AIF's main VD treatment centre. They even had specialist venereologists.'

'Is that who you were talking to just now?'

'I will never reveal my sources, Tilly.' Dear Agatha played at being horrified, positioned her fingers over her typewriter keys and began. 'Dear Worried of Woolloomooloo. How dreadful for you that you have suffered in silence but the time for silence is over. I would urge you to seek medical advice from a friendly doctor immediately for your own health.' She turned to Tilly. 'I'll write her a note with the name of my pox doctor. He's offered to help.'

Tilly wondered about the secrets men kept. Who would want to admit to a wife or a family that they'd been laid up in hospital in Palestine with the clap? Where was the honour and courage in that? So a soldier's secret becomes his wife's and then Dear Agatha's and the doctor's and so on and so on. It was indeed a tangled web, in which everyone was the prey.

She had been complicit in keeping the secrets of men. The indiscretions she'd overheard in the newsroom all the years she worked up on the third floor. The stories she'd heard on the women's correspondents' tour about important men in Sydney, those in positions of power and authority who had abused it.

And nothing looked about to change, Tilly thought. The war might well be over but all around her things seemed the same as they ever were.

Strike settlement talks were continuing between BHP and the Federal Government, with miners claiming BHP was deliberately inflicting a black Christmas on the Australian people, and BHP countering with claims of industrial thuggery on the part of the communist unions. Chifley was refusing to order the striking miners back to work, winning acclaim from other unions, while Sydneysiders and businesses were enduring electricity rationing to cope with the reduced supply. Hospitals had discharged more than five hundred patients in case of power failure. Paddington housewives were drawing up rosters for their neighbours to share their fuel coppers so the washing could still be done. An immediate ban had been placed on the sale of car tyres because power restrictions had stopped production. Supplies of canned meat were running low, half the theatres in New South Wales were closed and Berlei, the corset manufacturer, was predicting that the tremendous demand for foundation garments would go unmet as production had also been closed down. Word was that Chifley's office at Parliament House was being powered by hurricane lanterns and candles, in solidarity with the strikers, and the *Daily Herald* was producing smaller, emergency issues of the paper to conserve light and power.

Some forms of rationing were still in place, including petrol, which had put a dampener on many families' plans for a holiday on the coast or to the country. And those who were travelling by train were now having to contend with train cancellations and crowded carriages and restricted timetables due to the coal shortage, so Sydneysiders had decided to stay home for a quiet one.

Many diggers still hadn't returned home and others remained in hospital. There were funerals for those who'd succumbed to their wounds. The idea of celebrating Christmas, this first festive season in which she and the world finally knew she was a widow, seemed like an anathema to Tilly. Her grief was still too fresh and her feeling of loss too profound and complex to want to celebrate anything. Her city was looking to Christmas in a similarly subdued fashion, not feeling comfortable showing joy when so many were experiencing grief. What did she have to drink to?

The idea of offering toasts to absent loved ones was too much for some to bear, and who could blame them for not wanting to celebrate at all. Tilly knew her mother was already planning her traditional Christmas lunch. She'd been carefully feeding one of her young chooks to fatten it up for roasting, and it was only a couple of days away from its demise. When Tilly had exhibited a distinct lack of enthusiasm for the prospect, her mother had been horrified.

'We'll celebrate because Archie can't, love. We'll drink a toast to him and all you've lost. We still have each other. That's what I'll be celebrating.'

Christmas lunch would be more important than ever this year with Martha and her boys living back at Argyle Place. At least in the bosom of her family, Tilly could spirit herself away if she needed to have a cry. Her father and his union comrades didn't have much to celebrate either, having been pilloried for their strikes and blamed when talks with Chifley had broken down. When it had been announced that there would be power restrictions in the lead-up to Christmas because the coalminers supplying coal to Bunnerong power station were on strike, the grumbles had intensified. A victory for striking workers looked further away than ever.

Tilly had ignored the turning of the days on the calendar as the twenty-fifth grew closer. In the years their husbands had been away, Tilly and Mary had created a Christmas tree from pussy willow branches Mary had collected from the streets around Potts Point. They'd wrapped the jumpers they'd knitted for Bert and Archie and sat them under their makeshift tree. In the months leading up, they'd made fruit cakes, bought aftershave and shaving cream and new toothbrushes and packed everything up in brown paper and sent them off marked with their husbands' names in clear print with the words *prisoner of war* underneath, to be sent off to the Red Cross for distribution.

Now Tilly knew that nothing had ever reached Archie or Bert. What had happened to all the clothes and cakes and love letters and declarations and heartbreak collected between each line of those letters? Were they in a warehouse somewhere, a collective gathering of pain and suffering, bleeding tears into the ground beneath? Had rats and mice devoured all the fruit cake or had she and Mary and tens of thousands of other Australian women been inadvertently feeding the Japanese instead of their husbands?

Tilly was struggling to find much to celebrate and the prospect of 1946 loomed, filled with nothing but a series of obstacles she would have to overcome. What to do about her new job. Mary and Bert. Where she might live if they found a place of their own. Martha and her boys and their future. Her father's ailing health and his prospects of ever finding work again. Her mother's determined stoicism, which Tilly knew couldn't last forever.

Out of the corner of her eye, something caught her attention. She stopped staring out the streaked windows across the newsroom and saw Mrs Freeman take up position by Vera's desk. The editor cleared her throat and it sounded portentous.

Her reporters, as well as Maggie and Frances, looked up from their typing.

Mrs Freeman held her hands together at her waist waiting for everyone to listen in. 'I have an announcement to make.'

'I hope it's to do with Christmas and that extra week off we've been promised,' Vera called out. There was a general murmur of approval at that idea. It was the end of a long year and before that, a long war, and so many had been looking to Christmas to put a firm full stop on all of it. It should have been an exhale of breath for all those who'd been holding theirs for so long, but it hadn't brought the immediate new chapter people had been hoping for. The first peacetime Christmas was shaping up to be anything but peaceful.

She realised with a start that she hadn't been listening to Mrs Freeman and focussed her attention on her editor.

'Is she unwell?' Dear Agatha asked.

'There's something going around,' Vera added. 'A nasty cold, I hear.'

Tilly whispered to Dear Agatha, 'Who's unwell?'

'Kitty,' Mrs Freeman answered Tilly directly. 'She's needing to take some time off.'

'She's not in trouble, is she?' Maggie called out, blowing the smoke from her Woodbine into the air. She and Frances exchanged knowing glances.

Trouble? Tilly studied Maggie and Frances and their suddenly solemn expressions. Was anything about human behaviour a shock to them?

Mrs Freeman's mouth twitched and she pursed her lips to hide it. 'For goodness sake, Maggie. She's not wanted by the police. She'll be back in six months. About May. Or June. She's not certain yet. My point in telling you is that I need someone to fill her position doing Talk of the Town. I thought I'd offer it to everyone here before I look outside the paper.'

Tilly wanted to shrink under her desk. She looked around at her colleagues. Maggie would never be moved from her police round, neither would Frances from courts.

Vera's cookery column was more popular than ever and the flood of letters to Dear Agatha surely would keep her safe. That left Tilly as the most likely candidate to temporarily fill Kitty's role.

'No volunteers?' Mrs Freeman asked. Everyone seemed suddenly fascinated with their notebooks. Talk of the Town was a gossip column and it had suited Kitty perfectly, moving as she did in Sydney's fanciest circles. The idea of being assigned to it filled Tilly with utter despair. When Mrs Freeman glided up to her desk, Tilly looked up at her with resignation. She needed this job. She would do what she must, even if she couldn't tell the Marquis of Milford Haven from the Duke of Gloucester.

'I'll do whatever you need, Mrs Freeman.' Tilly bit the inside of her lip. She couldn't take the words back now.

Mrs Freeman considered Tilly for a moment. 'Thank you. I appreciate that.' She patted Tilly on the shoulder. 'There will be a few things I'll need you to attend to while we find someone to fill in on a longer-term basis.'

'You mean it won't be forever?' Tilly asked.

'For goodness sake, no,' Mrs Freeman scoffed.

Tilly couldn't hide her enormous sigh of relief.

'Do you know anyone around the traps who perhaps might be interested, Tilly?' Mrs Freeman paused. 'From one of the other papers, I mean? Perhaps a girl looking for an upgrade?'

Tilly's mind whirred. 'As a matter of fact, I know Denise Stapleton from *The Sun* pretty well. I can ask if she knows anyone over there.'

'Terrific. Let me know as soon as you have a name or two. Now tell me, what are you working on?'

Tilly reached for her notebook and stood respectfully.
'There's a rush on for tinned food with a photo from a
grocery counter showing a long queue of housewives, and
Miss Australia, Rhondda Kelly from Queensland, and the
other finalists will be riding through the city this afternoon
on an amphibious duck from the aircraft carrier *Implacable*.'

'Do as good a job as you can,' Mrs Freeman said as she
rolled her eyes and turned to Vera. 'What's cooking, Vera?'

She tucked a strand of hair behind her ear. 'A Christmas
Garland Cake and an assortment of savouries. Cheese toasted
savoury rolls, salted crackers and devilled bread crisps.'

'Can I have copies?' Dear Agatha asked. 'Anything will
be better than boiled mutton.'

Mrs Freeman crossed the newsroom to Frances and
Maggie. 'What about you two? What's happened in general
news?'

Maggie butted out her Woodbine. 'This yarn about
Ethel Livesey is only getting more interesting. So, she cancels
her lavish wedding here in Sydney two weeks ago and then
disappears off the face of the earth. The coppers think she
might be in Adelaide and that she might know something
about a certain Mrs Florence Elizabeth Ethel Gardiner, alias
Anderson, alias Stevens Lockwood, who absconded from
bail back in '33 while waiting to answer charges of false
pretences.'

'Intriguing,' Mrs Freeman murmured. 'This Mrs Livesey
… isn't she the cotton heiress who was supposed to marry
the man from the Treasury? Beech?'

'That's right,' Maggie nodded excitedly. Prickles rose on
the back of Tilly's neck. She wished she'd been in a position
to chase that story. It sounded like a cracker of a yarn.

'Kitty Darling wrote it up in Talk of the Town. Five hundred guests. Something about changing the venue from Woollahra to the Australia Hotel because all the publicity had made her ill?'

'It seems Mrs Ethel Livesey and this Gardiner Anderson Lockwood woman might be one and the same.'

'Oh, dear.' Mrs Freeman shook her head. 'Poor Mr Beech.'

Mrs Freeman went to Frances's desk. 'Frances?'

'I have a cracker here, Mrs Freeman. Upstairs says I've got page five. A fellow posed as a war correspondent ...' Frances waited for the laughter and it came heartily. Which of their male colleagues upstairs had he impersonated? 'He proposes to this young lass and then not only does he steal her trousseau, but it turns out he has a wife and child.'

'Vile!' Vera shouted.

'Off with his head!' Maggie laughed.

'He told the poor woman that he'd covered the war for the American Associated Press and he convinced her to sell her frock shop before they got married. So he not only gets the proceeds from that, but a diamond ring worth eighty pounds and all the furniture she moved out of her flat.'

'What a devil,' Tilly said to herself as she thought of Martha and her husband's betrayal.

'Keep at it, girls. Well done.'

Mrs Freeman returned to her office and Tilly couldn't shake the guilty feeling she'd had a narrow escape.

Chapter Thirty-one

'Do you think three chooks will be enough?' Elsie stood by her kitchen table, which was groaning with the dressed birds, peeled potatoes ready for boiling, a bowl of shelled peas, and turnips and half a pumpkin ready to go in the wood stove with the chicken. 'There's a glut because of the coal strikes so I nabbed an extra two for cheap.'

Martha elbowed Tilly in the side. 'Lucky there's a strike on, hey? How many of us are there? Mum and Dad, me and the boys. That's six.'

'Mary and Bert and me. That's nine.' Tilly cleared her throat. 'Oh, and Cooper. That makes ten.'

Martha whistled low. 'George Cooper, hey?'

Tilly's face heated. 'Oh, stop.'

'For goodness sake, Tilly. It hasn't been half obvious. Well, at least to those of us who want to see it.' Martha nudged her sister playfully. 'Of course, the wilfully blind might not have noticed.'

Tilly huffed. 'He only landed back in the country yesterday and he couldn't get a seat on a train to Canberra to see his father—it's hell getting a train anywhere at the moment—so I invited him here. If that's all right with you.' The idea of letting Cooper spend Christmas alone was unthinkable to Tilly. How could she explain to Martha how close they'd become in the past few months? Martha had had her own troubles to contend with—not to mention her boys—and hadn't needed to be burdened with Tilly's. Mary was struggling with Bert, and Elsie had been looking after her husband and the whole neighbourhood, from what Tilly had heard. Cooper had devoted every spare minute he had to being her confidante, her company, her refuge in the storm that had been raging all around her. With Cooper, she had felt she was in the eye of it. Safe.

Elsie exhaled and surveyed the table. 'I don't think we have enough plum pudding.'

Martha slipped an arm around her mother's shoulders. 'Of course there's enough plum pudding, Mum. It's going to be a feast.'

Elsie and her daughters had spent the morning cleaning the house and preparing for lunch. Martha's boys had been warned to be on their best behaviour and had been banished upstairs to their bedroom to read quietly while all the preparations were underway. Tilly had brought her father a copy of the day before's paper and had taken it upstairs to him when she'd arrived.

She'd tried to hide her shock at his appearance, as he lay under a knitted blanket on his bed. He'd seemed shrunken and pale yet had still managed to give her a warm smile.

'Tilly girl. Merry Christmas.'

She'd gone to him, kissed his cheek and lingered there. 'Hello, Dad. Thought you might like to read Chifley's message to members of the Labor Party. Here,' she gave him the folded newspaper. 'Page three.'

'Thank you. The capitalist press running a message to members of the Labor Party? Well, well, well.'

'And I see that power restrictions have been lifted for today.'

He'd cocked an eyebrow. 'Funny about that.'

Tilly had laughed. 'See you downstairs for lunch. Everything's almost done. You won't need to lift a finger.'

'I wouldn't want to get in the way of my girls.' And when he winked, Tilly saw a hint of the man he used to be, of the man he still was. And she thought of all the good men she knew, of whom he was the best of all.

By midday, the table was set, every spare chair in the house was crowded around it and Bernard, Brian and Terry were hovering, as anxious as labradors who'd sniffed out a bone. Tilly had put some finishing touches on the Christmas tree in the corner—a new angel for the very top branch—and hoped the boys would be able to resist tugging at the little wooden trains she'd bought new this year just for them and the paper lanterns she'd made from instructions in the *Women's Weekly*. They didn't have sparkling gold and silver baubles or fancy tinsel—they never had—but it didn't matter. Under the tree, a pile of presents wrapped in brown paper and tied with string were already tempting small and curious hands and Stan had warned the boys from them more than once.

Just as Tilly checked the time, she heard Mary calling from the street. She looked up to see Mary and Bert descending the steps and she rushed to the door, quickly glancing at Bert to judge his mood. His wide smile was a relief. He held a bottle of champagne in one hand and his hat in the other.

'Merry Christmas, Tilly!' Mary cried and threw her arms around her friend.

'And to you. How was Melbourne?'

'We had a wonderful time, although we started to panic at the thought we might not get a train home. But we're here now.'

'Merry Christmas, Tilly.' Bert stepped forward and kissed Tilly politely on the cheek before giving her the bottle.

'And you, Bert. Thank you for this. Mum, look. Champagne.'

Mary stepped forward. 'Hello, Mrs Bell. This is my husband, Bert. Bert, Mrs Bell. It's just lovely of you to have us here for Christmas. Thank you.'

Elsie was chuffed. 'The more the merrier, I say.'

As they hugged each other hello and shook hands, Tilly put the champagne in the icebox. There was so much commotion going on all around her, exclamations and cheerios, that when she felt a hand on her shoulder she startled.

And when she turned, the sight of Cooper made her heart swell. He was there, exactly how he'd promised he would be. Home for Christmas.

'You made it.'

'I wouldn't have missed it.' His blue eyes sparkled like the harbour.

It was so good to see him and the realisation about just how good was a surprise. His cheeks were smooth and his hair freshly cut. He looked as handsome as ever in his navy pinstripe suit and his smile was exactly what she needed to see. And just like that, the tension eased out of her. He was safe. He was home. He was here.

'Safe trip back?'

He nodded. 'The Indonesians say hello, by the way.'

Tilly chuckled. 'There's a certain father of mine who'll no doubt interrogate you for all the latest news from Batavia.'

'I look forward to it.'

'He's upstairs at the moment. He'll be down shortly.'

They looked at each other for the longest time, a silent understanding passing between them. They had both made it to the end of the year. He was safe and she had survived the deepest loss. In that moment, she realised that there had been no one more steadfast, after her parents and sister and Mary, than this man.

'Well … Merry Christmas, Mrs Galloway.'

'Merry Christmas, Cooper,' she replied, wrapping her arms around herself to quell the almost irresistible urge to cling to him.

He cocked his head at the paper bag in his arms. 'Where can I put this?'

She'd barely registered that he was holding anything. Tilly stepped in closer, pressed her palms against his biceps and went up on tiptoes. 'What's in there?'

He peered inside. 'MacRobertson's chocolate. Some Pascall fruit bonbons and lemonade for Martha's boys. A bottle of whisky for your father in the hope he'll pour one for me. And … some other things.'

Tilly kept her hands on him but met his gaze. 'Anything for me?'

Before he could answer, Mary was beside Tilly. Tilly lowered her hands and stepped back.

'Merry Christmas, George. It's so lovely to see you. You remember Bert?'

'Of course I do. Merry Christmas, digger.'

Half an hour later, with the boys so ravenous they were about to gnaw off their own arms, Christmas lunch began. Stan sat at the head of the table, Elsie at the other end. Martha and her boys were along one side, and Bert, Mary, Tilly and Cooper were on the other. Tilly had strategically placed Cooper next to her father, a move that was keeping the both of them highly entertained.

Between them all, the vegetables were steaming and the roast chickens' delectable scent filled the room.

Elsie cleared her throat. 'Stan?'

'Yes, love?'

'You were going to say a few words?'

As Stan slowly rose to his feet, Tilly whispered in Mary's ear, 'Sorry about grace, Mary.'

Mary whispered back. 'I prayed in church this morning. I don't mind.'

'Well.' Stan looked at each of his guests in turn, respectfully and considerately, welcoming them to his table and his home and to the embrace of his family. A wink at his wife. A smile at Martha and Tilly, a salute to Bert and Mary, a lift of his chin to Cooper and a cheeky grin for his grandsons. 'Welcome to you all and thank you for sharing our table today. We've had six Christmases at war. It's hard to think about that, isn't it? And finally we have peace.'

'Amen,' Mary whispered under her breath.

'The world has come through a time of terrible darkness. Our country has made enormous sacrifices to secure victory over the Germans and the Japanese. So has our own family. Boys, your father served for four years. Bravely.'

Across the table, Bernard, Brian and Terry looked solemnly at their grandfather. Terry turned to his mother and whispered, 'Is Daddy coming home soon, Mummy?'

'Soon, sweetheart,' Martha replied, biting her lip, her eyes filling with tears.

'And, of course, Archie. We mourn our son-in-law. We will never forget him.'

Tilly breathed deep as grief rolled over her in a wave. 'Thank you, Dad.' Under the table, there was a hand on hers. She looked down. Cooper.

'We thank Bert Smith for his service and for his courage in enduring the Japanese.' Bert nodded his thanks and Mary sniffed.

'Elsie. You've been a rock all these years. I couldn't have married a better woman.' Tilly could see by the tears welling in her mother's eyes that she knew how much this man loved her and appreciated her. It wasn't the first time Tilly thought how lucky she was to have been born to Stan and Elsie; how privileged she was to be their daughter, to have seen a love like theirs up close, to have been nourished and sent out into the world with the expectation of what she should strive for.

'And let's not forget we lost a prime minister in our John Curtin. He was the best of Labor men. He stood up to Churchill and MacArthur and was worn out by the burden of what he asked our young boys to do for their country.'

'Hear, hear,' Elsie said quietly.

Stan pulled back his shoulders and his voice grew louder. 'Our losses can only make us more aware of the losses of others in this war. The Londoners during the Blitz. The millions and millions of people in Europe crushed by Nazism. Those of the Jewish faith singled out by Hitler. And yes, those killed in Hiroshima and Nagasaki. They all made the ultimate sacrifice for warmongering men. To them we say, we will never forget.'

'Hear, hear.' Tilly pushed back her chair and got to her feet. All around her, the scrape of chairs and the shuffle of feet. 'To Archie.'

'To Archie,' everyone called in response.

'To my family,' Elsie said through her sobs. 'The most precious things in the world to me.'

'And to friends,' Tilly added. 'May the new year bring you hope.'

The adults clinked their glasses and the boys spilled their lemonade as they copied the move. Martha didn't fuss. Not today.

And as Bert offered to carve the first chicken, as Mary passed the plates around the table and Bernard poured the gravy, Tilly finally felt a flicker of hope, of the possibility of a new beginning in the first year of peace, and a surge of love for the people in her life who had helped her through.

She felt a light shining down on her, as if she was out in the bright summer sunshine, and it warmed her heart. Her Christmas wish for everyone at the table was that it would shine just as brightly for them, too.

After lunch, Tilly took charge of washing the dishes while everyone else scattered to the four winds with satisfied appetites and Christmas cheer on their faces. The boys had raced to the tree and Martha had skipped after them. It had been a long while since Tilly had seen her sister smile so broadly. After the excitement of his speech and the dinner conversation, during which, just as Tilly had predicted, Stan had launched into a deep discussion with Cooper about Batavia and the Indonesian Independence movement, he was now resting on the couch. Mary and Bert were in the stairwell which led from the kitchen up to the street, deep in conversation, the puffs of smoke from Bert's pipe curling up to join the clouds in the sky above. Beside her, Cooper was drying the dishes she was stacking on the draining board.

He'd offered to help her and she hadn't brushed him off. She had wanted to have him to herself for a moment and, anyway, men could wipe as well as women, couldn't they?

'I think your father likes me,' he said with a grin as he ran a tea towel over a saucepan and set it on the wood stove. His smile made the corners of his eyes crinkle and the colour shine bluer than she'd ever seen.

'Did he ask you about the Indonesians? About Soekarno and the People's Army?'

'Of course he did. He has some interesting views about colonialism and the Dutch. Can't say I disagree with him, actually. The Indonesians led the fight against the Japanese in their own country and then we expect them to welcome their colonial masters back again? Not likely.'

'I knew he would. When are you going back?' Tilly tried to make it sound like an innocent question. It wasn't. She had missed Cooper and would have to steel herself against missing him again if he was heading overseas for another posting. There had been talk at the paper, according to Maggie and Frances, that the newspaper's postings in London and Tokyo were open. The reconstruction in Japan was expected to take years and there had already been talk that a British Commonwealth Occupation Force, comprising some Australian troops, would be established in Hiroshima. And where the army went, a war correspondent was sure to follow.

'I have news on that score.'

Tilly shot a look at him. Her heart sank.

'I'm not going anywhere.'

'You didn't get London or Tokyo?'

'I told Sinclair I didn't want to go. I withdrew.'

'When?'

'Yesterday, when I got back.'

'Why?'

'Aunty Tilly.' Three pairs of arms were suddenly around her waist and she turned, her hands dripping water on three blond heads.

'Thank you for the book,' Terry said earnestly. 'I haven't read *The Magic Pudding.*'

'Glad to hear it. And what about you, Brian? Have you read *Seven Little Australians*? It's about mischievous children. I thought it was right up your alley.'

'I haven't but does this mean I have to now?' he moaned.

Tilly pretended to cuff him under the chin. 'Yes it does. Reading makes you smart.'

Bernard sidled up to his aunt. 'Thank you for the book about the robbers,' he said, somewhat sullen.

She turned to Cooper. '*Robbery Under Arms.*' And then back to Bernard. 'I thought you might like to read about a bushranger. His name is Captain Starlight.'

'A bushranger?' Bernard's eyes widened and he darted back to the Christmas tree.

'There are presents here for you, Tilly,' Elsie called and Tilly untied her apron. Cooper followed her into the living room and past the piles of brown paper and string covering the floor. Stan was already sniffing his bottle of whisky; Elsie was smoothing Tilly's gift of Helena Rubinstein Pasteurised Face Cream on her neck, and Martha seemed to love her new beauty case, which Tilly had filled with powder, hand cream and a pair of sheer stockings.

Elsie passed Tilly a package. The card tied to the string said *Merry Christmas. From George.*

'And here's yours, Cooper.'

'You first,' he said.

'You first.'

'No, you.'

'I insist, you.'

Martha interrupted. 'Someone open a bloody present. I'm dying to see what's inside.'

Tilly tore open the paper. It was a bottle of French perfume. She couldn't speak. Mary was by her side, her mouth open wide in surprise. 'It's not Jean Didier, is it?'

Tilly laughed, almost speechless, full of joy. 'No it isn't. It's … it's Chanel No. 5.'

Elsie, Mary and Martha stared at Tilly. She stared at the box and then at Cooper.

'Where did you …?'

He didn't answer her question but stepped closer to her and their eyes met. She held her breath as he leant forward and kissed her on the cheek. His warm lips met her blazing skin. She gripped his arm to steady herself as he whispered, 'Merry Christmas.'

She nodded to her gift, still in his hands. 'Your turn.'

He unwrapped the paper to reveal a leather writing compendium in deepest brown, with sheets of off-white paper and envelopes inside.

'Thank you. So I can write to you?' he asked, an eyebrow raised.

'I didn't know you were staying,' she replied, just to him. 'It seems pointless now, I expect.'

'Doesn't mean I won't write to you.'

'Excuse me.' Bert tapped a knife against his champagne glass and slipped an arm around Mary. 'We have an announcement to make.'

Mary shot a look at Tilly, and her face fell and Tilly knew that it wasn't a baby.

'Mary and I have a new home. My name was called in the Housing Commission's ballot last week and we've finally got somewhere to live.'

A rousing cheer went up in the room.

'It's a house in Avenue Road in Mosman,' Mary said laughing. 'It's ready for us to move in. This is my way of saying that I'm moving out, Tilly!'

Tilly rushed forward, hugged her friend and congratulated Bert.

'I can't believe it.'

'It has been a little squeezed with the three of us,' Mary said. 'You've had the patience of a saint.'

'Stop. I'm going to miss you dreadfully. You know that.'

'I know. But it'll be 1946 soon. Our whole future is ahead of us.' She whispered in Tilly's ear. 'For you and me both.'

Later, after Martha had taken the boys out for a walk to burn off all their pent-up energy from being on their best behaviour, Tilly waved goodbye to Mary and Bert and returned to the living room, where her mother sat with a cup of tea and Cooper. Stan had gone upstairs an hour before for a lie down, the excitement of so many people and the boys having worn him out, and Tilly was glad of a break. She wanted Cooper to get to know her mother better and the reverse was true as well.

She made herself a fresh cup and sat on the floor by the tree, surveying the paper and string and packaging and her bottle of scent. It was the most glamorous gift she'd ever received.

'So you've lived all your life here at Millers Point, Mrs Bell?' Cooper asked.

'Born and bred. I grew up on High Street. My father was a watersider. That's how I met Stan.'

Tilly listened while her mother told her story, her own mind drifting off as she stared through the back door into the yard. One less chicken was scratching in the dirt that day and Tilly's belly was all the better for it. She thought over Mary and Bert's news and what it would mean for her and her flat at Potts Point. She had been through so much upheaval that year that one more stone in the pond, rippling the surface of her life, was simply something she was going to have to bear. She couldn't afford it on her own so perhaps she might put an advertisement on the noticeboard in the staff canteen at the newspaper and see who might be interested. Or perhaps she would find somewhere new to live.

As it was, she didn't want to think about those choices right at that moment. She was finding it altogether more fascinating listening to her mother's proud storytelling and Cooper's genuine questions. She loved the sound of his voice, the deep timbre of it, the way it seemed to echo in his mouth when he laughed, and as she let her head fall back on the armchair, and fluttered her eyes closed, she let it soothe her.

And then a wail like nothing she had ever heard took its place and when she bolted upright, it was Cooper shaking her awake.

'Tilly. It's your father.'

Chapter Thirty-two

More than five hundred people from all over Sydney turned out to bury Stan Bell on 29 December 1945. Stan's comrades Arthur Black, Bob Bailey and Walter Rose were among the pallbearers at the funeral and afterwards led a rousing and emotional rendition of 'The Internationale', which would have made Stan proud.

Elsie Bell remained brave and strong throughout, taking her place at the front of the gathering at the Abraham Mott Hall across Argyle Place—the Coal Lumpers' Union having put aside any internecine workplace rivalry on account of it being Stan—and she had held the hands and accepted the condolences of grown men completely unabashed at shedding their tears. Tilly knew her mother would never be forgotten by the Waterside Workers' Federation. She would be held in the bosom of that community of workers for as long as she lived.

'It's too bloody young', was the most common refrain at the funeral, followed by 'Those bastards worked him to death', a sentiment that seared through Tilly like the hot rivet had through Billy McCartney's eye when the bridge was built back in the twenties.

Death had wrapped itself around Tilly like a cloak.

Her husband and now her father—the two men she had loved the most in her life—were gone.

Those last happy moments with her father had been at the Bells' kitchen table, the scene of so many lessons about family and their hard-scrabble life and the realities of work for men like him and families like hers. Stan Bell had stood proudly at the head of the Christmas table, looking across at those he loved and who loved him to reflect on the year—and the war—they had endured. He had exhorted them to never forget those who had made the ultimate sacrifice for warmongering men. How could Tilly ever?

The union paid for Stan's funeral and ran an open bar at a nearby pub afterwards for the men. Back at the house, Tilly and Martha made tea and accepted the many generous gifts of cakes and slices from their neighbours, union wives and others who were strangers to them, but who had known and respected their father.

Tilly held herself together as best she could. She poured tea. Sliced and served cake. Collected dirty dishes. Washed them and filled them all over again. She read *The Magic Pudding* to Martha's boys in the private eyrie of their attic bedroom when they were in tears, consoled Martha when she found her sobbing in the bathroom, fed cake scraps to the chooks in the backyard, and tried to smoke a cigarette for the first time in months, but she quickly discovered she'd already lost the taste for it so she stomped it out with her shoe and then watched the chickens peck at it in the dirt.

The screen door opened and closed with a clatter. The chooks flapped their wings and made a half-hearted attempt to take off but quickly changed their minds and continued to scratch.

Elsie slipped an arm through the crook of Tilly's elbow and sighed deep and weary. There was a lifetime of exhaustion in that exhalation. 'You all right, love?'

Tilly lifted her chin to rest on her mother's head and pulled her in close. Tilly had been a head taller than her mother since she'd been ten years old and this pose was familiar and comforting. It made Elsie chuckle and Tilly let herself smile.

'Don't you worry about me, Mum.'

'Of course I'm going to worry about you. And you don't need me to tell you why.'

The chooks *bawk-bawk*ed and gathered around Elsie but she flicked a foot at them to shoo them away. It was quiet in the backyard and Tilly wanted to hold her mother there in that moment, just the two of them, for as long as she could. They were the two widows of the family now; she was just thirty years old and her mother fifty. They were both far too young for what life had dealt them.

'People said lovely things about Dad.'

'That they did.'

'And when they burst into song ... well, that was hard.'

'I know, love.'

'And they also said nice things about you. Things I didn't know.'

'What didn't you know?' Elsie asked, perplexed.

'That you've been cooking for striking families. Looking after their children. Forgiving the rent of boarders if they're on strike.'

Elsie shrugged. 'That's nothing to write home about.'

'You don't think?'

'It's what you do for your comrades. It's what you do for the union, Tilly. We stick together. Plain and simple. The bosses want to divide us. They always have and they always will. Pitting one of us against another like these bloody chickens scratching here in the garden fighting over a carrot top. They want us to be weak, to be fighting each other, so we don't have the energy to fight them.' Elsie managed a chuckle. 'You can't be married to your father for more than thirty years and not have that sink into your noggin.'

Tilly's lips quivered and she breathed deep. Her dear mother. She had held this family together forever.

Elsie went weak in her daughter's arms. 'I don't know what I'm going to do without him, Tilly. I just don't know.'

Tilly held her mother's shoulders and met her sad eyes. 'You've got me and Martha and the boys. We'll see you right, Mum.'

Tilly didn't leave Argyle Place until the boys were already fast asleep and she and Martha had tucked Elsie into bed with one final cup of tea. Tilly waved goodbye to Martha, promising to call by the house the next day to see their mother, and went straight to Cooper's in a Legion cab.

He'd come to the funeral but they'd only exchanged a few quick words afterwards on the footpath in front of the Abraham Mott Hall, when he'd quickly told her he'd been invited to the pub. She'd had to hide her sudden envy that he was already welcome into the world from which she would forever be excluded because of her sex. She had lost her dear father, but Cooper would get to drink with his friends and be a part of the conversations she so desperately wanted to hear. The stories, the tall tales and true, the elevation to sainthood they would inevitably bestow on a dead union man.

Perhaps he'd seen her crestfallen expression, because he'd held back as the solemn crowd moved off to begin a long afternoon of drowning their sorrows, reaching towards her to rest a hand on her shoulder.

'I'll see you after.' It hadn't been a question.

Her answer was direct, demanding, urgent. 'When?'

He'd moved to her then, quickly pressed his cheek to hers, cool on her warm skin. 'Tonight. Come to my flat. When you can. I'll wait for you.'

The cab dropped her off on Darlinghurst Road and she walked the rest of the way, every step in rhythm with her quickening pulse, the burden of her grief feeling heavier and heavier the closer she came to Cooper's dingy bedsit. It was on the second floor of a red brick apartment building in a laneway off a backstreet and when she'd climbed the stairs she stood by his front door for a moment before knocking. She closed her eyes, laid a flat hand on her chest and felt the thud against her ribs.

She was standing on a threshold and she was about to step over it. Would she be judged for what she was about to do? And would she care about the judgement of someone who looked down on her for being lonely and filled with grief? How could anyone else ever understand what she had lived through? She was thirty years old and so much of her life and her dreams had been packed away in her camphorwood chest when Archie went to war and they were still in there, buried in letters and sorrow and in the knitted cardigans Archie would never wear and in her punishing anguish.

She had once been someone's loving and patient wife. But she was no longer that wife. She would forever be a widow and would carry the scars of that every day for the rest of her life. But wasn't she still a woman? That essential part of her had been packed away in a box, with her dreams, when Archie had gone to war. Was it wrong to want comfort and tenderness and even love again?

There was a man behind that door who wanted her. She hadn't let herself believe it—hadn't been ready to believe it—before that day, before his invitation, before the urgent press of his lips to her cheek in the street after her father's funeral. Before the tingling desire she'd felt watching him leave, and the expression on his face when he'd turned to look back at her. And right then, in that moment, she'd known that she would go to him and she would finally let herself want him too.

She lifted a hand. Made a fist. Knocked. The door opened quickly and Cooper didn't speak. She met his eyes. He took a step towards her.

She crossed that threshold.

Chapter Thirty-three

The next morning Tilly and Cooper lay together, tangled in the sheets on Cooper's sagging mattress.

They had fallen asleep that way, him on his back with his arm around her; she on her side, tucked up against him, one leg draped over his. But now they were awake, listening to the early morning sounds of the room and the world outside. A ticking clock. Footsteps from the next flat. A whistling kettle. Doors slamming from the hallway and the odd shout and curse.

Cooper entwined his fingers in her hair, messed and unruly. Her curls had been rubbed flat on his pillow during the night and he pushed her fringe back from her forehead with gentle fingers, his touch so light it was like a whisper of breath on her skin. She turned her face to him and lifted a hand from where it had been resting on his chest to trace the stubble on his chin, prickly and rough and real.

He'd always been objectively handsome, the kind of man women looked twice at as he sauntered past. 'He's a catch,' they might have said to each other, a lifted eyebrow and a pursed lip shaped for a whistle if they were the kind of girls to do that sort of thing. Tilly had always appreciated that about him in a superficial way—the cool sweep of his cheeks and his strong jaw, his commanding height and his charming smile. When had she suddenly lost her immunity to all of it? Why had she suddenly craved him so?

She pressed her nose into his neck and inhaled the cigarette and pine smell of him. There were no curtains nor a blind on the window but there was nothing to see anyway except dust and grime streaked with summer rain drops, long since dried, and beyond that a small and dim lightwell in the centre of the block of flats. Only the merest rays filtered in, making it feel like the earliest sunrise although it was most likely later. In that half-light, Tilly held on to Cooper, watching the shadows on his cheeks and his eyes, her breath catching when they disappeared as he turned towards her. Was this a dream? Was she still asleep or awake in a world that had changed in just twelve hours? She had long been denied the early morning comfort of being in bed with someone, of sharing their warmth, of feeling muscles move under skin, and he was right there and she ached with an unsated desire all over again. She pressed her intimate parts against his hip.

For the first time in so long, she felt alive.

Every nerve ending flared and fired at the feather light touch of his skin, his long arms and thighs; his narrow hips and curved calves and rounded buttocks; his sweet and soft lips and bony jaw and bristled cheeks. And she hadn't realised just how much until that morning.

Cooper turned to her. She felt him move but tightened her grip on him, pressing her thigh harder into his leg, slipping an arm across his chest and tucking her hand under his armpit.

'You hungry?' he murmured drowsily. 'Do you want something to eat?'

'No.' The truth was that she was famished but she wanted this more.

'Tea?'

'No.'

'For god's sake, give me an excuse to get out of bed.' He played at pleading with her. 'I need a cigarette, Mrs Galloway.'

She reluctantly let him go. He flipped back the sheets and strode across the room, his buttocks pale above tanned and lean legs, heading for the bathroom. Tilly lay back, her limbs akimbo, and stared at the ceiling.

She hadn't smoked a cigarette since the news about Archie and hadn't missed it at all. Cooper had tasted like cigarettes when she'd kissed him that first time the night before, right there on his doorstep, but the taste of Woodbines on his mouth hadn't made her want a cigarette. It had made her want him.

Tilly threw her arms above her head.

Cooper padded across the floor and slid back into bed next to her. He lifted an arm and she moved in beside him again.

'I didn't really need a cigarette.'

'I guessed.'

He pressed his lips to her forehead, gently, slowly.

'Tell me something,' she murmured.

'Depends.'

'On what?'

'Your question.'

'Where did you get those condoms?' She and Archie had never used one. No one she knew ever had. Archie had withdrawn from her at the last minute in the hope that would prevent her from getting pregnant and it had worked, although they had barely had a sex life before he'd enlisted. Six months in all.

'It pays to know Americans,' Cooper said. 'They used to get rubbers handed to them like lollies during the war. "Put it on before you put it in", they used to say. They were all scared witless of taking diseases home to their wives. A bit hard to hide what you've been up to when you go home with the clap.'

'So soldiers got condoms while women were told to abstain. Somehow those two things don't fit together, do they?'

'Did you …?' Cooper didn't finish his question but she knew what he was asking.

Tilly nodded against his chest. 'Yes. The whole time. Four years.'

He pulled her closer.

'I didn't marry a soldier. I married an insurance clerk. And back then, we had our whole life planned out, when it was all so new and we were in love and so, so naive as it turned out in the end. Remember how things were back in 1940? Everyone was saying the war would be over in a few months. I thought Archie would come back and we'd go back to that life. We thought the most exciting thing that would ever happen to us would be a train trip to the Blue Mountains for a holiday. I wanted to see the Three Sisters, you see?

'You know what's so awful?' Tilly felt her lips trembling and pressed them against Cooper's skin in a kiss to make them stop. 'Without the war, I never would have become a reporter. The newsroom would never have needed someone like me to fill the void left by all the blokes. And I have loved my job. Really loved it. I'm really good at it.'

'There's no doubt about that,' Cooper said.

'What's hard to reconcile is that the war blessed me and robbed me at the same time.'

Cooper was silent. The strength in his arms around her never wavered.

'I just don't know what comes next, Cooper. I need to know how my story ends.'

Chapter Thirty-four

'Tilly? A word if I may?'

'Of course, Mrs Freeman.' Tilly followed her editor across the floor to the enclosed office and waited by the guest chair while Mrs Freeman closed the door behind them, rounded the table and sat.

'Tilly. I'll come right out with it. You know what we reporters are like. I'm not going to bury the lead.' Mrs Freeman crossed her fingers on the desk. 'We've had a complaint.'

Tilly startled. 'I beg your pardon? A complaint about me?'

'I'm afraid so.'

Mrs Freeman passed a newspaper to Tilly, folded to highlight a story, a fashion parade Tilly had covered the day before at Mark Foy's Piazza. The headline read 'Summer Frocks Enthral Crowd', which she had to admit wasn't the most interesting slug line she'd ever written but the subeditors upstairs had gone with it.

She had always loved Sydney's magnificent department store with its bright white and glimmering golden frontages on Liverpool, Elizabeth and Castlereagh Streets. It had aimed to look Parisian when it had been built but Tilly had always thought of it as a castle with its gold highlights and its rooftop turrets. When the renovated building had opened in the late twenties, all of Sydney had stepped inside to soak up the glamour of the lavish woodwork, the enormous staircases and Sydney's first escalator. Her mother had dressed Tilly and her sister Martha up in their finest and they'd walked to the drapery store, beyond excited. They'd waited in a long queue and when Tilly had stepped on the moving stairs for the first time, she had gripped the moving handrail and quivered with excitement and thought that travelling in this fashion had felt like flying.

And she had shopped there before the war, mostly for little things—handkerchiefs for her mother's birthday, a new slip, some face powder—but she had never covered a fashion parade. They had always been Kitty Darling's to cover, but since Kitty wasn't at work and a replacement had yet to be found for her, Tilly had been despatched. She hadn't figured out why this particular fashion parade was so important, but calls had come down from Mr Sinclair to Mrs Freeman who had personally assigned the story to Tilly.

At the parade, she'd assumed Kitty's regular position in the front row next to the head of Ladies' Fashion and had fired questions at her about every frock and hat, scribbling furiously during the whole event.

The glamorous parade was held right under the domed glass roof in the centre of the ground floor. Red carpet had been rolled out to form a long catwalk and seats were set out in rows right along it. Above them the skylights captured Sydney's bold summer light that bounced from mirror to mirror, illuminating the ground floor like a stage.

Austerity was most definitely over. The parade had been filled with elegant models in dramatic long-stemmed American dresses in matt black crepe, with wide satin sashes swathing their hips in the style of a bustle to create a bottom where there wasn't one. Tilly had had to ask the head of Ladies Fashion to describe to her the details on the frocks so she would get them just right. She wrote pages and pages of shorthand notes. There were gowns with long sheathed sleeves and upswept hairdos that sat like American donuts on their heads. There were cap sleeves that left arms bare, coupled with long Lauren Bacall side-swept fringes that looked romantic and glamorous.

There were black satin and marquasite and hibiscus-pink crepe dresses, and sheer mist-grey chiffon, and peplums embroidered with glittering dew-drop bugle beads. Tilly couldn't imagine ever being able to afford any of the creations and would have nowhere to wear them in any case, but she had found herself spellbound by how beautiful they were.

And how they were symbolic of a different life. And as Tilly had looked on in awe, she imagined herself lighthearted and young again. For a few brief moments she was a woman in the first chapters of something interesting with a man she rather liked; on the brink of discovering where it might lead. All the endless possibilities of the days and nights ahead glittered like the dew-drop bugle beads catching the light on the catwalk.

But it didn't last long. Reality snapped at her like fresh elastic on her cheap underwear. She'd looked around her at the women in the audience and realised she wasn't one of them: the matrons, the ladies who had spent the war lunching, their daughters with their primped film-star blonde hair and sparkling blue eyes with just the right amount of shadow on their lids, and envied them for the simplicity of the decisions they were making about the right choice for the perfect debutante ball gown. They would wear their mother's pearls and be escorted by the sons of the families their own families had grown up with, young stockbrokers and doctors and lawyers and businessmen, whom they would later marry in a wedding which would feature in Kitty's society news page, and the virtuous and privileged circle would continue.

They had had a different war to the one she had endured. They moved in a different universe and she wondered how it was possible they lived in the same city, caught the same tram, drank the same tea. But she'd come back to the newsroom and written her story in the same way she tackled every other one: with a commitment to the facts, with a dedication to telling the story and with her opinions in her cheek.

'"Summer frocks enthral crowd",' Tilly read aloud. She couldn't imagine what on earth was incorrect about that. She looked to Mrs Freeman for guidance or a reprimand. 'Was it Betty Grable?'

Mrs Freeman stared at her blankly. 'I beg your pardon?'

'I swear that's what the head of Ladies Fashion told me. I can check my notes. The chiffon dress in delicate mist-grey was based on Betty Grable's dress in *Billy Rose's Diamond Horseshoe*.'

Mrs Freeman rolled her eyes. 'For Christ's sake, Tilly. I don't give a fig about the models or Betty Grable's dresses. *This* is your error.' She jabbed a perfectly manicured finger at Tilly's second paragraph.

Tilly read it aloud, muttering to herself. '"Seated front row at the parade, as a special and honoured guest of the retailer, was Mrs Robert Fowles of Rose Bay, in a pastel-pink rayon crepe-de-chine blouse with a high tie neckline and a fluted jabot front. Her suit was the palest grey and her shoes a stylish grey kid heel. She wore a miniature coachman's hat of strawberry straw covered with lilies of the valley. The fine balibuntal straw, with upswept sides and dinted in the crown, was designed especially for her by a Frenchman, and it gave a luxury note not seen since Sydney's pre-war days."'

Tilly read it twice and stared in bewilderment at her editor. 'I do know how to spell the name of the chairman of the board's wife. I arranged Mr Sinclair's appointments for years.'

Mrs Freeman pinched the bridge of her nose. 'Tilly, it's not the name. It's the colour of her crepe-de-chine blouse with the fluted jabot front.' She picked up her notepad and held it at arm's length, squinting just a little. '"It was most definitely not pastel pink. It was salmon pink. What standard of woman reporter are in your employ these days, Mrs Freeman? I'll be speaking to my husband about this. You can count on it."'

Tilly sat back in her chair, speechless. She had been chastised by the wife of the chairman of the board of the paper—and one of Sydney's most illustrious charity matrons—for inaccurately describing the colour of her blouse, which had probably cost more than Tilly's monthly wage. Tilly tried not to be furious. She remembered her interview with Daphne Teale two weeks before, the Red Cross worker who'd walked into Belsen. Such anger over the colour of a blouse when millions had been murdered. The incongruity was enraging.

Tilly swallowed her fury. Mrs Freeman had been nothing but professional and accommodating and the last thing Tilly had wanted to do was embarrass her editor. 'I'll personally apologise to Mrs Fowles, Mrs Freeman. And I apologise to you for my error.'

Mrs Freeman leant forward on her desk, her elbows crossed. She searched Tilly's face, looking for signs of nerves. Tilly knew the look: the pursed lips, the narrowed eyes, the question about her state of mind sitting there on the tip of her tongue, about to be asked. The cock of the head to one side. She'd been studied in such a way by everyone, like a specimen on a glass slide under a microscope. She shrank a little inside. Since she'd returned to the newsroom, her colleagues had been treating her with kid gloves, as if she might break like a sparrow's egg tipped from a nest.

'How is everything with you, Tilly?'

Her work? Her mind? Her life? Her desk? Her heart? 'I'm getting on with things, Mrs Freeman.'

The editor shared a kind smile. 'That's all you can do, I expect, isn't it? Get on with things? In my experience, grief is a long journey with no clear destination. It may not seem possible now, but one day you'll find comfort in the simple things again and then before you know it, it will be Easter and then spring and Christmas and 1947. Distance helps, if that's any comfort to you.'

'Yes,' Tilly replied, wondering where Mrs Freeman's particular understanding and sympathy had been born. 'One day at a time. That's my plan.'

'What you've been through …' Mrs Freeman's lips parted on a sad smile. 'Don't be too hard on yourself, that's all.'

'Thank you but I'll own up to my mistake, even if I find it to be petty and ridiculous. My failure to understand the importance of the difference between pale pink and salmon pink has nothing to do with what happened to my husband. It wasn't professional of me and I can only say I will do better next time.' The heat in her cheeks confirmed everything that the girl from Millers Point had always believed about herself, that even though she was smart as a whip, there would always be places in Sydney a watersider's daughter would never belong. She had observed the crowd at the fashion parade, but had never been one of the young women choosing their debutante gowns. While one might have thought the war had been a great equaliser, given death knew no class or rank distinction, Tilly realised that the war had only cemented Sydney's social strata, not shattered it. That was the reason why the waterside workers were fighting the shipping companies and the government, why men and women were on strike, fighting for a pay rise and fair working hours. Her anger at the inequality made bile rise in her throat.

'I'm aware this isn't your dream job,' Mrs Freeman started and then paused.

'It's not that, truly.'

'I do understand it wasn't your choice to come under my aegis, to report on fashion parades and the comings and goings of society matrons. The women's pages isn't hard news, as I'm sure you've noticed. New season hats can't compare with state parliament or the latest breaking news, can they?' Mrs Freeman's tone could have been belittling, but wasn't. Tilly's interest was piqued.

Tilly tried to find the right words to express her disappointment in her demotion and her exile from the newsroom, in a way that wouldn't insult the woman sitting opposite her who had been nothing but accommodating. 'A job's a job, Mrs Freeman. A woman ...' Tilly paused. 'A widow needs to pay the rent and put food on her table. I know the situation facing so many others and I really am very grateful to have a job at all. But ...'

Mrs Freeman raised a perfect eyebrow. 'But?'

'But ...' Tilly waited, wondered if she should be so forthright and then realised she had nothing to lose. 'I'd rather be writing about what women are doing and not what they're wearing.'

Mrs Freeman's lips pulled together in a firm line and Tilly couldn't shake the intuition that she was trying to hide a smile.

'How are you getting on financially, Tilly?'

'I received a bereavement payment from the army and I saved most of Archie's pay when he was, well, when we thought he was alive. I won't go without, at least for a little while.' It felt like blood money and Tilly would have gladly sent it all back with interest if she could have Archie instead. 'But I'm going to have to find a new flat.'

'Why is that?'

'My flatmate is Mary Smith from classified ads and she and her returned serviceman husband have won a Housing Commission house in the lottery. They found out just before Christmas.'

'Good luck to them. And how is Mary?'

There were secrets but they weren't Tilly's to tell. 'Mary is kind and patient and she loves her husband very much.'

Mrs Freeman saw through Tilly's words. 'I don't think there's a woman in Sydney whose life hasn't been changed in some way by the war.'

Tilly muttered under her breath. 'Some have faced more hardships than others.'

Mrs Freeman's eyes lit up. 'Exactly. And they're the ones who need us the most. I have some news, Tilly. And it involves you.'

Mrs Freeman walked to the window on her elegantly turned-out dancer's feet. She pointed through the dusty glass to the street below.

'Steel mills are making bathrooms and kitchen appliances now instead of planes and ships. Uniform manufacturers are turning production back to suits and frocks and children's clothes and sheets. I can't wait for new sheets myself. Mine are so thin I can see the springs in the mattress.' She chuckled and turned back to Tilly. 'Factories that made bullet casings are now making lipstick. Hooray to that, I say. And who buys all those things, with their husband's pay or with their own?'

Mrs Freeman threw the question to Tilly.

'Women?' Tilly offered.

'Exactly. We're the shoppers in households and for the first time women have had money of their own. Now that austerity and wartime manufacturing have come to an end, the whole economy is gearing up to sell things to us again, instead of to the government. They want to sell more fabric, shoes, soap, perfume, cigarettes, cleaning products, make-up, shoe polish and even push carts for children's birthday presents.'

'I'm not sure I understand what all this has to do with me,' Tilly said, perplexed.

'There have been discussions going on at board level for almost a year and they've finally agreed.' Mrs Freeman beamed. 'We're going to have a bigger women's section in the paper, a weekly lift-out every Thursday instead of the measly half a page a day we have now. Think of it, Tilly. Six whole pages full of news for women each week, and more if we get the advertising to support it. Vera will continue to write her cookery column. We're going to expand Talk of the Town because who doesn't love gossip, except when it's about oneself. We'll be answering more Dear Agatha letters and we're finally going to let her off the leash and print some of the hardest questions women are asking. If we receive a frank letter about marriage, we're going to answer it frankly. She'll be giving fearless—and mostly uncensored—advice to Sydney women about their sex lives. Even if we have to make up the first few letters ourselves, just to get things going.'

Mrs Freeman crossed her arms and stared into the distance. 'Do you know what the war has done to marriages in this country, Tilly?'

In her mind, Tilly saw Mary cowering in the bathroom, sobbing. She heard her begging Bert to come back to bed.

'Aside from my own?'

Mrs Freeman's face fell. 'Yes, of course. I'm talking about the ones who were lucky enough to come home.'

'Not really, no,' she lied.

'When women talk to each other—I mean really talk to each other—they tell the truth. Their husbands and boyfriends and sweethearts are not the men who left wearing a fresh uniform and a smile. Whether it's nerve disorders or the sufferings from battle or captivity, there has been a toll on their sexual power.'

So it wasn't just Bert?

'And wives are desperate for help. They're beside themselves about what to do. We can be that place for them, Tilly. We can, as you put it so succinctly just now, not just write about what they're wearing, but their lives and their challenges. What do you think?'

'I think it sounds marvellous.'

'I'm pleased to hear that because you're going to be the new editor.'

There was a buzzing in Tilly's ears and her vision blurred and then settled.

'I beg your pardon?'

'You heard me.' Mrs Freeman sat on the edge of her desk and stared at Tilly. 'Did you know that I worked hard to poach you from Sinclair?'

'I didn't know that. And now I'm completely perplexed.'

'I'm not surprised. Sinclair made it known that he wanted you to return as his secretary. I was infuriated and when I heard I marched into his office and told him that was not going to happen. As soon as those important men returned from the war—'

'Poncing around as if they were Ernest Hemingway.' Tilly smiled and Mrs Freeman laughed.

'Precisely. They thought we would all step back into the shadows, where no doubt most of them think we should have always been. But the shadows are full of secrets.' Mrs Freeman's mouth curved into a sly grin and she raised her eyebrows in mock surprise. 'And I know many of them.'

'Secrets?' Tilly asked, shocked.

Mrs Freeman nodded.

'You don't mean Mr Sinclair?'

Mrs Freeman laughed. 'Goodness, no. He goes home every night to kiss his wife and goes to church on Sundays with his ten grandchildren. I'm talking about Mr Robert Fowles.'

Tilly's thoughts raced. She was frantically trying to put together a puzzle without all the pieces.

Mrs Freeman sat at her desk, crossed one leg over the other and settled in.

'I was a dancer before I got into the newspaper business. Ballet. I was never quite good enough for the Ballets Russes or anything like that, but I was perfectly adequate for the JC Williamson company. My sister Maud auditioned and was accepted too. Oh, we loved those years. We were paid, a pittance but we were paid. We danced in theatres all over the country, the Tivolis, the Royals and the Roxies. I'd always loved the theatre. We were both Lovelies.' A wicked glint appeared in Mrs Freeman's eyes. 'We had to stand on stage, draped in white robes but topless for all intents and purposes. If we moved, you see, we would have to be paid as dancers, so we were as still as Greek marble statues until the curtains closed.' She stood, extended her arms and gazed up at the ceiling, and then became completely still. Tilly wasn't even sure she had blinked.

'It was all tremendous fun while it lasted. The boys in the chorus were all queer as quinces and such wonderful company. We could go wherever we wanted with one of them on our arm and no one blinked an eyelid.' She was lost for a moment in her memories. 'And then it all ended.'

Tilly was transfixed. 'A dance injury?'

Mrs Freeman returned to her chair. 'There was a pregnancy, you see, to a man who lavished gifts and promises and who had even rented a lovely little apartment in Rose Bay overlooking the water.'

'And that young woman was you?' Tilly asked, afraid to but desperate to know.

'My sister. Maud. She was two years younger than me and we looked so alike people thought we were twins. When Maud died in childbirth, I raised her daughter as my own. Started calling myself Mrs instead of Miss and gave up the theatre.' Mrs Freeman reached for a photograph in a wooden frame and passed it to Tilly. 'This is Lucille. Lucy.'

The woman in the photograph had dark eyes, upswept wartime hair and an impish smile. She wore a nurse's uniform.

'She works at the Concord Military Hospital, has done throughout the war.'

'You must be very proud of her.'

'I am. She's a wonderful young woman. Smart as a whip. I like being surrounded by smart young women.'

Tilly took the compliment with a nod and a smile.

The story hadn't come back around to the secrets from upstairs and when Tilly raised her eyebrows in a question, the older woman smiled conspiratorially. 'Her father is Robert Fowles.'

'Bloody hell.'

'I raised his daughter and I kept his secret.'

Tilly's mind whirred as she remembered the gossip that had swirled in the newsroom for months about Kitty Darling and her affair with an Important American. 'Kitty Darling? She's in the same boat, isn't she?'

'She has a secret, too. But she won't wear the shame of it as much as other women have. Women from your neck of the woods, or mine. It's all being taken care of. Knowledge is power, as I'm sure you know. And I have a certain power that I wish I'd earnt in a more traditional way, but they were the times I lived in and I had to survive for Lucy's sake. I owed that to my sister. But now, I've decided I've spent too many years in the shadows of powerful men, keeping their secrets. I'm retiring.'

'You can't do that—' Tilly began.

'I most definitely can. I've met a lovely man and I'm going to retire to the south coast. Bermagui. Lucy is on her feet and I'm looking forward to the companionship of a gentleman who seems to love me. I've waited a long time for this kind of happiness, you see. Anyway, my time here is over. I wouldn't have fought for you if I didn't think you were up to the job.'

'I'm delighted for you, Mrs Freeman. But I'm not certain about your offer.' Was Tilly giving up any chance of being taken seriously at the paper if she relegated herself to the section that had always been the laughing stock of the newsroom?

She corrected herself: the men's newsroom.

'Just like Sinclair, Tilly, I'm a relic of another era. Do you know I was born when women weren't allowed to vote? Who knows what I might have been able to achieve if I'd come into the world a little later. I've been honoured and proud to be editor of the women's pages for the *Daily Herald* for as long as I have. We've come a long way but there's a long way to go, and women of your generation, and perhaps the next, will bring the change we desperately need.'

The honour she was being asked to accept felt like a double-edged sword. Mrs Freeman obviously sensed her doubt.

'You'll get a pay rise. A decent one. You'll be able to hold your head up high when you go upstairs as a section editor. You'll be part of the editorial conferences. You will be able to make your mark in any way you choose.'

Tilly thought on it. 'Did you say we'll have more space?'

'Yes.'

'And how much leeway will I have to run the kind of stories I think are important?'

'As much as any other section editor at the newspaper.'

'My problem, Mrs Freeman, is that I don't see in our pages the stories of women that I know. We're not giving our readers the truth. We're giving them a box of chocolates when they are surviving on porridge and weak tea.'

'Some might say our readers want hope and escapism.'

Tilly heard the clear challenge in Mrs Freeman's words and she rose to it. 'Yes, sometimes we want fashion and frolics, just like the men want *The Phantom* and the sports pages. But I believe women want more. They want to recognise themselves in our stories. If they are able to get a window into the real struggles women are facing, it may well help them understand and cope with their own. To know they're not alone in their suffering. Imagine what a service we could do for those women?'

Tilly thought of Mary.

'And what about women raising children on their own? Having to cope with husbands who've abandoned them without a pound, trying to survive on a woman's wage that can be half of what men earn for doing the same job, the threat of poverty at their door every waking minute?'

Tilly thought of Martha.

'And older women who have kept their families together, never having worked a paid day out of the home, but every waking minute within it. Caring for broken-down husbands who've been worked to death? Looking after other people's children when they can't or so they can work to earn just enough to pay the rent?'

Tilly thought of her mother.

'Women who gave their all during the war, making uniforms and bullets and canned food, picking grapes and turnips and digging potatoes, creating maps to keep an eye on the enemy and to keep us safe. Women who served as nurses and even doctors and Red Cross workers. I'm not reading about them and what they will do now the war's over and their husbands may or may not have come back from the war in one piece, if at all. Where are they in our pages?'

Mrs Freeman smiled proudly. 'I knew there was something about you I liked.'

Tilly felt stronger and clearer than she ever had. 'Will I have a travel budget?'

'Why? Where do you want to go?'

And the idea arrived fully formed in her head. 'Japan.'

Mrs Freeman sounded as shocked as she looked. 'Are you certain?'

'I've never been surer of anything.'

Mrs Freeman gave Tilly a wry smile. 'Leave it with me.'

Tilly reached out a hand. 'Yes. I'll take it. Thank you, Mrs Freeman.'

'For god's sake, call me Dorothy.'

Chapter Thirty-five

'I think that's everything.' Mary looked over her possessions and laughed. 'It's not much, is it?'

There were two suitcases. A tea chest and a cardboard box filled with a few books, her shoes, some dishes from the kitchen she'd brought to the flat when she'd moved in, and lying on top, her heavy winter coat. Next to it, Bert's kit bag and another cardboard box filled with his civvies. The measly possessions of lives interrupted but more than many had.

'Just think,' Tilly said. 'Your new place is a blank canvas. You can buy a houseful of new furniture for it. You won't be sorry to say goodbye to those creaking old things that came with the flat.'

'I've heard built-in robes are popular. With sliding doors.' Mary's face lit up. 'Imagine all the space!'

Tilly gestured to the suitcases. 'You're going to have to buy some more clothes to fill them.'

'And I plan to, Tilly. Bert and I have talked and I'm going to stay in the Classified Advertisements department for a little while longer. There's no point quitting just yet.' Mary's mouth trembled. 'Just until we get on our feet.'

Tilly went to Mary and clasped her hands. 'You love each other. Surely that's got to count for something.'

'I do love him, although my faith in him and in God has been tested, which you know better than anyone. Perhaps this is what God has had in mind for me all along. To be Bert's wife. To help him get through this. I've thought a lot about it. Prayed a lot about it. When he went to war, I think I did too.'

'We both did,' Tilly said.

'I'm lucky in so many ways. He came home.' Tears welled in Mary's eyes and Tilly understood that this wasn't a boast. Mary had always been humble and she was humble now about her good fortune, even when it had been so hard to bear. During the years Bert was away, she had remained a bubbling fountain, a wellspring of hope for Tilly, but she'd been hollowed out since Bert's return. The war had sucked life and hope and her future away, had stolen the bright dreams of a woman who had not wished for much for herself, just a little life, enough happiness to get her through a day and a week and then a month and a year. She hadn't expected a bounty, an unfair proportion, or a share of anyone else's. Just hers.

It had never seemed that much to ask.

'Life is a gift, Tilly. And with existence comes pain as well as love. I'm grateful for my life. All of it.'

With existence comes pain as well as love.

Tilly had had enough pain for two lifetimes and yet she was still standing.

'I see that smile on your face. Cooper?'

Tilly felt heat in her cheeks. 'Pain as well as love. I'll remember that.'

'I would ask if you're going to be all right here by yourself but I think I know the answer.'

'Now that I'm an editor I'll be able to afford the rent on my own. Doesn't life work in mysterious ways?'

Mary enveloped Tilly in a hug and held on tight. 'I wouldn't have survived the war without you. You'll always be my best friend. My dearest friend.'

'And you mine.'

When they let go of each other, Tilly dipped her chin and met Mary's eyes directly and intently. Her words were almost lost in a sob. 'Promise me you will look after yourself as well as Bert. I will always be here if you need me. When things get hard, come to me. I understand like no one else can.'

Mary nodded. 'I promise.'

From the street, a car horn sounded and Mary darted to the window. 'It's Bert.'

Mary hoisted Bert's kit bag over her shoulder and lifted a suitcase. 'I'll be back with Bert for the rest in a minute.' She laughed. 'My carriage awaits!'

'Your prince is downstairs, m'lady.'

They held their smiles for just a moment longer.

'He's loved you for a long time, Tilly.'

'Cooper?' His name quickly spilled from Tilly's lips with a gasp of surprise that Mary had been paying attention all this time.

'Who else do you think I'm talking about? Bing Crosby?'

They giggled and that made Tilly so happy. They'd laughed so much in their earliest days in the flat and it felt so good for it to be filled with it once more.

'Why wait? That's all I'll say. The people I go to church with will tell you it's a sin, but you live your life the way you want to live it. Bugger what anyone else thinks.' Mary surprised even herself with that expression and covered her mouth with a hand. 'Life is short. You know that better than anyone. Live, Tilly, for those who can't.'

Later that night, Cooper and Tilly sat at the kitchen table eating midnight toast. They'd just got out of bed, suddenly hungry for something other than each other, and while Tilly had toasted the bread, Cooper had poured whisky into two glasses. He was dressed in his trousers, she in his shirt. The windows overlooking Orwell Street were wide open to capture the summer breeze coming off the water and the sounds of the crowd at the Roosevelt drifted up to them.

Cooper lifted his glass and nodded at Tilly to do the same. She tapped hers against his.

'To the *Daily Herald*'s newest section editor.'

They upended their glasses and Tilly waited for the warmth to seep into her bones.

'I'm so bloody proud of you, Mrs Galloway.'

'Call me Tilly.' She wanted to hear the sound of it on his lips, in his baritone.

He looked away. 'What kind of a name is that for a girl anyway?'

'It's short for Matilda. The waltzing kind.'

No one had ever called her Matilda, not even her mother or father when they'd been cross at her which, if Tilly was honest, wasn't often. Martha was the one who got into scrapes, who fought with the other children in the street, who skived off at school and bossed around the other children. Then, she became Martha Elsie Bell. 'Martha Elsie

Bell, you come right here.' Or 'Martha Elsie Bell, you put that down.'

'Matilda Galloway,' Cooper said, slowly, as if he were rolling those six syllables around in his mouth to taste them, holding her gaze for every syllable.

She had never been Matilda Galloway and wasn't sure she would turn at the sound of it if anyone were to call out that name out in a crowd. Matilda Galloway had never existed. And Tilly Galloway seemed like someone she used to be.

'So you grew up as Tilly Bell?'

'That was my name until I was twenty-five.'

'Bell,' Cooper repeated. 'Miss Bell. It sounds like a schoolteacher's name, don't you think? I'm sorry, Miss Bell. The dog ate my homework.'

He still hadn't said it. Cooper could evade like the best politician. But she was a reporter too and she knew his tricks by now.

'Say it.'

'I need a cigarette. Don't happen to have any, do you?'

She waited. She'd learnt to listen and she was listening now. Her heart was beating strong and fast in her chest. His breath was frustrated and his fingers tapped on the table. He poured himself another shot and it glug-glug-glugged into his glass. After he swallowed it, he let out a small hiss between his teeth.

'Say it,' she repeated.

He met her gaze. 'Truth?'

'Truth.'

'Calling you Mrs Galloway always reminded me, and I've needed reminding for a long time, that despite what I wanted you belonged to someone else.'

She knew what he needed to hear. It was what she needed to say to him and to herself.

She held on to her empty glass. When Cooper moved to fill it, she shook her head. 'Archie was a good and decent man. And that had nothing to do with being polite to the grocer or holding the door open for me or anything like that. He had an innate goodness to him. He didn't have big dreams, didn't want to change the world. When we met, we wanted a good marriage, children and a house, and to give them the life our parents couldn't give us. That was going to be enough for him. And for me.'

'I can tell you loved him very much,' Cooper said and there wasn't bitterness or envy in his voice, simply a weary resignation.

She nodded. 'I did and I will miss him forever and I want you to know that I will never get over losing him. How it happened made it worse, too. It was so, so cruel to live in hope all those years. What kind of a way was that to end the war? To realise that he'd been dead longer than I ever knew him?'

Cooper exhaled a deep breath. 'You can't know how I've suffered for you.'

'But he's gone, Cooper, and I want to go on living. I couldn't bury two people.'

If he understood the implications of what she was saying, he didn't seem willing to acknowledge it. 'Tell me something. Your husband enlisted to fight and suffered tragically for it and all I did was write about his sacrifices and those of so many others like him. What kind of a man does that make me? I'm not fit to shine his shoes.'

'What kind of man are you?' Tilly repeated, hardly believing he'd asked her.

'I'm the worst kind. I'm a man who's been in love with a woman whose husband was a soldier and a prisoner of war. That's who I am.'

Tilly's fingers trembled on her glass. Mary had been right. 'You love me?'

'How could I not? You're beautiful and smart and you write like a dream.'

Tilly waited as his compliments sunk in. She was a writer and an editor. She was so far from the girl who'd left Millers Point but in many ways she was still that sixteen-year-old girl, full of questions and ambitions and desires for a life bigger than her own to that point.

'Well, I'm no Ernest Hemingway. Or should that be Martha Gellhorn?'

Cooper smiled at her and there was hope in his expression, a question.

'You and I are alive,' she said quietly. 'We mourn the dead. We weep for them. We will never forget them. But still we live. Twelve million are dead, Cooper, but you and I are here. We need to go on living for all those who won't ever have the chance.'

He stood and went to her, reached for her hand and pulled her to her feet. He slipped his arms around her waist and pulled her in so their bodies were touching, thigh to hips, breasts to chest. He pressed his lips to her forehead and murmured so softly she barely heard it. 'Tilly.'

'Again.'

He kissed her closed eyes, her cheekbone, the soft plump of her cheek. 'Tilly.'

'Again.'

His lips were a breath away. 'Tilly.'

And when she tilted her head back to meet his mouth, she whispered into it, 'I'm yours.'

In the morning Tilly woke to silence in the flat. She roused, listened for sounds of Cooper but there were none. On the pillow next to her, she found a folded piece of paper. She opened it.

Dearest Tilly,
I wish I had a goddamn typewriter but this will have to do.
   This is our story.
   The who is you.
   The what is my love for you that for so long felt like a punishment for something I might have done in a past life, if I believed in that idea and I think you know me well enough to believe that I don't.
   The why is you. The where is everywhere you are.
   The when is slowly, then with a wham, and then every goddam waking minute of every goddam day since we first shared cheese and pickle sandwiches at Circular Quay. And every day since, more and more.
   I don't yet know the how of our story. I hope that's because we haven't written the end.
   I'll always be, yours truly,
   George

Tilly read it twice. Three times.

'Since Circular Quay?' she whispered to herself. Who had she been all those years ago and what had he seen in her that she hadn't even seen in herself? Newly married, a husband away in the army, a Millers Point girl, a secretary trying to make a life for herself. He had fallen in love with the young woman she had been and no longer was, and he still loved her? A woman broken with grief and clinging to hope?

He'd loved her when she'd been married, widowed, bereaved, broken, unloved, silent, dark and angry. He'd loved her when she was a secretary, when she was a war correspondent and when she was writing about flowers and frocks and frippery. He'd loved every part of her and her life, all this time and she hadn't known. She hadn't let herself know.

She hadn't been blind. She just hadn't been looking.

She was never going to let go of his letter. It would join Archie's in the camphorwood box of her most treasured things, all of which marked some turning point of her life. For this was indeed a turning point.

It was 1946. She was ready to lift her eyes to the horizon now, to imagine a new life for herself. She was determined to live for all those who couldn't.

The future we promised ourselves is here, but—

The woman's view—by one of them

The Sydney Morning Herald, 12 January 1946

Chapter Thirty-six

'How on earth is it right that the first child of a living soldier is allowed twenty-one shillings living allowance weekly but if their poor old dad is dead, has given his life for our country and the king, that fatherless child only gets seventeen and six? I mean, where's the fairness in that, I ask you?'

Tilly sat at the table in her mother's kitchen, a place for sharing injustices for as long as she could remember.

'Mrs McCartney, how do you know this is the case?'

The grandmother leant forward, her face reddening, her large bosom resting on the table. 'Because it's happened to my poor daughter, Geraldine. Her Barnie was killed in Timor—wherever that is, I don't know—and she has four mouths to feed. Do those little ones eat less now their father is dead?'

Elsie comforted her neighbour. 'It's just dreadful. How is Geraldine getting on then?'

'She's taking in washing and mending, and her father and I and all her brothers are doing as much as we can for the poor lass. But it's not like we all have much to spare. Not with the strikes. You know how it is, Tilly.'

Tilly nodded. 'Do you think the government thinks that war widows are embarrassing? A reminder that blokes were killed and it was sometimes the fault of those bloody generals like Blamey? They want to sweep them all under the carpet and pretend everything's the way it used to be. They don't seem to care a toss about Geraldine and others like her reduced to penury. And Geraldine's not the only one. There're thousands and thousands of them and I—' Mrs McCartney covered her mouth. 'Of course you know that, Tilly.'

'It's all right, Mrs McCartney. Archie and I had no children. I'm in a very different spot to poor Geraldine.'

'You all have your burdens to bear,' Elsie said, passing a plate of fruit cake to Tilly, who passed it straight on to Mrs McCartney.

'The other thing to hit poor Geraldine? All Barnie's pay that had been saved up, what do they call it …'

'Accrued leave pay?' Tilly offered.

'Yes, that's it. It's all gone! The widows don't get a penny of it. Barnie and all those boys earnt every pound ten times over. It's shocking, it is. And you ask about the pension, too, Tilly. It's pitiful.'

'I will. Thank you, Mrs McCartney. And please send on my condolences to Geraldine.'

'I will, love. And I'm sure she'd want me to send them right back to you.'

Tilly stomped across the women's newsroom to her office and tossed her handbag and notebook on her desk.

'You all right, boss?' Vera Maxwell popped her head in, a look of concern in her knitted eyebrows.

Vera and Dear Agatha and the newest reporter for the women's pages, Denise Stapleton, had given her the moniker and she had embraced it with good humour. She liked being reminded that she was the boss because as soon as she left the floor she was still treated by the other men at the paper as the ex-secretary. Funnily enough, no one called Cooper the ex-copyboy.

Denise had been tickled pink at being offered the job, lured by an upgrade, which meant more pay and something else worth far more than money.

'You came along at just the right time, Tilly. I've been looking for a way out of that newsroom for twelve months.'

When Tilly had asked why, Denise had rolled her eyes and frowned. 'Let's just call him the octopus. The married octopus.'

Denise stood at the doorway to Tilly's office. 'What's got your goat?'

Tilly told Denise what she'd learnt from Mrs McCartney and Denise's appalled expression revealed she was in total agreement with Tilly.

'I'm going to dig a little deeper.'

'Boss, there's something I'm interested in taking a look at. Can I run it by you?'

'Of course.' Tilly had given Denise a wide brief when she'd enticed her over. She trusted her judgement in knowing what a good story was.

'A number of women's organisations are holding a meeting to talk about their role in the new peace and reconstruction movement. I'd like to go along to the meeting tonight. I spoke to one of them just now and she said that men are intimidated by women en masse and women should make a good deal more use of that power. I liked her right away.'

'Sounds like I would, too. I look forward to reading your story.'

Denise left and Tilly worked her phone. Mrs McCartney had been correct. The more she investigated the story, the more certain Tilly was that Australia was failing its ten thousand war widows and its 11,240 fatherless children. Not only did they have to cope with the loss of their family breadwinner and loved one, but they were at dire risk of falling into poverty. A war widow without children received two pounds and fifteen shillings a week. How was a woman who had given her husband to the nation expected to live on half the basic wage? And a widow with two children was only entitled to four pounds, twelve shillings and sixpence, which was still less than the basic male wage of over five pounds.

Tilly sat back in her chair and thought about women in Martha's position. Martha wasn't a widow but she faced the same threat of poverty and homelessness. She hadn't seen a penny from Colin in the months since he'd told her he wanted a divorce. She was going to strike first, but the process was convoluted and infuriating. Martha had gone to a sympathetic lawyer the Waterside Workers' Federation had recommended, who had advised her she would first have to file a decree of restitution of conjugal rights. In other words, she would have to convince a judge that she wanted the lying, cheating sod back. Then, when he refused, she would be able to get a petition for dissolution right away.

Tilly slipped empty copy paper into her typewriter, cranked the platen knob and began.

Chapter Thirty-seven

Cooper tilted back the cap of Tilly's uniform and pressed his lips to hers.

Their kiss was long and gentle. It would have to last them a while and they both knew it. They'd prepared themselves for their separation by spending every minute of the past four weeks together.

His charming eyes sparkled at her. 'You'll have to marry me when you come back, you know.'

She laughed at his presumption. 'You call that a proposal?'

'I'm being practical. Think about it, Tilly. It's 1946. The war changed a whole lot about this country but a man and a woman still can't live together without being married.'

'We're not living together,' she clarified. 'You're taking care of the flat while I'm in Japan for three months. And also because your bedsit was a cesspit.'

Tilly stood in her living room in her freshly dry-cleaned war correspondent's uniform, a suitcase and Cooper's portable typewriter in its case at her feet. He held her in his arms, touched his forehead to hers.

'You've rescued me from squalor, I can't deny it. And a whole lot more.'

'And as to what people think of me? You may have noticed that I don't tend to care, George Cooper. I am a commie's daughter, after all.'

He chuckled and straightened her cap. 'But you're also the editor of the *Daily Herald*'s women's pages. Sydney's matrons will black ban you if they think you're a woman of low morals.'

'Funny you should say that. I want more of those women with supposedly low morals to be reading the paper, so perhaps I'm on to something. And anyway, they'll still have society favourite, their very own Kitty Darling, to cover what interests them. They've always loved her.' And Tilly knew they would continue to, even after she returned to Sydney having born her child out of wedlock in a secret place in the country. Once it was delivered into the arms of an adopting couple, she would return to work, like thousands of women all over the country, as if nothing had ever happened.

'Are you sure you have everything?'

'I'm sure.'

Tilly was sailing that day on the hospital ship *Manunda* with members of the Australian Army Medical Women's Service and the Australian Army Nursing Service, the first contingent of Australian women being sent to occupied Japan. They were heading there to care for the ten thousand Australians serving as part of the British Commonwealth Occupation Force, part of the Allied occupation of Japan.

Tilly had held Mrs Freeman to her promise that she would have free rein to run the women's pages however she chose and had informed Mr Sinclair that she believed they should report on the post-war reconstruction of Japan and what it meant for the women of the mysterious country to the north.

'Japan?' he'd muttered, chewing on the end of a pencil as he'd considered her request. 'I don't know which man I can spare to sail away to Tokyo.'

Tilly had planted her hands on his desk, stared him down, and replied, 'I don't need a man for this assignment, Rex. I'll be going.'

Since the war was over, and Japan still occupied, Tilly had discovered she would be free to move around without a military escort. The city she would be living in, Kure, was near Hiroshima. How could she be so close and not want to try to understand the devastation wrought on that city and its people?

And most particularly, she wanted answers to the question that had haunted her: whose suffering was more worthy or more honourable in war? Wasn't everyone a victim in one way or another? Was her grief at the loss of Archie somehow sadder than the grief of a Japanese war widow?

Her father's words on the day he died would never leave her. *Our losses can only make us more aware of the losses of others in this war.* When she closed her eyes she heard him singing, loud and proud, 'The Internationale', 'On tyrants only we'll make war'.

She would carry his principles and his commitment with her in her heart. Always. They would be her north star during the next three months on assignment.

Tilly checked the time on the carriage clock on the mantel. Archie's photo wasn't there any longer, and it wasn't because Cooper had been spending so much time with her.

She had packed it away with her letters and telegrams in the growing archive of her life. Each artefact another chapter. Another piece of her story. And an excitement coursed through her at all the possibilities that the next chapters would bring.

Would she marry Cooper? Possibly. He would be waiting for her when she returned home and that was enough for now.

She had some life to live first.

'Tilly!' Mary burst into the flat with wide arms and a smiling laugh the size of which Tilly hadn't seen in a long while. It gladdened her heart. By her side, Bert, a flush of colour in his cheeks, which were healthy and filled out now. He looked a lot closer to the man he had been in his photograph.

'We couldn't let you leave without saying goodbye. And to give you this.'

'What is it?' Tilly exclaimed. 'A farewell gift?' Mary handed her a small package wrapped in brown paper. She tore off the wrapping to reveal a box brownie camera, three rolls of film and a knitted scarf and hat.

'You've been knitting?' Tilly laughed. In that very room, they'd passed night after night creating garments for Bert and Archie and for donating to the Red Cross. Their friendship had grown and strengthened over knit one purl one, had helped them endure and survive. Mary's love was in every stitch and Tilly held the scratchy wool to her face.

'I hear it snows this time of year in Japan. You'll be absolutely freezing.'

And they held each other's attention for just long enough for Tilly to see hope in Mary's expression, a reassurance from a dear friend that life with Bert might be on an upward swing. That was better than any gift.

'Bert,' Tilly said, turning to him, reaching a hand out, and he placed his in hers and she gripped it firmly. 'I hope you understand why I'm going. Why I need to go. I thought you, perhaps better than anyone else, would understand.'

Bert's smile died on his lips. 'Safe travels.'

Tilly nodded. She understood. She didn't need to hear apologies from the Japanese—that wouldn't bring Archie back—but she needed answers. She needed to figure out the *why* of it. Why it had all happened in the first place. What had driven men to commit such horrendous acts in the name of their leader and their honour?

From the street, a car horn sounded. Mary kissed Tilly's cheek one more time and then reached for Bert's arm. 'We'll go. See you when you get back.'

Mary and Bert left with another wave and Tilly knelt down to open her case, finding room for the gifts. She clipped it closed and Cooper lifted it.

They stared at each other, barely hearing the car horn beep again from the street.

'Without fear or favour,' Cooper told her, his eyes soft, his voice low and rough. 'You'll be able to do that now the war's over. Find the truth and write it well, Tilly.'

They went down the stairs and out to the street. Cooper packed her bag and his typewriter into the boot and Tilly slipped in the back seat.

'Number six wharf, Darling Harbour, please.'

Cooper closed the car door. 'Say hello to your mother and Martha and the boys for me,' he said, leaning down to talk to her through the open window.

They kissed one more time.

'I will.' She leant out, her hand on her cap as the cab waited for a break in the traffic. 'Just in case you're wondering what I'll say about your offer …'

'My offer?'

She laughed. 'Don't pretend you don't remember, George Cooper. I've never known you to waste a word.'

His eyes held hers and he smiled. Damn him, he already knew the answer.

As the cab moved off she shouted back to him, 'I'll think about it.'

He grinned and saluted her and she watched him until the cab veered into Darlinghurst Road and he was out of sight.

The cab drove Tilly through the city towards the place her story had begun. The *Manunda* was berthed along the Hungry Mile, the place her father had tramped every day when he was alive, looking for work.

Now, his daughter was to tramp that same wharf, a suitcase and a typewriter in her hand, on her way to the other side of the world. Elsie and Martha and the boys were waiting there, a few streets from home, to say their goodbyes to their daughter and sister and aunt.

Tilly looked out into the clear blue Sydney summer sky. It no longer threatened her. It was the horizon, her future, which, for the first time in a very long time, seemed bright and filled with possibilities.

And stories.

She had so many stories to tell.

Author's Note

Tilly Galloway is purely a creation of my imagination, but she wouldn't exist on the page if it weren't for the trailblazing careers of the real-life Australian women war correspondents of World War II, as described so thoroughly in Jeannine *Baker's Australian Women War Reporters: Boer War to Vietnam* (NewSouth, Sydney, 2015).

In 1941, the *Australian Women's Weekly*'s wartime editor, Alice Jackson, became the first Australian woman officially accredited as a war correspondent by the Australian Army, and in 1946, one of its journalists, Dorothy Drain, reported from occupied Japan.

Anne Howard's *You'll Be Sorry: How World War II changed women's Lives* (Big Sky Publishing, Newport, 2016) is a fascinating insight into the real lives of women of the era, and *The Girls They Left Behind* by Betty Goldsmith and Beryl Sandford (Penguin, Ringwood, 1990) is full of poignant stories of women who lived through it, of wartime Australia and the burdens they bore.

For stories of the history of Sydney's waterfront and the appalling conditions those workers endured before and during the war, I turned to Margo Beasley's informative and comprehensive *Wharfies: The History of the Waterside Workers' Federation of Australia* (Halstead Press in association with the Australian National Maritime Museum, Rushcutters Bay, 2011) and Rowan Cahill's article in the Queensland Journal of Labour History, *Home front WW2: myths and realities* (19 September 2014).

I recommend Michael Duffy and Nick Hordern's *World War Noir: Sydney's unpatriotic war* (NewSouth, Sydney, 2019) for a glimpse into that city's seedy wartime underworld.

A special thank you to Carole Worthy. We met in Brisbane when I was on book tour with *The Land Girls* and she shared her own personal interest in the sinking of the *Montevideo Maru*—an event in Australia's history I had just begun researching. She introduced me to Andrea Williams of the Papua New Guinea Association of Australia and both women helped fill in the blanks for me about the families who were left behind when so many Australians tragically lost their lives on the ship.

Acknowledgements

Thanks once again to my family for supporting, feeding and watering me in the darkest depths of my deadline when it seemed, as Douglas Adams once described, it might go whooshing by.

To the best friends a gal could ever ask for—Debbie, Peter, Sally, Andrew, Anita and David—who patiently waited while I wrote this book and took me at my word when I said that one day I would come out to play again.

Thanks to Mark Corcoran for his insider's tour of Potts Point and Kings Cross.

I am indebted to Sarah Tooth for having the foresight to buy a secondhand bookshop at the exact moment I needed all kinds of old and unusual books for research.

At HarperCollins, thanks once again to Jo Mackay (something about the wind beneath my wings comes to mind) and to Annabel Blay for your eagle eye (glad I made you cry—in a good way). To Sue Brockhoff and James Kellow, I can't thank you enough for your continuing support, and a million thanks to the design team and sales team who make my books look beautiful and ensure they're on shelves all over the country.

The women war correspondents of the 1940s (and all those who had come before them) broke new ground, not just for themselves but for women everywhere. I studied journalism and began my career in the 1980s and I knew nothing of their place in our media history. I hope *The Women's Pages* sheds some long overdue light on them and their tenacity to report the truth when the hurdles seemed insurmountable. Women in the media have come a long way but there are so many battles to be won. I take my hat off to my former colleagues, those I admire from afar and those starting out their careers, all of whom continue to push new boundaries each and every day.

Other books by

Victoria Purman

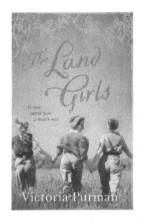 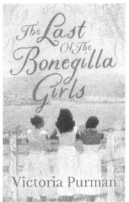

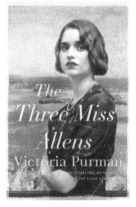

talk about it

Let's talk about books.

Join the conversation:

 facebook.com/harlequinaustralia

 @harlequinaus

 @harlequinaus

harpercollins.com.au/hq

If you love reading and want to know about our
authors and titles, then let's talk about it.